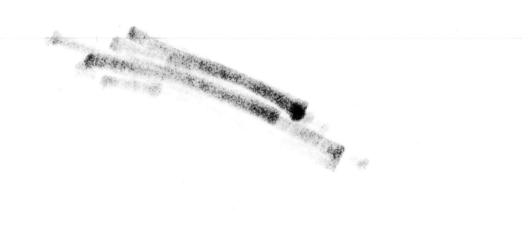

TAKING CHARGE

Recent Titles in
Contributions in Criminology and Penology

Children and Criminality: The Child as Victim and Perpetrator
Ronald Barri Flowers

Intervention Strategies for Chronic Juvenile Offenders: Some New Perspectives
Peter W. Greenwood, editor

Bandidos: The Varieties of Latin American Banditry
Richard W. Slatta, editor

America's Correctional Crisis: Prison Populations and Public Policy
Stephen D. Gottfredson and Sean McConville, editors

The Structure of Criminal Procedure: Laws and Practice of France, the Soviet
Union, China, and the United States
Barton L. Ingraham

Women and Criminality: The Woman as Victim, Offender, and Practitioner
Ronald Barri Flowers

Police Administration and Progressive Reform: Theodore Roosevelt as Police
Commissioner of New York
Jay Stuart Berman

Policing Multi-Ethnic Neighborhoods: The Miami Study and Findings for Law
Enforcement in the United States
Geoffrey P. Alpert and Roger G. Dunham

Minorities and Criminality
Ronald Barri Flowers

Marijuana: Costs of Abuse, Costs of Control
Mark Kleiman

Doing Time in American Prisons: A Study of Modern Novels
Dennis Massey

Demographics and Criminality: The Characteristics of Crime in America
Ronald Barri Flowers

TAKING CHARGE

CRISIS INTERVENTION IN CRIMINAL JUSTICE

ANNE T. ROMANO

Contributions in Criminology and Penology, Number 25
Marvin Wolfgang, *Series Adviser*

GREENWOOD PRESS
New York • Westport, Connecticut • London

Library of Congress Cataloging-in-Publication Data

Romano, Anne T.
    Taking charge : crisis intervention in criminal justice / Anne T.
Romano.
        p.   cm.—(Contributions in criminology and penology, ISSN
    0732-4464 : no. 25)
    Includes bibliographical references.
    ISBN 0-313-26890–8 (alk. paper)
    1. Police social work.   2. Assistance in emergencies.   3. Crisis
intervention (Psychiatry)   4. Leadership.   I. Title.   II. Series.
HV8079.2.R76   1990
362—dc20   89-37995

British Library Cataloguing in Publication Data is available.

Library of Congress Catalog Card Number: 89-37995
ISBN: 0-313-26890-8
ISSN: 0732-4464

First published in 1990

Greenwood Press, Inc.
88 Post Road West, Westport, Connecticut 06881

Printed in the United States of America

The paper used in this book complies with the
Permanent Paper Standard issued by the National
Information Standards Organization (Z39.48-1984).

10 9 8 7 6 5 4 3 2 1

Dedicated to the memory of

Rose Mary Rivera

CONTENTS

TABLES AND FIGURES ix

PREFACE xi

ACKNOWLEDGMENTS xv

INTRODUCTION xvii

Chapter 1   An Integrated Approach to Crisis Intervention 1

Chapter 2   Defining and Identifying Crisis 11

Chapter 3   Communication in Crisis Situations 29

Chapter 4   Crisis Intervention: Theory and Practice 49

Chapter 5   Crisis Intervention with Victims 61

Chapter 6   Specific Groups 77

Chapter 7   Victims of Violence 113

Chapter 8   Crisis Intervener Crises 157

BIBLIOGRAPHY 169

INDEX 179

TABLES AND FIGURES

TABLES

1.1 Major Conceptual Models Involved in Crises 3

2.1 Erikson's Psychosocial Stages 16

2.2 Post-Disaster Stress Behavior 22

2.3 Crisis Behavior 24

4.1 Techniques of Crisis Intervention 56

7.1 Developmental Stages 132

FIGURES

1.1 Integrated Model for Crisis Intervention 2

3.1 Communication Skills Flow Chart 32

5.1 Victimology Flow Chart 63

7.1 Playing the Game of Courtroom 145

7.2 Switching Roles in the Game of Courtroom 146

7.3 Impact of Intervener's Personal Biases and Past Experiences on Domestic Violence Incidents 152

PREFACE

The Chinese use two brush strokes to write the word "crisis." One brush stroke stands for danger; the other for opportunity. In a crisis, be aware of the danger—but recognize the opportunity.

—Richard M. Nixon

Chinese philosophy teaches that a crisis situation represents a point of choice between a fortunate and an unfortunate change. Accordingly, while the person who is caught in a crisis may indeed be in some form of danger, within that same dangerous situation there is also an opportunity to learn something about one's self and to make changes that improve one's situation. To successfully weather a crisis, therefore, it is essential to recognize the opportunity inherent in the crisis situation and utilize it as a turning point in life.

The crisis situation also presents an opportunity for persons who are employed to assist crisis victims. Crisis interveners are primarily involved in people-oriented professions, whose primary function is service. The criminal justice system is unique among the human service, people-oriented systems in that it becomes inevitably involved in the atypical and stressful events that profoundly affect all people. One important attribute of emergency response jobs within the criminal justice system is the necessity of responding immediately to crisis situations. This responsibility falls on all personnel—auxiliary police, state and local police officers, highway patrol, investigation personnel, juvenile justice agents, ambulance workers, probation officers, parole officers, corrections officers—including city, town, and county police, sheriffs' deputies, federal agents, state troopers, and others—who are actively involved in law enforcement. The responsibility to respond to crisis combined with the authority accorded them by their positions gives these officers a role set replete with crisis management potential. They are the rescuers who are called on time and time again to become involved in crisis intervention. They are the crisis interveners who are expected to take charge of situations that few others are capable of managing.

The crisis situation may represent a danger plus an opportunity for those experiencing it, according to Chinese tradition, but it also represents an opportunity for the crisis intervener who is working within the criminal justice community. The opportunity is to take charge of a situation in which the person in crisis has lost control; an opportunity to help that person toward a healthy adaptation and resolution, with a return to normal life. This approach places the crisis intervener in the position of a crisis-solving consultant or a partner who will use the least amount of control necessary for the situation yet just enough to provide help to the person in need. The goal of this intervention is to return the person to his or her prior state of functioning as quickly as possible; to take charge temporarily without "taking control" of the situation. Most people in crisis are in need of assistance, which the criminal justice crisis intervener can provide. Crisis interveners can act at the moment of crisis when people are most receptive to change. People look to the criminal justice person as a take-charge kind of person with the ability, knowledge, training, and experience to step in at times of crisis; someone who has a confident, alert, calm demeanor, yet is compassionate and understanding—necessary and valuable skills in a crisis situation. While people expect the intervener to assume control in many situations, this is particularly true in emergency situations. Knowledgeable, well-trained criminal justice interveners can transmit a special confidence that comes from professional maturity: accepting who they are and knowing what they believe. Other people sense this. Particularly during periods of confusion and doubt, people are drawn to those who seem in control.

People also look to the criminal justice person for guidance when they are involved in what they perceive as a crisis. In their opinion, the criminal justice crisis intervener has the training and experience to evaluate crisis situations as well as the ability to intervene and access the other social agencies that are available to help. In fact, the perception of criminal justice personnel in the take-charge role is itself a major factor in promoting speedy resolutions. When experiencing crisis, most people are more receptive to the intervention of someone they perceive as a helpful, authoritative figure than they would be to the intervention of others. These factors place the crisis intervener in an opportune position to effectively decrease the trauma and aftereffects of a crisis event.

However, the ability to be calm, confident, and decisive in a crisis situation is not inherited. It is the direct result of training and preparation. Therefore, an understanding of crisis theory and crisis intervention techniques is essential. Acquiring crisis intervention competence creates a greater sense of security and facilitates the safe and successful fulfillment of any crisis situation. Traditionally, the criminal justice professional has most often been the first person to be in direct contact with the individual who is experiencing a crisis situation. Criminal justice professionals are faced with the task of helping people deal with a variety of traumas, losses, and crises. The acknowledgment that they often cannot wait for a mental health professional to provide mental health services requires that the criminal justice personnel themselves be professionals in crisis counseling skills.

Crisis intervention is the process of actively intervening to influence someone's functioning during an event that may have caused disequilibrium in that person. The underlying premise is that help provided at a critical time can make the difference between an adaptive and a maladaptive resolution to change. The underlying theme of this book is that criminal justice work is "people work" and that most of the help that is requested involves assistance with stressful events in people's lives. As crisis interveners, understanding the person, the predicament, and the appropriate response can not only make our job more effective and self-satisfying but can certainly help that person toward adaptive resolution. Well-developed crisis intervention skills that include knowing what to say and how to respond are imperative. The understanding of specific crises, what causes them, how people react, and how the type of crisis may affect crisis intervention efforts will help the intervener temporarily take charge of situations for those persons while they are unable to help themselves.

ACKNOWLEDGMENTS

As the director of a crisis center located in the emergency room of a large metropolitan hospital, I was in the position to witness and interact with many people in different kinds of crises. Incorporated in this book, these crisis situations are utilized to illustrate certain points. In presenting the case histories I have tried not to intrude on the personal lives of those who have shared with me some of the most painful experiences of their lives. These pages reflect the anger and frustration as well as the rationalizations of the people who have trusted me enough to allow me to take charge of their lives for a short time, until they were able to take charge themselves. My sincerest gratitude is extended to them.

Many people have assisted me in the course of my work at the crisis center and subsequently on this book. More than anyone else, however, I am indebted to the late Rose Mary Rivera, who had enough confidence in me and my abilities to place me in my position at the crisis center. I have dedicated this book to the memory of this vibrant, energetic lady who fervently advocated for her clients and in the process turned around many a dismal, hopeless situation. Many of the individuals whose lives she impacted owe her a great debt of gratitude, as do I.

INTRODUCTION

During the past several years, social scientists and mental health practitioners have been studying the effects of crises on individuals, families, and communities. There seems to be an increasing public awareness of and support for specially victimized groups in crisis (e.g., battered women or victims of sexual assault or other crimes, disabling diseases, or natural disasters), and to develop programs dealing with uncontrollable events that come with advancing age (e.g., the "empty nest syndrome," mid-life crisis, retirement, relocation, or unemployment). There also seems to be a general understanding that it is "O.K." to have problems with changes in life that precipitate crisis. Seeking help for crisis reactions is increasingly viewed as a part of the normal life experience and is to a lesser degree than ever associated with the stigma of mental illness.

These changes in popular attitudes have been accompanied by increasing recognition within the criminal justice community of regularly occurring transitory crisis reactions, as well as crisis reactions to castastrophe, disaster, accidents, and to the violence associated with victimization. It has become clear that exposure to stressful life events that strain an individual's coping capability has negative consequences both psychologically and physically. Research studies have indicated that the degree to which someone is exposed to changes in life events is associated with the occurrence of the onset of accidents and major illnesses as well as a range of more minor medical complaints. Given the debilitating effects of exposure to stress and crises, crisis intervention training has become essential for professionals in all fields. However, the term *crisis intervention* represents varied strategies and evokes many different images. For some, the term signifies a hotline worker providing telephone counseling to individuals with a host of problems, ranging from a battered woman needing information on women's shelters to individuals with more complex emotional problems of perhaps psychotic proportions. For others, the term might bring to mind visions of a police officer attempting to defuse a hostage crisis situation, intervening in a violent marital fight, or attempting to dissuade a peer from a suicide attempt. However, in practice crisis intervention plays a major role in the jobs of many other criminal justice personnel including auxiliary police, probation or parole agents, and correctional personnel. They may be confronted by a rape victim, be the first at the scene of an accident, be called on to deliver death notices, deal with hostage situations, be confronted with child abuse victims, call at the scene of a domestic violence situation, or intervene in a potential suicide. For example, part of a probation officer's job may be to go to the home of a client to talk to a troubled teenager who has been expelled from school or is addicted to drugs. Another client may be the mother of six young children who is having difficulties coping with an abusive and alcoholic husband. Perhaps the probation officer will find it necessary to intervene in a situation in which a client is accused of sexual assualt by one of his children. A corrections officer may find himself providing crisis counseling to a prison sexual assault victim. A juvenille justice worker may intervene in a violent confrontation between two youths, or find herself providing crisis counseling to a young rape victim. Crisis intervention thus takes on different forms depending on the setting in which it occurs, who does the intervention, and whether the intervention is intended to help people deal with an ongoing crisis or help them recover from the effects of exposure to the crisis.

Crisis theorists have begun to attempt to systematically define the differences between the various types of crises and the different forms of intervention. There are certain concepts that are basic to understanding crisis behavior, however. While crisis is sometimes associated with stress, panic, catastrophe, disaster, violence, or potential violence, adherence to a philosophical model suggests that crisis may be defined as a turning point between a fortunate and an unfortunate change. In the medical world, crisis may be a turning point for better or worse in an acute disease or fever. In decision-making analysis, it is a "one-of-a-kind" situation or event.

The concept of crisis is also used by historians, sociologists, writers, political scientists, and psychologists to refer to critical events within their own particular discipline or frame of reference. For example, a political scientist or historian might use the term to refer to the economic crisis caused by an oil embargo or the international crisis precipitated by the violent overthrow of a foreign government. A sociologist might refer to the urban crisis, and a psychologist might refer to a personal crisis, indicating an emotionally significant event or radical change in a person's life. The writer may indicate the crisis as a similar point in the course of action in a play or other work of fiction. For the criminal justice worker, the term would most likely be used to refer to people who are having extreme difficulty coping with a personal problem, event, or interpersonal situation.

The first part of this book will underscore the integrated approach to crisis intervention. A multidimensional model for crisis intervention will be presented to provide the criminal justice intervener with the necessary knowledge and tools to be effective. In this day of multiple human problems and the growing awareness of the interrelationship of human service systems, mental health workers and criminal justice personnel have found the need to understand and collaborate with each other. Crisis diagnosis and mental health consultation are important concepts in the overall practical framework for handling crisis situations. For those professionals working within the community with victims of crisis, this portion of the book will assist in understanding how multiple theories of intervention in human life events are necessary in community practice.

Increasingly, people in crisis face a multitude of problems requiring multidimensional interventions. To underscore this concept, consider the following scenario: A rape victim who is brought to the hospital emergency room for medical intervention begins to exhibit erratic behavior requiring psychiatric intervention. When her family is notified of the rape, they refuse to come to her assistance because they believe she invited the attack. Furthermore, they refuse to accept her back into their home.

In this scenario the victim requires criminal justice intervention for the crime that was committed against her, medical intervention for injuries and the collection of evidence, psychiatric intervention for her emotional problems, counseling and advocacy to compensate for the absence of a support system, and social service intervention for help in securing temporary shelter and funds. In chapter 1 this multidimensional approach to crisis intervention is presented. Five major models are applied to one situation in order to clarify the approaches of the different models and at the same time help the criminal justice crisis intervener understand their perspectives. These conceptual models are the counselor, medical, psychiatric, psychological, and sociological approaches.

In chapter 2, concepts and patterns of crisis are presented. Basic to these concepts is the awareness that crisis is not an illness but rather a normal reaction to a perceived threat. There are four interrelated factors that can produce a state of crisis. These include (1) the hazardous event, (2) the vulnerable state, (3) disequilibrium, and (4) the state of active crisis. Coping mechanisms are also discussed in this section. Coping mechanisms are those aspects of ego functioning designed to sustain psychic equilibrium by regulating and controlling the intensity of anxiety-producing perceptions of real or fantasized external dangers that involve loss or threat of loss.

Individuals are considered to be in a state of crisis when faced with a threat they believe they do not have the ability to cope with effectively and for which they do not think they can get the needed help from their support system. While in this state, individuals will exhibit certain behaviors that can be quickly identified by the intervener. A two-dimensional table with five categories of crisis behavior is presented to enable quick identification. They are: tone of voice, verbal expressions, physical movement, decision-making ability, and display of confidence. Also in this chapter different typologies of crises are presented within the conceptual framework of homeostasis, stress theory, and coping. Within the typology of crisis, internal crises theories of both Freud and Erikson are juxtoposed with external crises events to illustrate the variety of possible crisis situations.

Explanations of human styles of communication and the difficulties of these styles are offered in chapter 3. Barriers to effective communication are identified as well as a number of practical methods that can be employed to improve communication skills. Basic flow charts are introduced to enhance the intervener's ability to conceptualize the complexity of the communication process and to avoid the pitfalls inherent in communication.

The same two-dimensional table with five categories of behavior that was presented in chapter 2 to identify and analyze crisis behavior is again presented in chapter 4 along with suggestions for resolving and restoring equilibrium to the person in crisis. Crisis intervention and psychological first-aid techniques are discussed and explored as ways of effectively communicating with people in crisis.

Chapter 5 focuses on communicating with victims. Victimology, the study of victim behavior, is outlined in a practical, observable fashion. This chapter focuses on the behavior and attitudes of victims and how the trauma of becoming a victim affects psychological and emotional stability. It differentiates between various types of victims and the intensity of the trauma for each. It further explains how this trauma affects the psychological and emotional stability of each victim. Chapter 5 also illustrates how several social institutions exhibit their reluctance to believe in the innocence of the victim; therefore, an explanation for the social blaming element when communicating with victims is presented.

In the second half of the book, specific groups are addressed individually. The framework already presented is used to study and understand different groups of people whose needs for crisis intervention have been previously neglected both in criminal justice practice and in the professional literature. Criminal justice interveners are committed to care for these populations by way of the humanistic traditions of their professions. The bereaved individual, the substance abuser, the suicidal person, the victim of violence, and the sexually abused are all citizens deserving of considerate and intelligent intervention. Within the chapters that deal with these target populations, the conceptual framework presented in the first half of the book will serve to present a new model of care for these groups.

Chapter 7 continues to examine target populations and the new model for treating victims of sexual abuse. Rape victims and children who are sexually abused present special needs for crisis interveners. Different styles of intervention may be essential for the successful resolution of these kinds of crises. Domestic violence situations also present a myriad of problems to the intervener. This chapter deals with crisis intervention in these types of situations.

In chapter 8 the focus will shift from the victim to the crisis intervener. While we would all like to think we are competent professionals who do the best job possible, it is also extremely difficult to be fully aware of our own crisis reactions. In this chapter, job-related stress is discussed. Due to the nature of criminal justice work, the probability of job-related stress is high. Working with people in crisis is difficult and involves emotionally draining activities. When this stress is coupled with the stress of an individual's personal life, the result can be overwhelming. Helping professionals themselves may at times need assistance to deal effectively with stress and to avoid burnout. This chapter will deal with job and personal life stress and will offer solutions for both.

While criminal justice interveners may incorporate all the assistance provided in this book, it is important to note that an individual's success will depend to a great degree on knowledge but combined with flexibility, creativity, and good judgment. With all these elements combined, the crisis situation can be treated as a challenge that can be effectively and competently met with a minimum of stress to the crisis victim and the crisis intervener.

TAKING
CHARGE

Chapter *1*

AN INTEGRATED APPROACH TO CRISIS INTERVENTION

Evidence is accumulating to indicate that knowledge of a multidimensional model for crisis intervention is imperative for the criminal justice crisis intervener. Large numbers of persons present multiple human problems along with their presenting complaints when they are referred to criminal justice agencies. These problems do not easily lend themselves to simple explanations or resolutions. In this day of multiple human problems, the growing awareness of the interrelationship of human service systems, mental health workers, medical personnel, and criminal justice personnel has resulted in the need for collaboration (figure 1.1). Along with this need to collaborate comes the need to understand the technical jargon of each of the separate disciplines, their methods of evaluation, their orientations, and their methods for determining treatment. Criminal justice people may find it difficult to understand, for example, why a psychiatrist needs so much time to evaluate a situation before selecting a treatment program. The psychiatrist may, on the other hand, be critical of the criminal justice worker's pressing need for information to solve a case while seemingly ignoring the client's mental distress.

Social workers may wonder about some of the language of criminal justice interveners. They may have difficulty understanding the relevance of some of the police procedures and the apparent insensitivity of their interviewing techniques. Criminal justice interveners, on the other hand, may be snickering at the "do-gooder" orientation of the social workers who, in their opinion, "do not know what the real world outside is like." Each of the disciplines that may intervene in a crisis situation will confront the client

Figure 1.1
Integrated Model for Crisis Intervention

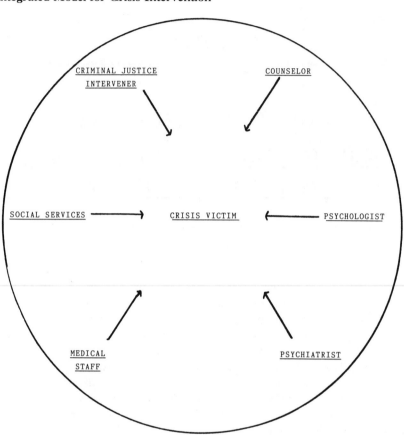

from differing perspectives, which are sometimes critical or just barely tolerant of each other. Each discipline has its own orientation, each has its own ideology or system of ideas subscribed to by the profession as a whole (table 1.1). One of the major reasons for the difficulty in understanding differing perspectives is that there is little communication or cooperation between the disciplines. While each discipline will allow the other to do its own job without interference, the lack of cooperation works as a deterrant to helping crisis victims integrate what is happening. The resulting confusion further victimizes the already overburdened victims, leaving them to coordinate their own treatment, which they are obviously unable to do for themselves.

There are five major conceptual models besides the criminal justice model that are implicitly involved in the treatment of crisis victims. These are the

Table 1.1
Major Conceptual Models Involved in Crises

	Training/Education	Responsibilities
Counselor	May have a bachelor's degree (B.A./B.S.) with some experience in his or her area of expertise (e.g., crisis, rape, sexual assault, domestic violence or elderly).	Deals with special problems under supervision. Crisis counselors provide support for victims, rape, domestic violence, elderly, and crime victims. May serve as advocates in court or police system.
Social Worker	Master of Social Work (M.S.W.) and several years of graduate training. May be state certified (C.S.W.) or Ph.D.	Trained to deal with social aspects of human problems: for example, housing, medical care, treatment of emotional problems, food stamps, or income maintenance.
Medical Staff	Medical doctors, registered nurses, and nurses aides. Specializations such as gynecologists (Gyn) for rape, gerontologists to care for the elderly.	Concerned with medical health and care of those in crisis. Physical examination, including weight, height, blood pressure, and referral for special problems.
Psychologist	Usually has a degree in education or counseling (Ph.D.). Graduate training in counseling for emotional problems and psychological testing.	Provides therapeutic intervention to establish degree of trauma to mental stability. May prescribe follow-up counseling for emotional problems.
Psychiatrist	Degree in medicine (M.D.) plus graduate training in mental health.	Trained to deal with medical problems involving mental difficulties and neurological damage. Emotional difficulties, diagnoses and treatment of inappropriate behavior symptoms and personality disorders. Can prescribe medication.

mental health advocacy model, the medical model, the psychiatric model, the psychological model, and the social model. While a person in crisis may not become involved in all five of the models presented, he or she is sure to become involved in several of them. When someone in crisis is treated, the kind of history obtained, the meaning assigned to specific historical facts, and the treatment modalities chosen depend on what model or combination of models is employed. It is important for the criminal justice intervener to have a working awareness of the differing orientations. The differing orientations are illustrated by the following case histories taken by different clinicians of the same rape victim, Mrs. Reynolds, a 55-year-old widow who was raped as she was coming home from work one evening. Mrs. Reynolds returned to the crisis center in the emergency room where she was originally treated one week after the rape, in a severe panic.

CASE HISTORY—COUNSELOR APPROACH

Client was seen at this center last week. Client reported at that time that she was walking from the bus stop to her home when she was approached by two men with knives who dragged her into their car. They drove to an isolated area and raped and sodomized her. Client has bruises and lacerations over her body. Client was seen by medical staff and interviewed by police officers in the emergency room at that time. She has returned today reporting that she has been "feeling panicky," has not been able to sleep or eat, and has not gone to work. She expresses a need for some follow-up counseling regarding her feelings of loneliness and fear. She also states that she feels confused about what to do about the police and court process. She also wishes to see a doctor about her weight loss, her inability to sleep, and the anxiety she feels.

CASE HISTORY—MEDICAL APPROACH

The patient is a 55-year-old white female, who presents with feelings of depression, distress, and desperation. States she is "unable to handle anything since her rape last week." She cannot work, is unable to concentrate, and is unable to take care of herself. She expresses that she is unable to sleep or eat, and states that she "cannot stop shaking." She appears tired, her skin is flushed and warm to touch, and her hair and dress are disheveled. Trembling noted, rambling speech, and she is unable to keep still. Her blood pressure is 150/90, pulse 125 (tachycardic), respiration 28. Her weight is 125 pounds which is 10 pounds less than at her visit last week. Her height is 5 feet and 4 inches.

CASE HISTORY—PSYCHIATRIC APPROACH

Mrs. Reynolds, a 55-year-old widow, gave a history of a depressive syndrome. Since the rape she has lost 10 pounds in weight, has early morning awakening, and has a diurnaľ variation in affect evidenced by feeling better as the day progresses. She describes feelings of helplessness, hopelessness, and worthlessness. She presents no evidence of delusions, paranoid ideation, or suicidal intent. She describes herself as having experienced periods of depression throughout her life. The patient's mother was hospitalized for depression that responded positively to electronconvulsive therapy.

CASE HISTORY—PSYCHOLOGIC APPROACH

Mrs. Reynolds, a 55-year-old widow, has been depressed since her rape one week ago. She expresses no anger about the rape. Her husband died six months ago and she states that she has not experienced any grief over his death. She expresses feelings of self-blame and self-criticism for minor events of the past and the present. Mrs. Reynolds is the youngest child in a family of five older brothers. She states that she has had similar reactions to other times in her life when she felt oppressed and suffocated. She appears to be intelligent, articulate, and motivated for treatment. She expresses a desire to understand herself better.

CASE HISTORY—SOCIAL APPROACH

Mrs. Reynolds, a 55-year-old widow, has been depressed since her rape one week ago. Unable to return to her home, she moved to another apartment in a different neighborhood. Although she feels safer in the new neighborhood, she feels isolated. Since her husband's death six months prior she has not been able to visit old friends and children because she does not drive. This situation has been aggravated since the new home increases the distance between them. She does not have access to convenient public transportation, which would enable her to stay in close contact with friends and family.

EXPLANATIONS OF THE MODELS

Counselor Approach

Counselors and advocates may be found in many areas of the social service system. Crisis counselors or rape counselors may be found in emergency rooms of hospitals, where they provide immediate support for the victim of a sexual assault or domestic dispute. They will assist the victim throughout the medical examination, providing information about what will occur in the emergency room. They also will inform the victim about the interview with police representatives and the follow-up investigation and court process. Brochures and pamphlets providing telephone numbers and other general information about available counseling services, safe houses, shelters, income maintenance, and other social services will be offered and discussed. Other counselors may be encountered in other areas, for example, follow-up counselors at victim services agencies, shelter counselors, elder abuse counselors, child care counselors and advocates, court-based victim counselors and advocates who assist the victim through the court proceedings, and family counseling groups such as Prison Family Anonymous. (This particular group is a self-help, nonprofit organization whose purpose is to help families and friends of those who have a loved one in prison or involved in the criminal or juvenile justice system. It is the intent of this organization to provide a way to keep families from facing their fears and trauma alone. Their services, therefore, include counseling, advocacy, and referrals.)

According to this approach, clients are at a vulnerable point in their lives and need assistance in assuring that their safety and health needs are met, and that they receive the necessary information and help to get them through the criminal justice maze.

Medical Approach

According to the medical model, the patient's complete physical history must be taken to determine the immediacy of the situation. Reports of presenting symptoms, weight, height, blood pressure, and pulse rate must all be registered as indices of the patient's health. Knowing the symptoms determines the treatment. In Mrs. Reynold's situation, she would be interviewed, phsycially examined, and probably referred for consultation to the psychiatric emergency room for further evaluation.

Psychiatric Approach

According to the psychiatric model, mental illnesses are diseases just like any others. For each disease there will be a cause related to the anatomy of the brain. The psychiatric clinician is concerned with etiology, signs and symptoms, diagnosis, treatment, and prognosis. While addressing the victims with proper medical respect, this clinician finds it important to remain distant so that objectivity may be maintained. In this case, the clinician observes a group of symtoms consistent with the diagnosis of endogenous depression. The current syndrome, the earlier episodes of depression, and the family history determine the diagnosis of manic-depressive illness (depressed type). Antidepressant medication or electroconvulsive treatments will be the probable course of treatment. The patient will be told that she is suffering from a depressive illness which is not uncommon in her age group, and is due to hormonal or menopausal changes. This depression has been exacebated by the rape. The illness is time-limited and, with proper treatment, it has a favorable prognosis.

Psychologic Approach

The psychological model views the early childhood relations between parent and child along with other developmental issues as causes of adult neuroses and vulnerabilities to certain stresses. As a result of these psychological determinants, patients distort reality, are prone to depression, and may, for example, avoid heterosexuality or fear success. Although outward changes may be made and drugs prescribed, the abnormality continues because the personality is abnormal.

The course of treatment would consist of therapeutic sessions with a psychologist through which events, feelings, and behaviors could be reviewed and clarified through adult eyes. The patient would be taught how to experience feelings appropriate to real-life situations. Through analysis, forgotten events that may have impacted on adult behavior will be remembered, reexperienced, and then put into their proper perspective. As a result of therapeutic treatment, growth and maturity will be achieved. Most important to this treatment is the rapport between the patient and the therapist. It is within this safe relationship that the client gains the strength to make changes.

For Mrs. Reynolds, the therapist would pay special attention to the absence of either anger about the rape or grief at the death of her husband. This has psychological meaning and is probably related to her ambivalent feelings toward her husband. Since the primary modality of treatment would be psychotherapy, there is a sense of a favorable outcome because of her intelligence and ability to articulate her feelings.

Social Approach

The social view focuses on the way in which the individual functions in the social system. Symptoms are traced not to physical illness (medical), conflicts within the mind (psychological), or manifestations of psychiatric disease (psychiatric), but rather to the relationship of the individual to the social system. Accordingly, when a socially disruptive event occurs such as a husband's death, a rape, a geographic displacement, or an economic depression, the resulting symptoms are seen as stemming from the social disorder.

Treatment would consist of either reorganizing the patient's relation to the social system or reorganizing the social system around her. The clinician, using the social model to evaulate the case, would notice that the patient's social matrix had been altered in several ways. In the first place, she has permanently lost the one person to whom she was closest. Second, because of the rape she moved to a new residence, placing herself in a situation where she lost access to those with whom she had previously related. Simultaneously, the therapist would attempt to reestablish a social field in which the patient could be comfortable. To this end, she might be encouraged to move to a house where she could have better access to her family and old friends. Likewise, the therapist might suggest a return to work to widen Mrs. Reynold's social contacts. Continued individual or group therapy might help her to acquire social skills that she might never have developed or was losing due to her fear of social contact since the rape.

POINTS TO REMEMBER

Available services. The available resources for treatment are an important determinant of the choice of conceptual model. Walk-in and emergency centers, in responding to large numbers of patients on a daily basis, approach the client from the social and biological perspectives, which usually require less time from the clinician but are effective for many crisis conditions. The psychological model requires more time and is used as a follow-up treatment modality.

Immediacy of the situation. When the cause is obvious, pressing, and immediate, first consideration is usually given to medical treatment. If a domestic violence victim is beaten or suffers some other form of physical assault, the victim must initially be treated by the medical team. She then would be seen by the social interveners so that she might begin to make changes in her social system. If a victim of a mugging or a rape victim demonstrates symptoms of psychosis, the initial mode of treatment must be the psychiatric intervention. Psychological intervention during a crisis is usually unproductive. Interview attempts by criminal justice personnel at this point would also be unsatisfactory.

Complete explanations. None of the conceptual models offers a complete explanation for the phenomena to which it addresses itself. Each model by its own definition and orientation ignores a large part of the person's life and function.

Alternative explanations. Any two conceptual models may offer alternative explanations for the same behavioral events. For example, the psychiatrist may argue that the relief of Mrs. Reynolds's panic can be obtained by the use of an antidepressant drug. Contrariwise, the social worker may contend that in undergoing social reorganization methods coupled with positive reinforcement, Mrs. Reynolds will be relieved of her panic.

Contradiction. In applying more than one conceptual model in treating a given patient, we must recognize the possibility of apparent contradictions, and, therefore, confusion to the client. For example, Mrs. Reynolds may be simultaneously prescribed medication for her anxiety and be scheduled for electroconvulsive treatment for her depression by a psychiatrist (implying a biological basis for her anxiety), be offered psychotherapy (implying that childhood experiences account for her present dysfunction), be counseled by social workers about changing residences or neighborhoods, and be thoroughly interviewed by criminal justice personnel so that the perpetrator of her rape might be caught. As a result of these contradictions, the victim receives mixed messages: "Do I feel badly because of my brain, my childhood, my social milieu, or because someone did something to me that I didn't like?"

Confidentiality. Many medical professionals will rationalize their lack of cooperation by utilizing the issue of confidentiality. This can be frustrating to someone tyring to gather as much information as possible in order to provide proper assistance. This lack of cooperation further impedes the coordination of services leaving the victims with a feeling that they have to settle for whatever they can get rather than what is rightfully theirs.

Referral. While criminal justice personnel will always refer the crisis victim to medical assistance, the reverse referral does not always occur. Some medical personnel are reluctant to get involved when there is a suggestion of criminal activity or when the situation may warrant law enforcement investigation and intervention. Again, this lack of cooperation is a detriment for the person who is in need of total crisis intervention services.

The conceptual problems described in this chapter reflect limitations that exist in the total picture of crisis behavior and crisis intervention. It is unfortunate that the conceptual models have remained so separate from each other. To the degree that this occurs, communication between professionals treating crisis situations is impaired, progress is slowed, and the victim, who is at the center of all this, is shortchanged. Whereas human beings are simultaneously biological organisms, psychological beings, and members of social systems, a comprehensive integrated set of guidelines that incorporate all these conceptual models fails to exist. The test of a skilled criminal justice crisis intervener is the assemblage and integration of the separate orientations. To accomplish this best, the crisis intervener should be aware of the various conceptual models that are likely to intervene at the same time, and be knowledgable of their orientation, the terminology unique to their discipline, the different evaulation techniques, and each treatment modality. The proper attention to each of the different disciplines that impact on the victim's life is essential to the resolution of a crisis.

SUMMARY

In this chapter the conceptual models that are implicit in crisis intervention have been identified and discussed. The five conceptual approaches commonly used are the mental health advocate or counseling, the biological or medical, the psychiatric, the psychological, and the social. Some of the variables that determine the choice of approach include the ideology of the clinician, the diagnosis, the effectiveness of available treatments, available services, and the immediacy of the situation. By recognizing the various approaches utilized, the decision-making process can become more rational, a broader range of treatment modalities can be made available, and communication between practitioners can be enhanced. The test of the skillful crisis intervener is the understanding of each of the models and the integration of all to achieve an effective, multidimensional model of treatment for the person in crisis.

Chapter *2*

DEFINING AND IDENTIFYING CRISIS

Once a situation is identified as being of a crisis nature, the intervener is faced with the task of effectively dealing with it. Crisis situations have certain important similarities. First, one or more highly emotional persons are likely to be involved, although the particular emotions expressed will vary according to the type of crisis and the personalities and cultural diversity of the persons involved. In order for the intervener to deal effectively with highly emotional people, the next important step will be to calm them down. Calming an aggressive, confused, or hysterical person is often a difficult task. Such persons, however, must be calmed, not only for their own comfort, but also to permit the intervener to get on with the job of resolving the crisis and restoring order. Once they are calmed, the important task of gathering relevant information can be started so that appropriate action can be taken. In the second part of this chapter a behavioral analysis chart is presented that illustrates the kinds of behavior precipitated by the stress of the crisis situation. Analyzed and presented are the five variables that can be used to make a quick diagnosis of behavior exhibited in a crisis call: tone of voice, verbal expression, physical movement, decision-making abilities, and display of confidence. These are easily discernible behaviors that the crisis intervener will have little problem identifying.

Understanding the primary behavioral principles in crisis situations and utilizing the procedures of the crisis intervention technique aid effective intervention. The steps of this technique are as follows:

- Identify the crisis situation;
- Calm any highly emotional persons;
- Gather the needed information, even under difficult circumstances;
- Take appropriate crisis-reducing action; and
- Restore order.

FLOW OF CRISIS

The best definition of a crisis comes from *Webster's Third New International Dictionary of the English Language.* It defines crisis as a psychological or social condition characterized by unusual instability and caused by excessive stress. It either endangers or is felt to endanger the continuity of the individual or his or her group. What generally happens to an individual undergoing a crisis can be conceptualized as follows: A state of previous equilibrium in an individual or a family's life is disrupted by an internal or external event, which disturbs the equilibrium in some way (a hazard is experienced) and results in a rise in tension in reaction to the impact of stress. The person experiences a sense of confusion and upset, he or she is bewildered and wonders what is happening, why it is happening, and how a situation so far beyond his or her usual experience can be resolved. Feelings of panic are not unusual. This disequilibrium is followed by a period of attempted resolution. During this period, habitual problem-solving mechanisms are attempted, and all resources are mobilized to deal with the situation. In the case of a divorce, the person may seek out friends for emotional support or validation. In the case of a disaster, the person may selectively perceive the situation in a more favorable light. If successful, such individuals are likely to resume functioning once more at the pre-crisis level, and in some cases will move into a growth adjustment phase. If unsuccessful, however, the person is likely to move into a decompensated adjustment phase. This phase may be characterized by withdrawal, depression, guilt, apathy, anxiety, anger, or any number of extreme psychological consequences.

Some people involved in a crisis may resolve their crisis by a general discharge of anger directed at the cause of their anguish and may thus reach some functional agreement, resolving their problem within the time it takes to make the call for help and the arrival of assistance. For other victims, it may not be so simple. As we know, certain circumstances might produce a crisis in some people and not in others. Whether change is good or bad depends on how it is experienced. Even Hans Selye, who developed the GAS model (for further information on the General Adaptation Syndrome, see chapter 8), has stated that certain kinds of stress, which he called *eustress*, are good for people. In addition, each person has a certain repertoire of responses or ways of dealing with situations including those of crisis proportions. The type of response is determined by the person's type, physical health, and personality. Some people actually are tougher than others in dealing with major problems. These types are also stronger when dealing with frustration. Various other factors may affect coping behavior to the trauma, namely, ego strength, social network support such as the influence of significant others, and the ways they are treated as victims. Other variables that determine the type of response may be the type of situation the person is in, or the type of crime the person experienced and the amount of aggression contained therein.

Another characteristic of a crisis is its recognizable stages. These proceed from the initial impact, with its highly charged emotions, through a recoil stage of denial, to a resolution stage where some type of solution or accommodation is found.

The following are a number of dimensions or characteristics that have been identified as occurring in a crisis:

Need for action. It is a situation in which the requirements for actions are high among participants, yet the ability to cope with the event is lowered.

Goals and objectives. It usually threatens the goals and objectives of those involved and is followed by an outcome whose consequences shape the future of the participants.

Loss of control. Once caught in a crisis, reduced control over the events and the effects of these events as well as heightened urgency often produce stress.

Time element. The crisis is acute rather than chronic, although its length is usually unspecified and limited.

Perception of crisis. There may be some difficulty in identifying and defining a crisis because what is a crisis event to one person may not be experienced as such to another.

Coping ability. Overall, a crisis is any event that reduces an individual's ability to cope with a given situation.

Opportunity. Crisis may also consist of a convergence of events that result in a new set of circumstances presenting an opportunity for change and growth.

People will request and accept assistance more readily when they are in a crisis situation, particularly if they have trust and confidence in the person offering help. The degree to which they will accept help is also dependent on the amount of distress they feel and the level of helplessness and loss of control they are experiencing. In terms of concepts of balance and equilibrium, it is known that a person in crisis will do whatever is necessary to restore the former state of equlibrium. This makes the acceptance of outside help easier and the cooperation needed for a quick resolution of the problem more readily available. Thus, the course that a crisis takes may be diagrammed in this way:

Equilibrium → Disorganization → Resolution → Equilibrium restored

Most people live their lives in some degree of homeostasis or equilibrium with accompanying stability. Homeostasis describes a physiological balance of the organism while stability describes a balance in behavior. Although daily problems contain stressors that create stressful situations, under usual circumstances, the person's emotional and physiological equilibrium returns to its previous level. Humans may be viewed as part of a complex adaptive system with a homeostatic or balanced nature. Equilibrium requires the presence of both physiological homeostasis and behavioral stability. An imbalance of either one destroys the steady state. In a crisis, either one may be absent; at times, both are disrupted.

Crises may be precipitated by disruptions in homeostasis caused by internal or external events. In the following pages these kinds of disruptions will be discussed and ways in which they cause an imbalance to physiological and behavioral states will be identified.

TYPOLOGY OF CRISES

Crisis experts have identified two main types of crises: the internal or maturational crisis of the life cycle, and the external or situational crisis. The first type is a threat involving the possible loss of a source of needs satisfaction, or a threat to one's stability or equilibrium. This may be a threat of loss of a loved object or person or the loss of equilibrium that accompanies transitional stages and life changes. This loss would result in the loss of self-gratification that was accomplished through the particular person, thing, or stage of life. The second type of crisis is not the threat of loss, but the loss itself. This may occur when one actually loses an object, a loved person, or a source of gratification, or when one loses integrity or belongings, or becomes injured.

Internal Crises

It was Sigmund Freud's theory of psychosexual development and, later, Erik Erikson's concept of the eight stages of psychosocial development in the human life cycle, that provided the theoretical base for analyzing developmental or maturational crises. Freud posited that human individuals pass through various psychosexual stages of development that correspond to the maturational stage of their bodies at various times in their lives. Each state is associated with a unique crisis of some kind. The first crisis is obviously birth, when one is thrust out into the world and becomes dependent on others for basic needs. The stages that follow are the oral stage, the anal stage, the phallic stage, and the latency stage. If specific needs are not satisfied during each stage the residue will remain locked away in the unconscious mind and resurface in adulthood by way of behavioral problems such as depression, dependency, schizophrenia, or hostility. Not receiving enough oral gratification during the oral stage will result in adult symptoms of depression or schizophrenia. Too much gratification usually results in overdependence on others. During the anal stage, the child's major source of pleasure shifts from activities surrounding feeding to those surrounding toilet training. If there was conflict between the child and the caretaker over toilet training, the child might become a hostile, rigid, and miserly adult. Thus, later personality development is influenced by what happends psychologically during these periods.

In contrast to Freud's psychosexual stages, Erikson conceptualized personality development as a succession of differentiated phases, through which one must pass on the way to complete maturity. Each of Erikson's psychosocial stages is characterized by its own type of crisis or conflict. Erikson saw these crises as being the eight great tests of human character. Typically there are two opposing tendencies operating at the time of each crisis. One tendency is negative in that it tends to retard development, while the other tendency is positive and promotes healthy growth. The crisis at each stage is resolved when the relative balance between the two tendencies swings either to the positive or to the negative pole. Out of these crises grow the strengths that people need in order to mature and survive in a healthy fashion.

Between each phase and the next, periods of transition are characterized by disorganized behavior. The person may be aware of minor mood swings as well as fluctuating emotions and thoughts. The solution from the previous phase is then applied to the next phase. Erikson's theory emphasizes the relationship between a person's social development and social environment. He also emphasizes the normal aspect of the stages of development. For example, he goes into considerable detail in describing the normal identity crises in the adolescent developmental crisis phase, stating that the phase includes multiple, increased conflicts with which the person must deal concurrently. Identity crises actually can arise at any point in life from the need to make decisions involving career choices, marriage, and involvement in political, social, and religious groups. Eventually a person arrives at some acceptable balance between personal identity (how we view ourselves) and social identity (what perception tells us about what others expect and how we are judged).

Erikson identifies these eight major developmental crises in terms of the tasks that must be resolved in each phase. In the following table, Erikson's psychosocial stages are presented along with the corresponding conflict of each stage, and a description of how the conflict should be resolved. For comparison, the Freudian stages are identified alongside the corresponding Eriksonian stages (table 2.1).

Internal or developmental crises are expected events occurring normally to most individuals in the course of their life span. Because they are expected,

Table 2.1
Erikson's Psychosocial Stages

Ages	Conflict	Accomplishment	Freudian Stage
0-18 mo.	Basic trust vs. mistrust	If child's needs are met with support, nurturance and love, child develops basic trust. If not, misturst develops.	Oral
1-3 yrs .	Autonomy vs. shame or doubt	Child develops bladder and bowel control and a healthy attitude about independence and self-sufficiency. Criticisms of independence cause shame and doubt to develop.	Anal
3-5 yrs.	Initiative vs. guilt	Child discovers ways to initiate own actions. If successful, guilt is avoided.	Phallic
6-14 yrs.	Industry vs. inferiority	Child learns competency, especially with peers. Failure results in feelings of inferiority.	Latency
12-17 yrs.	Identity vs. role confusion	Adolescent develops a sense of role identity. Must choose vocation and' life career.	Genital
Young adult	Intimacy vs. isolation	Close friendships and relationships with opposite sex are important. Otherwise feelings of isolation persist.	
Middle Adulthood	Generativity vs. stagnation	Helping and guiding the next generation is useful. Teaching or leading girl or boy Scouts may be ways to help for childless persons .	
Later Adulthood	Ego integrity vs. despair	Person reviews his or her life. If the life was well spent the person will have a sense of integrity. If not, he or she will suffer despair.	

an individual should have the opportunity during development to prepare for these events; however, most often because of the lack of proper identification of crises, people do not know they are in crisis until they are experiencing it. Mastery of these internal crises plays a large part in determining the ego strength of the individual. Coping skills are usually tried and tested to deal with the various maturational tasks. For example, in our culture adolescence is considered by many to be a period of conflict and stress. It is a time of changes, when self-concept and attitudes may alter considerably. Adolescents must also deal for the first time with sexual relationships, the choice of a career, political decisions, economic alternatives, and a host of other adult tasks. Erikson points out that during adolescence there is an important struggle to establish an identity, and to develop an acceptable, functional, and stable self-concept. Those who succeed will establish a sense of identity, and those who fail will suffer role confusion. With so many major conflicts and decisions to face, is it any wonder that for adolescents the journey from puberty to adulthood is turbulent and filled with conflict? For many adolescents the journey is a rocky one, while others never make it through those years. Some adolescents may cope in healthy ways, while others may cope by withdrawing through alcohol and drugs. Some make the final withdrawal by committing suicide. Since 1964, the rate of suicide among adolescents and young adults of ages 15 to 24 has more than doubled. It is during these turbulent years that many adolescents come to the attention of criminal justice agencies.

External Crises

A crisis may also occur when an unexpected traumatic external event is effective in disrupting the balance between a person's internal adaptation or homeostatic state and the environment. With few exceptions, people exposed to plane crashes, automobile accidents, explosions, ship and train wrecks, fires, earthquakes, tornadoes, sexual assaults, or other terrifying experiences show psychological shock reactions or some form of personality disintegration. The symptoms may vary greatly, depending on the nature and severity of the terrifying experience, the degree of the surprise, and the personality make-up of the individual. Reactions are painful, disruptive, and dysfunctional. Over half the survivors of the disastrous Cocoanut Grove nightclub fire, which took the lives of 492 people in Boston in 1942, required treatment for severe psychological shock (Adler, 1943). Similarly, when two commuter trains collided in Chicago in 1972, leaving 44 persons dead and over 300 injured, the tragedy also filled survivors with feelings of fear, anxiety, and guilt; more than 80 of them attended a voluntary session with psychiatrists (Uhlenhuth, 1973). The trauma of a natural disaster may also cause long-standing psychological scars. Adams and Adams (1984) reported that residents of a small town in Seattle, Washington, located near Mount

St. Helens, showed long-term psychological disorders as a result of the May 1980 violent eruption, volcanic flow, ash fall, and flooding.

Two examples from shipwrecks illustrate this syndrome further; the 1912 sinking of the *Titanic* and the 1956 collision of the luxury liner *Andrea Doria* with the Swedish liner *Stockholm* a few miles off Nantucket Island. In a report on the *Titanic* disaster, which took the lives of 1,503 persons, W. Lord (1955) stated that the terror-stricken survivors who were fortunate enough to secure lifeboats refused to let swimmers aboard, even though the boats were only half full. Boat occupants beat off the struggling swimmers with oars, and only 1 of 18 lifeboats returned to the scene to help others. Taking advantage of the law of the sea—"women and children first"—at least one man donned a dress in an attempt to save himself.

Another insightful account of the psychological reactions to catastrophes in the water was published by two psychiatrists who were on a rescue ship to the *Andrea Doria* sinking (Friedman and Linn, 1957) in which 52 persons died and 1,600 were rescued. They noted that the survivors appeared sedated; they moved extremely slowly; were passive, compliant, suggestible, emotionless, and showed amnesia concerning facts and personal information. After some time had passed, many of the survivors exhibited a preoccupation with the tragedy and a compulsive need to tell the story of the collision over and over with identical details and emphasis.

It also appears that one does not have to be a direct victim of a catastrophe to exhibit psychological problems. An observer or a rescue worker can also be affected. The collapse of the Hyatt Regency Hotel skywalk in Kansas City in July 1981 during a dance was one such event. It was estimated that some 2,000 people were present when skywalk bridges at the second and fourth levels collapsed, cascading an estimated 65 tons of steel and concrete onto the lobby floor, killing 114 people, and injuring 200 others. C. B. Wilkinson (1983) surveyed victims, observers, and rescuers in a follow-up study some five months later. Virtually all the subjects exhibited psychological symptoms, and only slight differences were observed among the victims, the observers, and the rescuers.

The Disaster Syndrome

The typical response to a catastrophe is called the "disaster syndrome" (Raher, Wallace, and Rayner, 1956; Wallace, 1956). It consists of three succeeding stages, or reactions, experienced by many survivors of such catastrophes. This syndrome is described in terms of the reactions during the traumatic experience, the initial reactions after it, and the complications that may be long-lasting or arise later—the chronic or delayed posttraumatic stress.

The initial responses typically involved the shock stage, the suggestible stage, and the recovery stage.

Shock stage. Individuals are stunned, dazed, and apathetic. They are frequently unaware of the extent of personal injuries and tend to wander aimlessly until guided or directed by someone else. They are unable to make more than minimal efforts to help either themselves or others. In extreme cases, they may be stuporous, disoriented, and amnesic regarding the event.

Suggestible stage. Individuals tend to be passive, suggestible, and willing to take directions. The survivors emerge from the state of shock and discover that although the danger may be over, life remains to be faced. Emotionality, ranging from sobbing and giggling to anger, hostility, irritability, and feelings of hopelessness, frequently results. Individuals often will express extreme concern over the welfare of others involved in the incident and attempt to be of assistance. Their behavior tends to be inefficient, however, even in the performance of routine tasks. During this stage, lamentations or tears are seldom seen unless physical injury is present. Sometimes, even with injuries, some victims may be unaware of the extent and seriousness of their physical condition.

Recovery stage. Individuals may be tense and apprehensive and show generalized anxiety concerning the memories of the horrifying experience. Sleeplessness, nightmares, and a need to repetitively tell about the catastrophic event are common. Intense emotional upsets, anxiety, and hypersensitivity are frequently seen.

These unexpected life events are usually chance events and unpredictable from the point of view of the person effected. It is the element of unpreparedness that triggers the crisis potential and reduces the person's control or mastery in the situation. In some cases, complications may enter because of feelings of grief and depression. Where the individual feels that personal inadequacy contributed to the loss of loved ones, the situation may be further complicated by strong feelings of guilt, and the posttraumatic stress may extend for a period of months. This pattern is demonstrated in the following example of an automobile accident in which an infant is seriously injured. The mother of the child, who was driving the car, might be exhibiting various behaviors. She might be calm and collected, she might be dazed and unresponsive, or she might be crying, screaming, or physically uncontrollable. No matter what the behavior, it represents her reaction to the crisis event and her way of coping with the overwhelming input of stress. Her behavior in a short period of time could and probably will change as she gradually adjusts to the accident. However, if her guilt about the accident produces stress with which she can not deal, anything said to her may affect her adjustment either adversely or favorably. Saying to her, "Would you like to give me your vehicle registration?" or "Would you like us to notify someone?" are favorable questions which are not inflammatory. On the other hand, "Why did you go through that red light?" or "Why was this baby riding in the front seat?" are adverse questions that can increase the guilt that the woman already feels, causing additional stress. This type of questioning may infer that she is to blame, making it more difficult for her to eventually adjust to the accident and its aftereffects.

Months later, this mother may be depressed and bored, have frightening dreams, and become easily confused and irritated. In some instances, the guilt of the survivor seems to center around the feeling that he or she did not deserve to survive the accident. This is called a posttraumatic stress reaction, and may include the following symptoms: (a) anxiety, varying from mild apprehension to episodes of acute anxiety commonly associated with situations that recall the traumatic experience; (b) chronic tension and irritability, often accompanied by fatigability, insomnia, and the inability to tolerate noise; (c) repetitive nightmares reproducing the traumatic incident directly or symbolically; (d) complaints of impaired concentration and memory; and (e) feelings of depression. In some cases, the individual may withdraw from social contact and avoid exciting experiences—such as avoiding interpersonal involvement, losing sexual interest, and requiring peace and quiet.

Characteristics of External Crises

An external or situational crisis has the following characteristics:

Sudden and unexpected. A crisis event can be any event that occurs suddenly; it interrupts normal life events, it is unpredictable, and it is arbitrary. The impact is unexpected; there is no warning. If, for example, a person knows he will unavoidably lose a great deal of money in his business this year or that his spouse will die of cancer within the next six months, he can be psychologically prepared for these events to some extent. The stress that will occur will not be sudden. However, if his spouse dies suddenly or he looses all his money in a burglary, he may experience a serious crisis because of the suddenness of the events.

Unpredictability. Unpredictable events usually cause a sudden psychological reaction. Events such as accidents, death, crimes perpetrated against the subject, and disasters are unpredictable events that interrupt normal lives and block some of life's pursuits.

Arbitrary. Such events may also be arbitrary. When one feels that an event occurred without apparent reason, is unfair, or defies an explanation, such an event is considered arbitrary. For example, a heavy object may fall from a high building and kill one pedestrian walking in a crowd. Why is that particular person harmed and others left unscathed?

Coping Mechanisms

When an event occurs that causes a sudden input of psychological stress, individuals will use whatever kinds of coping strategies are available to them. Everyone, when faced with a threat either internal or external, has a certain repertoire of responses or ways to deal with the situation. The type of repertoire will be determined by personality, frame of reference, and cultural background. A crisis occurs when a person faces a difficulty, either a threat of loss or a loss, in which his or her existing coping repertoire is insufficient, and he or she therefore has no immediate way of handling the stress.

When faced with stressful situations, people will attempt to problem-solve through a mechanism called coping. They may work out a way of dealing with their problems before they are over. They may try all kinds of things that were not tried before, in order to see whether they can handle the events. Coping strategies are immediate efforts employed by people attempting to meet and overcome the demands inherent in stressful situations. We have three basic choices for coping directly at our disposal: confrontation, compromise, and withdrawal. Some individuals can meet a situation head-on and intensify their efforts to get what they want (confrontation). This type of person may attempt to deal directly with the situation by appraising it and then doing something to change or avoid it. The response may consist of behaviors such as directly attacking the source of the stress (a burglar, purse snatcher, pickpocket, mugger, rapist, or other assaulter). Confrontation usually includes some expressions of anger. Another type of person may give up some of what he or she wants and perhaps persuade others to give up part of what they want as well (compromise). Compromise is one of the most common ways of coping directly with frustration or conflict. This response may lead a victim to offer something in exchange for not being physically hurt. Another type of individual may admit defeat and stop fighting (withdrawal). In some circumstances this is the most effective way of coping with stress. If one realizes that the adversary is the more powerful or perceives that there is no way to alter the situation or reach a compromise, and that any form of aggression would be self-destructive, withdrawal is a realistic adjustment to the situation. In seemingly hopeless situations, such as disasters, some people will give up, believing that there is nothing that they can do to save themselves. If the situation is in fact hopeless, resignation may indeed be the most effective way of coping.

APPLICATIONS TO CRIMINAL JUSTICE

Although research studies generally support the belief that severe stress and the crises of life changes can result in psychological disturbances, what is the impact of these disturbances on the criminal justice system? When Mount St. Helens erupted on Sunday morning, May 18, 1980, several local residents were killed, and the force of the explosion and the subsequent lava flow caused miles of destruction to vegetation and wildlife. In addition, the disaster sent tons of ashes throughout Washington, Oregon, and Idaho. In many communities, the ash fall was so heavy that it blotted out the sun, leaving residents in total darkness. This catastrophic situation placed a large number of people in the surrounding area of Washington State at great risk

Table 2.2
Post-Disaster Stress Behavior

Categories of Change	Increased Statistics
Marital and family problems	Increase in total of divorces filed, child-abuse reports investigated. police calls for domestic violence, juvenile court referrals.
Alcohol abuse	Increase in total of clients served in community alcohol program, citations issued for driving while intoxicated, other alcohol-related tickets or arrests, rate of auto accidents; police tests for intoxication ("breathalyzer").
Aggression and violence	Increase in police calls, criminal bookings, criminal cases opened in Superior Court.
Adjustment problems	Increase in psychiatric commitment investigations caseloads, mental health appointments, crisis-line calls.
Illnesses	Increase in total patient clinic contacts, hospital emergency room visits, sick leave, death rate, welfare caseload, absenteeism, diagnoses of illness aggravated by stress, diagnoses of mental illness.

for property loss and loss of life for a period of time following the eruption. Two researchers conducted a field study of the disaster to evaluate post-traumatic stress disorder (Adams and Adams, 1984). They defined the post-disaster period as the seven-month period following the disaster, and the identical seven-month period of the preceding year as the predisaster period. A comparison of satistics for both periods revealed that following the eruption, cases of mental illness increased by nearly 236 percent, psychosomatic illness increased by 219 percent, and stress-aggravated illness increased by 198 percent. The researchers concluded that a disaster of this sort is likely to increase not only physical and psychosomatic illness, but also alcohol-related problems, aggression and violence, and domestic violence incidents (table 2.2).

These statistics are understandable in light of a catastrophe such as the Mount St. Helens disaster, but internal life crises also increase the chances of criminal justice intervention. In adolescent rehabilitation environments and juvenile homes, counselors find themselves facing one crisis after another. Knowledge of the life span developmental stages, what can be expected of each life stage, and the factors that may affect people at each maturational level is helpful in providing crisis intervention and counseling.

IDENTIFYING CRISIS BEHAVIOR

Crisis reactions (i.e., feelings and behavior) may appear in any combination. The criminal justice crisis intervener will hear people say that they are experiencing feelings of:

Chaos	"Things are falling apart."
Confusion	"I can't seem to make a decision."
Helplessness	"I can't help myself."
Dependency	"Please tell me what to do."

Characteristic crisis behavior patterns will also be evident in various combinations, such as:

Regression	Reverting to childlike behavior.
Disruption of basic Functions	Failing to eat, sleep, and so forth.
Denial	Behaving as if nothing has happened.
Repression	"I can't remember anything."
Mistrust	"I don't trust anybody to help me."

In terms of behavior, the following table describes observable crisis behavior. Five different variables are utilized for this purpose (see table 2.3). Some persons may be overactive when in crisis, while others may be underactive. The behavior of each type is described. It is important to remember at this point that people become emotionally disturbed during crisis periods, but the anxiety, agitation, depression, tension, and anger and hostility are not to be confused with the symptoms of psychiatric illness, which they may superficially resemble. They are the signs of an active internal struggle that is in process within an individual who is attempting to solve problems and return to homeostasis.

Included in this table are the pitfalls to successful crisis resolution. These behavioral patterns are sometimes seen in crisis interveners who have gotten caught up in the contagiousness of crisis situations. Needless to say, they are examples of behavior to be avoided by the crisis intervener.

Tone of Voice

The tone of voice may be the first indication that someone is experiencing a crisis event. People tend to speak faster when under stress, causing speech disturbances such as missed words, stuttering, and mispronunciation of commonly used words. There may also be a quivering in the voice, or a break in the voice indicating heightened emotions. Other signs may include ex-

Table 2.3
Crisis Behavior

	TONE OF VOICE	VERBAL EXPRESSIONS	PHYSICAL MOVEMENTS	DECISION MAKING	DISPLAY OF CONFIDENCE
(Crisis Victim) **OVER-STIMULATED BEHAVIOR**	Demanding Rapid speech Missing words Quivering with emotion Breaking of voice Faltering Smacking of lips Searching for words Sputtering	Yelling and screaming Stuttering Unable to articulate Cursing Referring to God Reverting to wnd language Argumentative Uncontrolled weeping	Aimless Running around Waving arms Hitting Trembling Grabbing Perspiring Nausea/vomiting Mild diarrhea Frequent urination Pounding heart Hysteria	Indecision "What should I do?" Shifting of decisions "Maybe I should..." "Should I have?" Irrational decision making	Lack of confidence Sensitive Questioning of prior decisions Self-blame "Why me?" "What next?" Loss of judgement Blindness to reality
UNDER-STIMULATED BEHAVIOR	Shock Numbness Hesitancy Unemotional Very strained	Vacant expressions Emotionless Little or no response to questioning Fear Anxiety	Inability to stand or sit Immobility Moves slowly Catatonic Unaware of surroundings	Don't care attitude Unable to be decisive Can't make choices	Puzzled Confused cannot take responsibility without supervision Helpless
(Crisis Intervener)	Blame Ridicule Telling him to "Snap out of it" Arguing "You're acting abnormal" "You shouldn't feel that way"	Complete silence Shouting Use of jargon Use of codes "This guy sounds bad" Jokes Humor	Threatening posture Strutting Rolling of eyes Negative shaking of head Folded arms "It's all in your head"	Inappropriate assumptions False expectations Negative first impressions	Shifting of role Placing blame Unnecessary officious behavior

DISORGANIZATION AND CONTAGIOUS BEHAVIOR

PITFALLS TO SUCCESSFUL RESOLUTION

cessive amounts of lip and tongue movement, faltering, hesitancy, and searching for words.

At the other extreme and not to be ignored is the person who is very unemotional. This person may be restrained while relaying information that would ordinarily evoke more anxious responses. The voice may sound detached, as though the person does not care about the incident; however, this is just a defensive response to the overwhelming stress that the person is actually experiencing. Behaviors the crisis intervener should avoid include ridiculing the person or blaming him or her. Telling people in crisis to "Snap out of it," or that "You shouldn't feel that way," will not help them resolve their feelings.

Verbal Expressions

People caught in the grips of a crisis may verbalize in many different ways. They may yell and scream, cursing at everyone and everything including the person offering help. They may refer to or call on God to help them, or they may even revert to a native language that may be foreign to the intervener who is trying to help them. This type of behavior occurs because of the sudden, unpredictable nature of crisis, which initiates a regressive process. In an effort to restabilize the self psychologically, emotionally, and physically, individuals will regress to the point of their development in which they found satisfaction or felt most comfortable. This is the defense mechanism of regression at work. If the regressive process does not find a workable frame of reference, the victim may not be able to articulate what has happened. In some cases a victim may even regress to a silent, catatonic state and be incapacitated. The regressive element of a crisis situation is contagious. The responding intervener should be aware of this contagious element of the crisis event and avoid getting caught up in attempting to overshout the person. When someone is very angry, or very anxious and confused, he or she will usually be tuned in to his or her own feelings of the moment, and will often be unresponsive and unaware of the attempts of others to communicate. The intervener may find him- or herself repeating questions in order to "get through."

The crisis intervener who does not understand the various verbal expressions that are a response to crisis may tend to respond to hostile expressions by being too harsh in return. Other responses may be to lean too hard on the victim, pressing for information in an attempt to overshout and/or outcurse. The purpose is therefore defeated, and attempts to calm the person, get the required information, and resolve the crisis are unsuccessful. The intervener has then in fact gotten caught up in the contagiousness of the crisis situation, and the opposite goal may occur. The disturbance level may then increase, and threats and expressions of anger directed at the intervener may become more plausible.

Physical Movement

In terms of physical movement, the victim may be running around, waving arms, grabbing, or hitting, or conversely may be catatonic (i.e., frozen in an immobilized state). Victims may be trembling and feel very cold. In terms of physiological response they may perspire, feel nauseous or vomit, experience diarrhea or frequent urination, talk about a pounding heart that "feels like it's going to jump out of my chest," or be hysterical.

Whatever reasonable actions are needed to prevent injury or further harm to the victim should be undertaken. The victim is quite vulnerable to influences, negative as well as positive, at this point. Positive, helpful advice on the part of the crisis intervener will be readily accepted; however, negative responses such as shouting, rolling the eyes in disgust, impatience, or shaking the head can cause further victimization. Body language and facial expressions conducive to listening and empathy will assure the successful resolution of the crisis.

Decision-Making Abilities

To expect a victim to make sound and rational decisions is asking too much of the person caught in a crisis. Rather, what is more likely to be observed is a shifting of behavior. The person in crisis is not able to make decisions, and will ask, "What should I do?" The underactive crisis victim may adapt an uncaring attitude and appear confused. Responding interveners should avoid making inappropriate assumptions based on first impressions. To help the crisis victim overcome the physical and/or psychological trauma, the intervener should be decisive and firm. Those decisions made on the behalf of the crisis victim should be objective and considerate of their psychological effect. In addition, consideration could be given at this time to allowing the victim to make inconsequential decisions. The process of making simple decisions will help the victim regain the decision-making ability that was lost in the reactions to the crisis.

Display of Confidence

The nature of fact finding, information gathering, and report writing has a "blaming element" inherent in it; therefore, be aware that the crisis victim lacks self-confidence and will be sensitive to any display of blame. Crisis victims tend to question their previous decisions and will blame themselves for what has happened. What may be heard is an emotional questioning of the actions that led to the crisis: "Why me?" "What next?" "Why didn't I stay home?" "Why was I out so late?" "I should have locked the door." and so on.

Sometimes persons may exhibit guilt feelings for the incident, placing the blame on some past behavior for which they are being "repaid." Victims may make statements such as "I know. I'm being repaid for what I did to Helen!" or ask "What did I do to deserve this? . . . I was good. I go to church on Sunday. Why me?" and "I do the right thing for everyone; I didn't deserve this."

The underactive victim may appear puzzled, confused, and helpless. In these situations, an unprepared crisis intervener in an effort to gain control and initiate orderly behavior may shift from a helping role to a blaming role by responding to these questions. In fact, given the nature of crisis, there are no answers.

The crisis state presents complicated problems for the intervener. Most of the situations in which criminal justice personnel become involved are direct cries for help made by people who may be experiencing a critical, crucial moment in their lives. Even if a person properly adjusts to a crisis incident, its effect is indelibly imprinted on the psyche, as the event will never be forgotten. Proper adjustment to these permanent impressions and the incident itself will depend on the kind of help people in crisis receive at the onset of their trauma.

Most of these crisis moments concern actual occurrences. Unfortunately, others may be imagined or completely false. In either case, many of the persons simply require some sort of assistance in coping with a problem. These problems may at times seem very insignificant for the crisis intervener, but to the persons involved they are very real. The help needed may just be a kind word or a sympathetic ear; however, if rendered properly and to the best of the intervener's ability, it will be a job well done.

SUMMARY

In this chapter the research and clinical development in the field of crisis was presented. The definition of crisis as a change in life situation, in which there is a problem that cannot be solved through the usual coping strategies and that therefore upsets the subject's equilibrium, is offered. If the homeostatic balance is offset, the disruption in life style is termed a crisis. A typology of crises is presented to include developmental crises that are the internal tasks to be mastered as one progresses through the life cycle, and external crises that consist of situational events, unanticipated events, and victim events.

Chapter *3*

COMMUNICATION IN CRISIS SITUATIONS

It may seem unusual that a person whose professional career is devoted to criminal justice work should be interested in problems of communication. What relationship is there between providing crisis intervention in the criminal justice world and the business of communication? Actually, the relationship is very close. The whole task of crisis intervention is the task of communicating with people. People in crisis are in difficulty because communication within themselves and with others has broken down and they are unable to make any rational decisions. Consequently, there are distortions in the way they communicate with themselves and others. The task of crisis intervention is to help the persons achieve—with the assistance of the crisis intervener—equilibrium within themselves so that they can resume their normal activities.

In this chapter, basic communication theory is presented along with some of the major factors that block or impede communication, particularly in crisis situations. Once the communication problems are identified, some important ways of improving or facilitating communication will be presented. To illustrate the need for this chapter, consider the following scenario.

Two sex crimes detectives are leaving an initial interview with a rape victim. One turns to the other and states: "I don't believe her story. Anyway, 80 percent of alleged rape victims are lying!" Consider the possible responses of the other detective. Almost invariably the reply will be either approval or disapproval of the attitude expressed. Either the detective will respond, "I didn't believe her either." or he or she will tend to reply, "Oh, I don't agree with you, I kind of believed her. Besides, I think that the figure that you are quoting is inflated."

In other words, the primary reaction is to evaluate what has been said from one's own point of view or frame of reference. The major barrier to mutual interpersonal communication is the very natural tendency to judge, evaluate, approve, or disapprove what other people or groups are saying according to one's own frame of reference.

Consider another example. Suppose as a police officer you are in a hospital emergency room, interviewing a woman who has just been badly beaten by her husband. She proceeds to say with strong feeling, "I think that men are behaving terribly these days, beating up women the way they do!" What is the response that arises in your mind as you listen? The overwhelming likelihood is that it will be evaluative. You will find yourself agreeing or disagreeing ("She's right. There has been a large increase in domestic violence calls recently"), or making some judgment about her such as "She must be a man-hater."

This illustration raises another point related to communicating with people in crisis. Although the tendency to make evaulations is normal in almost all interchanges, it is very much heightened in those situations where feelings and emotions are involved. The stronger the feelings, the more likely that there will be no mutual agreement in the communication process. Since almost all crisis situations involve heightened emotions and feelings, it is important to be aware of the communication process and the barriers as well as the bridges to effective communication.

VERBAL COMMUNICATION

To understand the complexity of the communication process, let's review the steps involved when a person wants to send a message. First, a person must have an emotion, idea, or thought to express. How it is expressed will be governed by such factors as age, status, sex, education, background, cultural heritage, mental and physical health, environment, attitudes, and many other variables in the speaker's field of experience, or, as it is sometimes called, the frame of reference. Day by day these variables may change. The speaker must express him- or herself with words—the choice of which is also determined by another set of variables such as vocabularly, knowledge, situation, emotional state, person receiving the communication, and so on. These factors may also vary.

The speaker must then decide how the message is to be transmitted. When the message is oral, other factors are brought into play—voice tone, inflection, and body language—which often say more than words through nonverbal communication. If it is written, the speaker must realize that the message does not have the advantage of immediate feedback and nonverbal cues to clarify it.

Verbal cues can be very direct. For example, the individual makes a statement of fact, such as: "My child was just raped. Can you help me?" The crisis intervener must be alert not only to what the individual is saying, but to how; the tone of voice and general attitudes of concern. The direct statement, however, does not take too much interpreting to understand the concerns and the need for help in resolving them. Usually, time spent in direct questioning, listening, and information giving can help reduce anxiety and assist in problem solving. The channel of communication may also be altered by interference of various kinds such as sound or external noise.

David K. Berlo popularized the source-message-channel-receiver (SMCR) model of communication in his landmark volume *The Process of Communication*. Despite numerous attempts to improve on his SMCR model, it remains one of the most useful interpretations of the process of communication. Berlo introduced six constitutents of the communication model:

1. Communication source
2. Encoder
3. Message
4. Channel
5. Decoder, and
6. Communication receiver

Effective communication is the proper coding and decoding of a message. In Berlo's model, the source and encoder are the same, as are the receiver and the decoder. Some variables are missing in this simple model of communication. As human beings we experience communication via the five senses—visual, tactile, auditory, olfactory, and gustatory. Interpersonal communication allows the participants much more opportunity to be stimulated through all the senses than do other forms of communication such as the mass media, film, television, radio, or print. Interpersonal communication involves the simultaneous use of hearing, seeing, and touching. It also involves, for example, the social environment in which communication takes place, and the emotions of both participants at the time of communication, which will affect the interpretation of the message.

At this point it is apparent that communication is a process that centers on people, and that there are five elements basic to all human communication. Therefore, our simple model of communication has evolved. To better understand the process by which communication functions, and to help us visualize its complexity, a human communication skills flow chart is presented (fig. 3.1).

In referring to the flow chart, the five elements basic to all human communication can be identified as:

Figure 3.1
Communication Skills Flow Chart

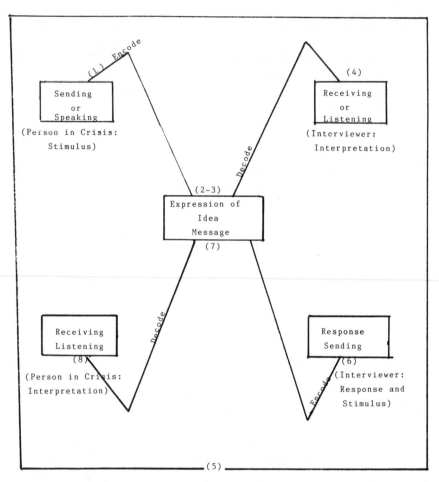

1. A person originates a thought or idea and the word or mannerism to convey the idea (encode).
2. The idea itself is expressed (message).
3. A medium or channel is used to express the idea (verbal, nonverbal, written).
4. A person receives and interprets the idea (decode).
5. There is a context or setting in which the transmission of the idea, attitude, thought, or emotion occurs.

Utilizing the five phases of communication, we have established one-way communication. The sender, or speaker, forwards a message intended to receive a receiver, or listener (no. 1). The message is expressed and a medium is used to express it (nos. 2 and 3). The receiver of the message decodes the message (no. 4). To be effective, however, communication must be two-way. There must be a response in some manner to assure the sender that the message was received and that the required action will be taken (nos. 6, 7, and 8).

Misunderstanding-Distortion

In any communication process there are three general sources of misunderstanding: first, the person communicating may not clearly communicate the intended message; second, the person receiving may not clearly understand the message; and third, the message itself may be ambiguous (because of conflict between the channels of communication or because of confusion within one channel), so that neither communicator nor receiver is certain about what is being said. Making the interaction better for the listener so that he or she will be more likely to hear what you are trying to communicate without becoming defensive is one way of assuring good communication. There are three mechanical conflicts or points of misunderstanding in a communication system:

1. What the speaker thinks he or she said;
2. What the listener thought was said; and
3. What the speaker actually said.

All three can be different and, consequently, can generate an environment of conflict or misunderstanding; this initiates the blaming process. People become defensive and begin blaming in their communication when they perceive a threat or possible threat toward them. When one is defensively aroused, it is difficult to pay accurate attention to the messages that are being sent. It is at times such as these that one is likely to misinterpret what the other person is saying or distort what is being heard. Nearly everyone has played the communication game in which one individual whispers a statement that is then passed from person to person around a circle. By the time the message returns to the originator, the context is usually distorted and sometimes totally different from the original. Each person in this communication chain has acted as a resister or booster, emphasizing certain aspects of the message while de-emphasizing others. In interpersonal communication, each of us receives, makes judgments about, and modifies messages before we pass them along. Each of us acts as a checkpoint in the communication process—we refuse to transmit some messages, overemphasize others, and play down still more.

Physical Conditions

Our perceptions can also be altered by both internal and external physical conditions, which help heighten, diminish, accept, or reject messages. Internal physical conditions refer to the well-being or health of the individual audience member. When physically ill, a person filters messages differently from the way he or she does when in good health. A migraine headache, a bleeding ulcer, or an abscessed tooth can radically alter message filtering. The pain of a smashed thumb affects the senses of touch so intensely that sight or sound can be impaired. In some individuals, physical discomfort may heighten the communication experience. For example, a beer commercial is reacted to in one way by a person who is hot and thirsty but in another way by someone suffering from a hangover. Also, inattention to physical impairments, such as partial deafness and fatigue, affects understanding, and the listener may interpret the message erroneously, attaching a different meaning to the speaker's words when decoding what was said.

External physical conditions refer to the environment or surroundings in which we receive messages. If the room in which you are located is too hot, too cold, too dark, or too noisy, it will affect your senses and the way you understand what you are reading or hearing. Background noises and other distractions can also distort the message. Physical noise contributes a possible error factor to the message received by the listener. A wailing siren or a loud vehicular engine may blank out a word or phrase, resulting in a message that either makes no sense or takes on an entirely different meaning.

Barriers to Effective Communication

Communication failures are stumbling blocks to good living. We hear examples of communication failures every day: "I didn't mean to say that!" or "He misunderstood me." and "He lied!" The resultant damage to human feelings, business, property and finance, and even international relations is inestimable. We can avoid this by communicating clearly, honestly, and effectively. The most frequent communication breakdowns occur in the encoding (selecting and speaking the words) and decoding (interpreting what was said) stages, because of the assumption that words have the same meaning to everyone. A word in itself is merely a symbol; the meaning is conditioned by past experiences, usage, and understanding. However, there are other barriers to communication that need to be taken into consideration. Consider the following barriers.

Prejudices-Attitudes-Stereotyping

A prejudiced intervener, although not actually reflecting this attitude in words, often conveys a prejudice by way of tone of voice or body language. Attitude also is an extremely important part of verbal communication. Voice inflection and personal demeanor contribute as much to conversation as the words spoken, and when coupled with words and an improper attitude, the result can be devastating. Stereotyping involves projecting one's perception of a group of people onto an individual member of that group. A stereotype is expressed in the form of a generalization. It is the assumption that the members of any group are all alike. However, we all have our personal likes, dislikes, and beliefs that have grown out of our individual experiences with people. Several are: redheads are hot-tempered, blonds tend to be dumb, fat people are happy, ruddy complexions reveal dishonest tendencies, short people all think that they are Napoleons (i.e., domineering), people with close-set eyes are unintelligent, and high foreheads mean intelligence. We tend to think these are "good" beliefs because they are our own, but all are usually completely unsupported in fact.

Because of these preconceived ideas about others we tend to select a mode of communication reflective of what we think of a particular group. For example, in a crisis, in which our ability to remain in control is challenged, there may be a tendency to get caught up in the contagiousness of the situation, causing our mode of communication to regress to one of anger and insults. These insults may encompass negative remarks about the ethnic group, race, or culture that the victim may represent. Too often minorities are referred to as "they" and opposed to "we." Likewise, expressions such as "your kind," "those people," and so on, may seem insignificant but can be highly offensive to others.

The crisis intervener comes to the job with fully developed attitudes, prejudices, and stereotypes about people and the difficult situations that may arise with some of the individuals he or she needs to help. These types of communication barriers are counterproductive to crisis intervention. The intervener may therefore stereotype crisis victims because of their accent, their manner of speaking, or their dress, and this affects the way the intervener responds to the victims' needs. If this bias is not realized and dealt with, a void will develop between the victim and the intervener.

Cultural Differences

All members in a given culture share certain common beliefs, customs, and values. While growing up, the child learns to behave in ways expected by the culture. Traditions, values, ways of looking at things, and the expectations one's culture has of its members vary from group to group. Rarely do people of different cultures think or act exactly alike. This difference becomes particularly observable in crisis situations.

Traditions, values, and cultural ways of acting in problem solving play a major role in crisis situations. Of primary concern here is the understanding that the very definition of a situation as one of crisis is partially determined by culture. This can be readily observable in the response of certain persons to pain. For some cultures pain is to be accepted stoically, with the sufferer playing the strong, silent type—a sort of "bite-the-bullet" response. For these persons, pain is best left unspoken—an ideal with roots as deep as Plato, who wrote that "It is finest to keep as quiet as possible in misfortune." Our culture admires many values that are heir to Plato's sentiment; the "stiff upper lip" we admire as the hallmark of English breeding; the athlete who "plays with pain" and without excuses; even the male child who suppresses his tears. For certain other cultures pain is not to be tolerated quietly, but rather to be expressed loudly and strongly. A good example of this difference was illustrated by Butcher and P. Pancheri (1976) in a comparison study of psychiatric patients from Italy, Switzerland, and the United States. The Italian patients showed an exaggerated pattern of physical complaints that differentiated them from both the Swiss and American patients, regardless of clinical diagnoses. This finding was consistent with earlier research by Opler and Singer (1959) and Zola (1966). For example, I. Zola examined symptom expression in two samples of second-generation American patients who were Italian and Irish. When patients were matched on the basis of actual physical disorder, Zola found that the Italian patients made more physical complaints than the Irish. He attributed the difference to a defense mechanism, which he called dramatization, in which the Italian patients, once identified as ill, tended to exaggerate or dramatize their physical problems to a greater extent than patients of other ethnic backgrounds.

Moreover, in certain cultures there are very clear-cut methods for dealing with particular circumstances. For instance, while for some cultures in death situations the grieving process is publicly demonstrated, for others death is just another life episode to be accepted quietly.

Ways of reacting are therefore prescribed by the norms and values of culture, and participants in a culture will generally follow these norms. Cultural definitions and solutions and the degree to which a crisis has been considered by a culture are thus likely to be significant factors in determining the outcome of a crisis. It is important to understand these cultural differences and their impact on communication in crisis situations to avoid misinterpretation. Since norms vary from society to society, the cultural meaning of the same act can have large differences in different places. These cultural differences can lead to serious misinterpretation, which can interfere with effective communication and crisis intervention. Therefore, listening, trying sincerely to get the crisis victim's interpretations and ideas, and acting on the basis of what the victim thinks, not what we think or what we wish the victim would think, are absolutely essential to realistic communication.

The meaning of words may also be a reflection of cultural differences. Many words and expressions accepted as proper and inoffensive within one group may have a degrading connotation when spoken in the presence of someone from a different group. Consider for example, the following case history:

A 10-year-old girl approached a radio car and reported to the police officers that while she was on her way to school she was pulled into an automobile by a man. While in the car, she reported to the officers in graphic vernacular, "He rubbed his hands all over my tits. He was touching my pussy and then he stuck his dick into it." The officers brought her and her mother to the hospital emergency room for examination. The responding sex crimes detective upon hearing from the police officers how the details of the story were reported to them responded sarcastically, "Well! I guess we have one street-wise little kid here." However, in later interviews with the mother, it became apparent that because they were from another culture, they thought that the words they had learned to identify these body parts were accepted and used by everyone. The mother, a very respectable woman, used the very same words.

Inferences/Observations

It is incredibly difficult at times for someone to discriminate between what he or she *knows* (i.e., what he has actually observed—seen, heard, read, and so on) and what he or she is only inferring or guessing. One of the key reasons for this lies in the character of the language used to express observations and inferences. To the already traumatized crisis victim, inferences about what other people think of them and their situation can destroy communication efforts. For example:

While the police officers and detectives were waiting for medical personnel to complete examinations on a severely beaten mugging victim, they were talking and laughing among themselves in one of the unoccupied rooms of the emergency room. When the victim was through with the medical examination, she approached the room in order to be interviewed and heard the laughter. Suspecting the worse (that they were all sitting around and laughing about her situation) she became infuriated and refused to cooperate with the officers. No amount of talking could alleviate her feelings that they would not be able to take her situation seriously. She angrily stomped out of the emergency room without being interviewed about her case. Caught in the grips of her crisis, she was unable to distinguish what she had inferred from what was actually occurring.

Disrespectful Modes of Address

Courtesy is a barrier breaker and a bond builder. The corollary of this is also true; discourtesy is a bond breaker and a barrier builder. Everyone appreciates being addressed in a polite fashion and resents being spoken to in an overly familiar or rude way. No matter what his or her station in life, every person is entitled to be addressed in terms that imply respect. Ladies, gentlemen, madam, miss, and sir are normally the proper titles for one to use. Words such as Yo, Hey You, Mack, Jack, or Jim, are insulting appellations. Addressing young adults as Kid, Boy, or Girl should also be avoided because such labels imply that the listener is immature, inferior, and ineligible for personal respect. Similarly, addressing a stranger by first name is

objectionable because he or she is at a decided disadvantage by being unaware of your given name. Moreover, one should not address others in such
a familiar way even if they are not strangers unless one expects or even wants
others to respond in kind. If one violates this norm, he or she is almost
certain to evoke a hostile response from the addressee.

Referring to a woman with whom one is unacquainted as Dear, Sweetie,
Honey, or Doll is invariably a breach of etiquette and an invasion of psychological privacy. These expressions also suggest familiarity and when they
are uninvited they become phony and insincere and create barriers to effectively communicating with the victim.

Communication is not always conducted through the use of words alone.
Many times the real meaning of what one is thinking is conveyed through
facial expressions, tone of voice, gestures, eye movements, or even silence.
These are examples of communicating through the use of nonverbal cues.

THE POWER AND INFLUENCE OF NONVERBAL COMMUNICATION

One of the most important insights achieved in recent years is our recognition of the importance of communication that takes place outside of the
spoken language. Dramatic new research discoveries have pinpointed the
crucial role of the silent signals of nonverbal communication. Everybody
"speaks" nonverbally usually without even knowing it. We transmit a lot of
information to others through our facial expressions, body postures, vocal
intonations, and physical distance. Consider, for instance, how silence itself
is a way of communcation. When someone says "Good morning" and we
fail to respond, we are communicating something. When someone asks us
a question and we fail to answer, this is also communicating. The silence
that occurs with a group of people, when the subject of their prior conversation enters the room, may tell that person a great deal about what kind of
things were being said about him in his absence. The skeptical person who
sits back, folds her arms and crosses her legs (indicating resistance) and lifts
her eyebrows (indicating disbelief) is communicating nonverbally.

In the average two-way conversation, it is estimated that the verbal band
carries less than 35 percent of the social meaning of the situation; more than
65 percent is transmitted by nonverbal bands. Many of the meanings that
are given to human encounters are given because of glances, touch, vocal
tones, gestures, or facial expressions, and with or without the addition of
words. From the moment of greeting to the moment of separation, people
observe each other with all their senses, hearing pauses, and tones in the
voice; observing the way other people dress and carry themselves, observing
glances and facial tensions, as well as observing the words spoken. The rest
of the body sends messages also, particularly through position and posture.
This has been called body language. When relaxed, people tend to sprawl

back in a chair; when tense, to sit more stiffly with their feet together. Slumping, crossing the arms and legs, and straightness of the back all supply clues about which emotion someone is feeling. Ray Birdwhistell (1952), professor of communications at the University of Pennsylvania, made the study of body language into a science called kinesics. He believes that every movement of the body has a meaning, that no movement is accidental, and that all our significant gestures and movements are learned. Moreover, these body gestures may contradict our verbal messages about what we are feeling. Another expert, Albert Mehrabian, professor of psychology at U.C.L.A. and author of *Silent Messages,* maintains that a person's nonverbal behavior has more bearing on communication than do words. Sigmund Freud noted that an actress who, in performing a role as an adulteress, used nonverbal actions to communicate her character's inner conflict by slipping her wedding ring on and off while speaking to her prospective lover.

The elements of nonverbal communication can be described as follows:

Shaking hands	How close you stand to others
Appearance	The way you stand
Posture	The way you move
Voice tone	How you touch other people
Smile	Confidence
Clothes	Breathing
Hair style	How you listen
Facial expressions	Expression in your eyes

Allan Pease, the author of *Signals,* writes of another kind of body communication; the distance that can be measured in four distinct zone distances, the Intimate Zone (6–18 inches), Personal Zone (1 1/2–4 feet), Social Zone (4–12 feet), and Public Zone (over 12 feet). The normal distance between people differs from situation to situation and from culture to culture. Two Swedes standing and talking would ordinarily stand much farther apart than two Arabs or Greeks, and lovers would stand closer than strangers. Within every culture there seems to be a distance that is thought appropriate for normal conversation. If someone is standing closer than usual to you, it may indicate aggressiveness or sexuality; if farther away than usual, it may indicate withdrawal or repugnance.

Although the spoken word is the main device through which people communicate, the power and influence of nonverbal cues cannot be ignored. The shrug of resignation, or doubt, the bowed head of despair or defeat, or the frown of anger sometimes are even more expressive than words. What one says with words can be controlled fairly well. One may tell the truth or lie or choose not to talk; however, it is much more difficult to control body language. Often the body will communicate feelings that may not be revealed with words. Other times, words will say one thing and the body another. It is more difficult to lie with the body. A person may say verbally, "I like you" yet say "Stay away" with his or her body; a person may say "I feel fine" with words but say "I feel terrible" with the body. These contradictory messages may be the result of insincerity or the consequence of simply not knowing how one feels.

In crisis situations it is important to remember that there are two sets of body language to be considered, the victim's and the crisis intervener's. These types of interpersonal communication are usually nonconfrontive and noninterrogative, as opposed to the confrontation that is associated with investigative kinds of criminal justice/civilian contacts. Therefore, styles of communication need to be adjusted. Several points regarding nonverbal communication in crisis situations follow.

- Avoid standing over the victim while talking. It implies intimidation. Try for equality.
- While eye contact is important, a direct stare is threatening.
- Refrain from threatening gestures such as pointing fingers or clenched fists.
- Too much visual attention to body language can create discomfort.
- Avoid placing inanimate objects between you and the victim. These act as an unconscius barrier to communication.

Although interpretation of nonverbal actions must be tentative and considered in the context of the interaction, there are some frequently occurring ways in which common messages are communicated nonverbally. For example:

Anxiety and tension may be reflected by increased rates of speech, decrease in the amount of silence, repeating phrases, failing to complete sentences, frequently changing stream of consciousness, shifting the voice volume, stuttering, frequent gestures, frequent eye blinking, sweating, shifting of seating position, flushed face, foot or finger tapping, dry mouth, and increased smoking.

Anger may be reflected by louder-than-normal speech, flailing arms, frowning, tensed lips, clenched teeth, chin and head thrust forward, and wide eyes.

Grief or sadness may be demonstrated through slow speech, frequent pauses while speaking, holding one's head in one's hands, and crying or sighing.

Depression or withdrawal may be demonstrated by slumping forward, head down with the arms tightly crossed in front of the body.

Coldness or distance may be conveyed by non-smiling expression, failing to make eye contact or closing the eyes while the intervener is speaking, leaning away, assuming a *closed* position (i.e., arms held across the chest, legs crossed high up, hand covering mouth, and wearing sunglasses indoors.

Warmth and openness may be communicated by leaning forward, turning the body toward the intervener, smiling, making eye contact, uncrossed legs, and arms not folded across the chest.

Hands also express feelings. You may cover your face with your hands to express shame, hunch your shoulders and turn your palms up to express puzzlement, or strike your palm against your forehead to express surprise or forgetfulness.

Crisis interveners can be perceived as sympathetically listening and attentive when they tend to incline their heads and upper torsos toward the speaker. Leaning back from the speaker, on the other hand frequently indicates disbelief or skepticism. When intervening in a crisis it is a good idea to monitor one's body posture to determine what is being communicated.

WORDS THAT TRIGGER EMOTIONAL RESPONSES

There are some people who exhibit emotional reactions whenever they hear certain words. Abortion, mistress, racial quotas, mother, welfare—the mere mention of such terms can produce visible alterations in demeanor. A person may stammer, blanch, turn argumentative, undergo erratic changes in blood pressure and pulse, and become violent—all in response to a mere word. Responses will vary dependent upon the person. For someone who had a happy childhood, words such as *family* and *marriage* have a slight but definitely pleasant feeling attached. If childhood was unhappy, the same words have a negative effect. The word *love* can arouse feelings associated with loss of freedom, manipulation, or smothering. To another person, the word love carries a positive emotional tone—feelings associated with affection, commitment, comfort, or solace. The same word has an opposite effect on two people.

With practice, it is possible to detect within others inward tension, elation, or dissatisfaction associated with certain words. Within a split second of hearing a word or phrase, there is a reaction to what was heard. At this very early point there is a tendency to demonstrate a personality change at the mention of a word or term. When persons are in an already fragile state as during a crisis, they are more vulnerable to emotional outbursts at trigger words. Emotional responsiveness to these words is difficult to control at these times.

INDIRECT VERBAL CUES

For the individual who has difficulty verbalizing feelings and concerns, crisis interveners may have to depend on nonverbal communication and indirect verbal communication for cues to levels of anxiety and concerns.

Like nonverbal communication, indirect verbal cues are subtle and take varying degrees of skill of interpretation to get at their meanings. Here the individual gives the intervener hints that he or she is feeling uncomfortable, tense, and anxious, and that he or she feels the need for help in clarifying these feelings. The individual also is describing difficulty coping. For example the individual may "wonder aloud" about some of the following issues:

"I wonder how I'm going to get home from the hospital emergency room!"

"I wonder how I'm going to tell my spouse that our child has been sexually assaulted!"

"I wonder what the results of the blood test will show!" (A particularly troublesome concern when one has been raped and the blood test will indicate the presence of veneral disease) or

"What if I've become pregnant from this incident?"

The individual may speak about a "friend who has a drinking problem," or say "I wonder what I can do about those broken locks?" (a burglary situation).

The client may wonder aloud about the cost of the medical care that is being rendered, saying, for example, "Boy, this hospital must be expensive!"

It is not only how and what is said, but what is not said in a specific situation that must be considered. The person in crisis may be experiencing anxiety and tension so great that the ability to directly verbalize feelings may be missing. Some persons in crisis may also be too embarrassed to ask for assistance. For example, wouldn't it seem unusual if the mother of a sexually molested child asked no questions on her first visit to a station house? Nonetheless, it happens sometimes. These are the unfortunate "hidden agendas" of crisis situations that a skilled crisis intervener can identify and respond to. They represent an ideal opportunity for the intervener to provide added support, reassurance, and comfort to someone in crisis.

TWO-WAY BARRIERS

Everything that is done by a sender and receiver is interrelated, and the resulting interaction creates the process of communication. Thus far, barriers to communication have focused on the crisis intervener's behavior. However, the receiver or crisis victim also has a strong impact on the message because he or she edits according to the variables generated by his or her own field of experience or frame of reference. When there is an overlap in the fields of experience of the two communicants, and the variables for both the sender and receiver are reduced, the communication process will be improved; this is the ideal situation. Communication, after all, must be a two-way process open at both ends. However, there are the communication barriers placed by crisis victims to consider in our model of effective communication. The crisis victim also has his or her own field of experience or frame of reference, prejudices, biases, stereotypes and attitudes that will get in the way of effective communication. The sex of the crisis intervener, the race or ethnicity of the intervener, and the image of criminal justice itself may all be variables that get in the way of intervention. Consider the following situations:

A call for help to 911 turns hostile when the caller insists on speaking to another operator. The operator inquiring as to the reason why hears the caller say that he "don't want to talk to any black person." This situation may also occur when the operator may have any hint of an accent, getting responses such as "I can't understand anything you're saying, give me someone else to talk to!" Operators in an effort to understand the callers' predicament and to offer assistance are often insulted and perplexed at this attitude. Their exasperation is exhibited when they state, "What difference does it make what race or ethnicity I am. All that should be important is that I'm here to help them!"

A male police officer responding to a rape situation becomes dismayed when the victim refuses to talk to him. Often, this occurs in calls for assistance by rape victims because the victim generalizes the fear experienced during the rape toward all men.

A female police lieutenant becomes angry at the caller asking for assistance, who insists on speaking to "the man in charge!" Implicit in this demand is the belief that because she is female she is not as competent and will not provide the same kinds of assistance as a male police officer.

THE CRIMINAL JUSTICE IMAGE

Every crisis intervener should be aware that certain groups of criminal justice personnel are threatening to many people. The police, corrections, and probation officers may be regarded as disciplinarians, wielders of power and authority, and people to be feared in many situations. The presence of the police constitutes a threat to many people even when they are not doing anything deserving police intervention. For example, many people will slow down while driving when they see a patrol car even though they are not exceeding the speed limit. Undoubtedly, many people will immediately make a behavioral inventory (did I do something wrong?) and become wary when they see a police officer approaching. This wariness, uneasiness, or apprehension is part of the aura of threat with which the police are surrounded. The officer is thus often seen as a person to be avoided.

The fact that some people may see the police department as a threat has undesirable consequences, and the tendency to avoid contact is one. Another is a lack of cooperation by some people even when a crime perpetrated against them is being investigated. Many a police officer or detective has been called to the emergency room in response to a call for help only to hear the victim tell them, "What do you want? You don't care about me. You're not going to do anything to catch that guy anyway!"

Such strained relationships are inherent in the criminal justice role. Some expect the relationship to be an adversary one, leaving the intervener to take special measures to relieve the strain. In a non-adversary contact the intervener can avoid appearing a threat or a major obstacle to an effective contact. Moreover, if the intervener avoids inflicting pain and can reduce guilt, treat the person with respect, and offer him- or herself as a helping and supportive person, then the person in crisis will be likely to develop a positive and trusting relationship with the intervener.

The very nature of police and investigate agencies makes it mandatory to provide assistance to others, even those who will not like or respect them. In order to promote and maintain a good image, it is of paramount importance that the intervener understand this. The crisis intervener must be tolerant under all conditions, even in the face of intense provocation, to offset a negative psychological effect on an already impaired psychological state. Bearing this in mind, the problem becomes one of creating the most favorable image possible; that is, being the most effective, courteous, and humane crisis intervener possible.

BRIDGES TO EFFECTIVE COMMUNICATION

Providing Feedback

The single most important method of improving communication and avoiding misunderstanding is to provide feedback. If the originator is of the opinion that all he or she has to do is talk and all the receiver must do is listen then there is a high risk that the communication will fail. False perceptions and small errors magnify into major distortion if the recipient does not have the opportunity to respond. The need for feedback can be observed by the person's reactions; nonverbal cues such as the facial expressions of puzzlement, anger, and so on; symbolic significance ascribed to the words; the adjustment of the tone of voice and rate of speaking, and so forth. In addition, limiting a person to a "yes" or "no" response is not an effective method of gaining feedback. You will want to allow people to comment on whatever they deem appropriate, even in casual conversation.

Explaining Actions

Most of us in ordinary situations want to know what is happening and why something is being done to us or in relation to us. This need for control is further exacerbated in an unfamiliar situation. A simple explanation by the intervener will satisfy curiosity and reduce anger and fear. Telling the person why you are there, what you intend to do for them, or where you will be taking them changes the situation from a threatening one to a comfortable one.

Effective Listening

Up until this point one side of verbal communication (i.e., talking) has been emphasized, and listening, the other side of communication, has only been mentioned. In the communication process, conscientious listening is just as important as speaking. People spend far more time listening than reading, writing, or talking, yet few know how to really hear what is being said.

To listen is to do more than hear. Hearing is a physiological function and involves receiving a message, while listening is a mental function that involves perceiving a message (interpreting and giving meaning to it). Skill in listening is dependent on how well the message is translated and understood. We are dealing with a mental process. Actually, there are two mental processes to be considered. Listening is part of two-way interaction between the person who originates the message and the person for whom the message is intended. To effect real communication, speaking and listening must work in concert; the two participants in the exchange must mentally engage one another in shaping the message. They cooperatively build thought and determine meaning and significance. If the listener invests nothing in the enterprise, communication will suffer.

Although people differ in their ability to listen well, recent research has shown that—barring organic dysfunction—listening ability can be improved through properly guided practice. In addition, any particular act of listening can be made productive if the listener will bring to it a correct physical adjustment and a proper mental attitude. Good listening requires an active effort to derive meaning from all aspects of the communication: from the speaker's tone of voice, movements, gestures, and facial expression, as well as from the words that are uttered. In addition, it includes interpretation and appraisal: a constant and critical consideration of the ideas presented, the materials by which these ideas are supported and explained, the purposes that motivate them, and the language in which they are expressed. In short, good listening is comprehensive, but, even more important, it is creative. Only the listener can provide the feedback necessary to enable the speaker to determine the degree to which the hidden message is being received or rejected and, consequently, the extent to which it must be modified or redirected.

We hear, but we do not really listen. Individuals spend 80 percent of their waking hours communicating in one way or another; of that time, about 45 percent is spent listening. However, the focus in our educational programs is upside down. We spend the greatest amount of time teaching people to do what they will spend the least time doing: writing. Furthermore, we spend the least amount of time teaching people what they will do most in life: listening.

This is lamentable because listening is much more complex than reading.

What we read is locked on the printed page. If people are distracted, they can put aside their reading and return to it later. If they do not understand the message right off, they have the means to repeat it. In listening, however, the message is written on the wind, it is transient. If we do not get the message the first time, there is usually no going back. It has been said that we hear half of what is said, we listen to half of that, we understand half of that, we believe half of that, and we remember only half of that.

Keep in mind that listening is a combination of what we hear, what we understand, and what we remember. The efficiency of listening for most people in learning situations is about 20 to 25 percent.

There are reasons for improving your listening skills. If you are alert and listen you will be better able to perform in the crisis interveners role effectively. You will be better equipped to answer questions and improve your self-confidence. You will be able to relate to and understand the people you come in contact with. When you listen carefully you improve your own vocabulary and language ability. Ideas and concepts can be heard more quickly and clarified more easily when one listens intently.

Improving Listening Skills

When you seek to improve a skill such as listening, it is well to identify the problem to begin with. Problems with listening may appear at any time but they are particularly evident in long conversations. Some problems are:

1. Viewing the subject as uninteresting or as bored and disinterested in what is being said.

2. Criticizing the delivery or appearance, instead of the message. Too often we get distracted by a voice, mannerism, ethnicity, use of slang, foreign accent, or other external factor that has nothing to do with the value of what is being said. One police officer in the forgery squad was interviewing a man when he noticed that the man had a gold tooth in his mouth with initials engraved on it. The officer later related that "I spent so much time trying to figure out what was engraved on the gold tooth, that after a while I realized that I hadn't heard a word he had said."

3. Getting overstimulated to the extent that we are more concerned with our own message than with what is being said. We become so eager to express ourselves that we do not even hear what is said.

4. Listening only for facts. Facts have no meaning by themselves; they must relate to an idea, concept, or principle.

5. Letting emotion-laden words interfere with listening. Trigger words like *liberal, radical, system, mother,* and ethnic slurs or curse words tend to grasp attention, to the distraction of what the speaker is saying.

6. Deep-seated opinions or convictions impair comprehension. Whenever your ego involvement is strong in a situation and there appears to be a threat to deeply held opinions, little real listening will take place.

Points to Remember

Limit your own talking. You can't talk and listen at the same time.

Think like the person in crisis. His or her problem and needs are important . . . and you will understand and retain them better if you keep this point of view.

Don't interrupt. A pause . . . even a long pause . . . does not always mean the person is finished saying everything he or she wants to say.

Concentrate. Focus your mind on what the person's saying. Practice shutting out outside distractions.

Take notes. This will help you to remember important points.

Listen for ideas—not just words. You want to get the whole picture, not just isolated bits and pieces.

Interjection. An occasional "Yes" and "I see" shows the other person you are still following—but do not overdo it or use a meaningless comment.

Turn off your own words. This is not always easy . . . but personal fears, worries, and problems not connected with the contact can alienate the crisis victim.

React to ideas—not the person. Do not allow irritation at things the person may say . . . or his or her manner . . . distract you.

Don't jump to conclusions. Avoid making unwarranted assumptions about what the person is going to say . . . or mentally trying to complete sentences for him or her.

Practice listening. Most important, make all of your human contacts tools for improving listening skills . . . "for sharpening your inner ear."

SUMMARY

In this chapter, communication theory is presented with emphasis on both verbal and nonverbal communication. The variables that damage the communiction process are identified, as well as ways of building good communication skills. The crisis intervener's primary communication tool is speech. By becoming aware of the impact of words, thoughtless statements, cultural and experiential biases, and misunderstandings, one can sharpen communication skills and avoid offending others. As we have seen there are many barriers to effective communication. For every barrier there is a bridge of expert/professional communication skills. It is essential for the crisis intervener to become aware of the important role that communication plays in the successful resolution of crisis situations.

Chapter *4*

CRISIS INTERVENTION: THEORY AND PRACTICE

When someone helps a victim to restore control and order to his or her life, that person is intervening in the crisis. Therefore, the initial contact in a crisis situation is an important one. The person is most often under considerable tension and stress and will be very sensitive to the attitudes and reactions of the intervener. During this initial meeting an opportunity is presented to:

- Observe the person in crisis (Identification),
- Assess the crisis situation and the amount of stress the person is experiencing (Investigation-Information gathering), and
- Determine the ways in which the needs of the person will be met most efficiently (Intervention).

Upon encountering the crisis situation, the criminal justice intervener must reduce the impact of the crisis event and build a solid basis for the required steps of intervention. Since crises are very disorganizing, a good response tends to put organization back into the emergency environment. The intervener can be considered a consultant to a situation. This allows for the objective response of the intervener, which facilitates an overall assessment of the crisis.

THE CRIMINAL JUSTICE INTERVENER

While one does not have to experience a crisis of a similar nature to be of assistance, the knowledge and understanding of crisis behavior and intervention are vital tools. Most events with which crisis interveners are involved have crisis implications for someone, and the key to the most effective completion of their tasks is in the nature of the intervention. The authority of the intervener is also critical. Most professionals in our society are seen as authority figures, and their ability to perform their duties is enhanced by this aura of authority. Professionals are expected to be competent; to be able to do their jobs skillfully. Therefore, those seeking their services will listen and follow directions to facilitate this competency. Similarly, criminal justice crisis interveners have considerable authority, both real and symbolic. Because of the nature of this position, they have immediacy and authority, and their behavior toward the individual in crisis will have impact on short- and long-term adjustment. In order to be effective in assisting others, help must come from an authoritative source; however, authority must be distinguished from authoritarianism.

Authority. This is exhibited by the individual's overall knowledge of his or her position, competence in his or her ability to recognize and deal effectively with individuals in crisis, and basic understanding of his or her role in the overall picture of the organization as a helping system. The more one knows, the more capable, aware, and competent one will be. This authority model gives the individual a variety of possibilities when intervening in crisis situations, whereas the power model (authoritarian) is just one answer with a limited number of responses to crisis situations. Authority is derived from knowledge and competence. Criminal justice interveners can transmit a special confidence that comes from accepting who they are and knowing what they believe. Others sense this. Particularly in times of confusion and doubt, people are drawn to those who seem to be in control.

Authoritarianism. Organizations such as criminal justice agencies tend to encourage this style of communication. The language of the police department, for example, is usually of an authoritarian nature. This type of intervention is characterized by a display of power (physically or vocally) or status, indicating control over everything because of one's position in this organization. It is unfortunate when this style carries over into the area of service, where the role is not an interrogative one. For example, during emergencies where there is not time for feedback, authoritarian communication is necessary.

The intervener who communicates from this position uses threats and intimidation to gain cooperation, uses the style of order giving, and seldom gives praise or positive feedback. This intervener handles conflict through controlling and oppressive methods. The direction of his or her communication is usually downward and one-way. The authoritarian intervener is constantly judging and evaluating, using phrases such as "You should know better," ... "You are wrong," ... "I'm in control here," ... "I'll do the thinking," and "You do just as you are told." This is the superiority style that is typified by a need for power and lack of interest in anyone else's needs or comfort. This type of communication has undesirable consequences. The intervener is regarded as someone to fear and, therefore, someone to avoid. It also generates in others feelings of accusation, guilt, anger, and resentment. A person's hostility tends to be contagious, stimulates defensiveness and counter-hostility, and raises barriers to communication. No one wants to be talked down to, and no one likes to be made to feel inferior. The dictatorial or authoritarian attitude impairs communication and destroys cooperation. Cooperation simply does not exist in an atmosphere of laying down the law of "take it or leave it" and "I know a lot more about this than you do."

Effective communication while intervening is the key to handling crisis events (see chapter 3). If the intervener communicates professionalism, confidence, efficiency, sincerity, and empathy—a sort of crisis-solving partnership—the crisis will dissolve more readily. Making a good impression and using common sense will promote confidence in the intervener's ability to handle crisis situations. Approaching crisis response with these general considerations will enhance the intervener's potential for accomplishing the self-satisfying, supportive, emergency role.

CRISIS-SOLVING PARTNERSHIP

A crisis-solving partnership allows for input and exchange of information and an active dialogue between the parties. Although authoritarianism may be more time-consuming, it is more respectful and allows for feedback and corrections that may be necessary to clear up any mistakes or misunderstandings. This exchange promotes harmony and understanding, and places the communicators on an equal footing. When one feels equal, confidence building and improved communication evolve.

People in crisis desire three things: Respect, recognition, and responsiveness.

Respect. The relationship between the crisis intervener and the person in crisis can be viewed as a partnership; each party has an interest in solving the crisis quickly.

Recognition. The intervener explicitly recognizes the situation and feelings of the person in crisis. This recognition includes:

Validation: communicating to the person that what he or she is experiencing and feeling is O.K. and appropriate.

Ventilation and catharsis: The crisis intervener by listening with interest can allow the person in crisis to relieve fears and anxieties through talking about what happened. This serves as a catharsis for the victim.

Responsiveness. An overwhelming sense of loneliness frequently accompanies crisis. The individual will feel less lonely after sharing thoughts and feelings with the intervener and being accepted and helped. The intervener increases his or her own sense of worth by providing assistance to the criminal investigation in return. Responsiveness may also include:

Giving information: The intervener can identify the precipitating event and define the effects of the crisis. The intervener can also clarify what can and will be done to assist in restoring equilibrium.

Giving hope: The crisis intervener should use his or her expertise and knowledge in exploring the crisis situation. The realization that other people have experienced similar events, thoughts, and feelings is a tremendous relief to many people in crisis. It diminishes their feelings of aloneness. In addition, the fact that others have experienced similar crises and have worked them out satisfactorily will offer hope to people in crisis.

Contacting social network: The lack of an identifiable support system is often a major factor in crisis intervention. The intervener can serve as a catalyst in reorganizing the crisis victim's social network, and as needed serve as a support system until family and friends arrive.

Imitative Behavior: The intervener can help the victim explore ineffective coping mechanisms and explore alternative ways of coping. This can be in the form of suggestions or in sharing the intervener's own past attempts at dealing with similar situations. The calm and controlled impression that an intervener provides can help serve as a model for the victim to emulate.

COMPONENTS OF INTERVENTION

The role of the criminal justice intervener is organized according to three major criminal justice functions: identification, investigation, and intervention.

Identification. This involves identifying the crisis and making an evaluation of the situation. By paying close attention to the behavioral analysis of the encounter, the crisis may well be identified. Sometimes it will be stated in the presenting complaint and at other times the crisis will be readily observable, but sometimes it will be less obvious and the intervener will have to listen carefully for the crisis issue. Of importance is the understanding of how the person views the crisis. What type of crisis is it? This must be defined: Is it an internal crisis (anticipated or unanticipated life event) or an external crisis event (or victim experience)?

Establishing an alliance or rapport as quickly as possible is important in helping the crisis victim understand that the intervener is there to help. In order for the person in crisis to trust the intervener and to be able to fully recount the details of the crisis, the person in crisis must realize that there is something to gain in the meeting. Without this trust or rapport, the crisis victim will be reluctant to talk. This point is especially important when the crisis intervener is attempting to interview children or adolescents in crisis. The crisis intervener may encourage trust by treating the person in crisis with respect, and by being honest, trustworthy, and empathetic. The intorvoner's ability to have a calming effect on the person in crisis will be the key to reducing his or her tension and anxiety to more bearable limits.

Investigation. Once the crisis has been identified, the intervener should remain focused on details of the crisis. The goal in crisis intervention is to understand as much of the incident as possible, as well as the reactions of the person. The intervener will want to know the circumstances under which the event occurred, the conversation, the thoughts and reactions displayed by those involved, and significant events since the incident.

The assessment also involves evaluation of the person's ability to function without being hospitalized, identification of significant persons involved in the situation, identification of significant others in the person's social network, location of the hazards that are threatening the individual, and reaching some type of final diagnoses or evaluation.

Intervention. The intervener makes plans for intervention bearing in mind the strengths and weaknesses of the individual, the situation, the severity of the crisis, the perception of the crisis by the individual, the social network of the individual, and the potential for resolving the crisis quickly.

The goal of crisis intervention is to offer help to the person in crisis so that the psychological equilibrium can be restored. This may follow one or more of several courses, such as fostering an understanding or awareness of the crisis and assisting in the development of new patterns of coping.

In general, the patterns of desired responses for an individual for healthy crisis resolution have been described as follows:

1. Correct understanding of the situation.
2. Awareness of one's feelings leading toward control.
3. Appropriate verbalization leading toward discharge of tension and mastery of feelings.
4. Development of patterns of seeking and using help with actual tasks and feelings by using interpersonal and institutional resources.

In crisis intervention, the individual is assisted in gaining cognitive understanding of his situation. The problem is clarified and the precipitating event is identified. Coping mechanisms that have been unsuccessfully attempted as well as existing support systems are explored. More adaptive coping mechanisms are then introduced. The individual may then choose and use the selected coping mechanisms. The coping mechanism can be a new way of behaving or thinking that will serve to change the way the individual feels.

Management of feelings is accompanied by using the coping mechanism technique. Management of feelings is also facilitated by the free expression of emotion in regard to the crisis situation. An individual in crisis often experiences disordered affect and becomes irrational. Individuals need acceptance of their feelings and confusion along with assurance that what they are experiencing is a normal reaction to the crisis situation.

EMPOWERMENT

What can be given to the crisis victim? What needs to be replaced in the person who has been involved in a crisis situation? In chapter 2, the psychological losses that were incurred during a crisis were identified: power, dignity, and security. The goal of crisis intervention is to empower crisis victims so that they can become actively involved in their own healing process. During a crisis, individuals feel unable to control their destiny in the face of what has happened to them. To be able to have some measure of control may in itself begin the healing process. Psychological data are emerging indicating that enhancing the feeling of being in control of one's life has positive benefits on health. In a series of experiments, laboratory rats implanted with tumors and then subjected to electric shocks rejected the tumors more frequently if they were able to end the shocks themselves. In another study conducted in a nursing home, if elderly residents were able to control even minor conditions of their lives, such as deciding on meals or whether they wanted their telephones plugged or unplugged, it lowered the mortality rate over a period of 18 months by 50 percent, compared to residents in the same homes who did not exercise such control.

The feeling of empowerment, of being able to do something for oneself, seems to be an important healing mechanism. Authoritarian methods of control have the effect of making people dependent, whereas empowering people by giving them something they can do for themselves gives them a sense of mastery over their environment that was taken away from them during the crisis. For the intervener, the major goal of crisis intervention is empowerment. Objectives of crisis intervention are: (1) to empower victims so that they may function as quickly as possible in their original state, as they were prior to the victimization; (2) to lessen the emotional intensity of the victims' reactions to the stress of the moment; and (3) to prevent the victims from harming themselves further while their judgment is impaired.

Elements of Empowerment

In order to replace what was lost to the crisis victim, the intervener may employ the following restorative techniques:

1. *Power.* All crisis victims lose a sense of power. The victim had few choices given to him or her by the assailant, who possessed all the power. The crisis intervener can give the victim power by enlisting him or her in decision making. A person cannot feel empowered when passively sitting. Empowerment can begin by the intervener

   a. Asking questions leading with: "Are you ready to . . . ? Are you able to . . . ?" or pertaining to a description: "Are you ready to give a description now?"

   b. Having the victims make some decisions on their own, such as where to meet someone, when to come to the office.

c. Asking the victim if he or she would like to make a telephone call.

d. Asking permission to sit. Have the victim decide where you should sit during the interview: "Do you mind if I sit here?" . . . "May I speak with you now?" . . . "Is this all right with you?"

2. *Dignity.* All crisis victims lose a certain degree of dignity and often blame themselves for being a victim. The intervener can restore dignity by:

a. Telling them, "You did the right thing."

b. Avoiding criticism of their actions.

3. *Security.* All crisis victims have a sense of insecurity after a crime has been committed against them. The intervener can restore security by:

a. Reassuring victims that you care enough to intervene and "I'm glad you're all right."

b. Telling them that you are there to help.

c. Emphasizing your concern and expressing empathy for what has happened to them, "I'm sorry it happened."

d. Shifting the blame for what happened off them and on to the criminal, where it belongs, "You did nothing wrong."

The following table illustrates the techniques of crisis intervention (table 4.1). The first part of the table indicates how supportive behavior on the part of the intervener is conducive to a successful resolution of the crisis. The second half of the table illustrates the behavior of the crisis victim after equilibrium is restored.

Recommended Intervener Behavior

The intervener's behavior, especially the first impression that the victim gets, will have a lot to do with how aggressively the person behaves or how cooperative he or she is with the intervener's efforts to calm the situation and resolve the crisis. People take note of the intervener's actions and behavior. Everyone pays attention to the intervener's facial expression, gestures, tone of voice, and verbal expression. An "in-charge" demeanor that is calm, unhurried, open, and nonthreatening, yet decisive and confident despite the sickening or shocking state of the situation or the heart-rendering or horrifying condition of the victim, is essential.

Studies have shown that people cope in a multitude of ways with crisis situations. Some people use thinking and planning to cope, while others use physical action or verbal strategies. How a person reacts is determined by personality, past experience, and the effects of the crisis itself. Some persons become emotionally disturbed during crisis periods, but it is important to remember that the anxious behavior, depression, tension, and hostility and anger are not to be confused with psychiatric illness, which they superficially

Table 4.1
Techniques of Crisis Intervention

RECOMMENDED INTERVENER BEHAVIOR — SUPPORTIVE OF SUCCESSFUL RESOLUTION

Tone of Voice	Verbal Expression	Physical Movement	Decision Making	Display of Confidence
Calm	Clear	Eye contact	Be decisive	De-emphasize blame
Reassuring	Free of cursing	Listening posture	Show firmness	Minimum use of officiousness
Gentle	Polite	Non-threatening	Safe decisions	Deal with crisis quickly
Empathetic	No derogatory remarks		Objectivity	Convey that victim did the right thing
Interested	Allow ventilation	Respectful distance	Provide decision-making tasks	"We are here to help you"
Compassionate	Don't interrupt	Assign tasks in harmony with ability	Ask permission of victim	
Establish rapport	Avoid firstname basis	Call family/friends		"We'll get you what you need"
	Encourage person to talk	No suggestion of force		"You did the right thing by reaching out for help"

PERSON IN CRISIS — EQUILIBRIUM RESTORED

Normal voice restored	Dignity and respect restored	Normal physical movements	Person ready to answer questions and offers information	Confidence restored
				Feels reassured
				Feels empowered

resemble. They are the signals that the person in crisis is engaged in an active internal struggle in an attempt to restore equilibrium to his or her life.

Achieving Equilibrium

By the use of supportive words and tone of voice, interveners can make it clear that they understand what the person is feeling and how intensely he or she is feeling it. Interveners should remain calm, speak softly, and carefully select their words. The person in crisis will respond to many of the hidden meanings of what is said; that is, attitudes, tone of voice, and double meanings of words in terms of his or her own background and previous experience. For example, a person will respond in a warm, friendly way to a speaker who uses the same tone of voice, while the reverse, a tone revealing distrust, may invoke an aggressive reply. In addition, a poor choice of words or phrases reflecting double meanings, and a lack of appropriate feedback might well result in the creation of a psychological gap between the intervener and the person in crisis.

The interview should be handled in a calm manner, with the intervener speaking clearly and remaining respectful towards the victim. With a careful choice of words and the correct tone of voice the intervener assures the victim that he or she is responding calmly to the crisis situation. This will frequently have a calming effect on highly emotional persons in crisis.

Reassurance

Use of reassurance aids in calming an emotional person because it indicates to the person the intervener's concern for his or her situation. For example, the intervener may reassure the person with statements such as "Don't worry, we'll take care of it for you," . . . "Everything will be all right," . . . "The ambulance will be there very soon" or "Try not to be concerned, we're here now!" Reassurance works particularly well in calming a situation if the intervener has established a first impression of concern and desire to give assistance.

Ventilation

Encouraging the person to talk is often an effective means for calming him or her down. It is difficult for a person to continue yelling, screaming, crying, or cursing while trying to answer a series of questions at the same time. This procedure serves a double purpose, as in the process of ventilation the person will give important information that the intervener will need anyway. To this end, it will prove useful to encourage talking about the crisis itself. Questions relating to the event regarding who did what, at what location, and the time involved can be helpful to the intervener. However, some people will remain upset when talking about the crisis itself because of the intensity of the feelings they are experiencing. In this situation, information that has no emotions attached to it can be sought, such as names of people involved, addresses, ages, phone numbers, occupations, and so forth. Whichever methods seem suited to the situation, the intervener should realize that ventilation allows the victim to recapture dignity, respect, and control. The intervener should not interrupt while the victim is telling the story.

Psychological Distance

It bears repeating that the intervener should remain aware of psychological distancing. The intervener should not jump to a first-name basis, which would position him or her too close to the victim. To go to the opposite extreme, however—, the position of acting disinterested in the victim's problem—would position the intervener too far away.

Display of Confidence

The intervener may help by avoiding blaming responses such as "You should have locked the door," or "What were you doing out so late?" The intervener's role is to de-emphasize blame of the person in the crisis, and all efforts should be toward that end. The intervener should exhibit minimum use of officious behavior. Finally, the idea that the victim did the correct thing by calling for help should be conveyed with statements such as "You did the right thing by calling us." It is important to restore confidence and feelings of self-worth to the victim. The intervener is, after all, there to help.

The Necessity of Feedback

The single most important method of avoiding misunderstanding in crisis events is by providing feedback. False perceptions and small errors magnify into major distortion if the recipient does not have the opportunity to respond.

We are in a much better position to evaluate the effectiveness of our communications with others when we are aware of the complexity of the process and how easy it is to be misunderstood. The process of feedback is a way to reduce misunderstanding. The receiver can paraphrase the message as he or she understands it and ask the speaker whether he or she received the message the speaker had intended. The paraphrasing technique should be used when you want to enhance clarity and understanding between yourself and another person. It allows you to know what the other person means and assures the other person that you understand.

Paraphrasing consists of restating in your own words what the other person's statements mean to you. With this sort of restatement, the other person can determine whether the message getting through to you is the one that was intended. The paraphrase technique is based on the premise that when an individual expresses an idea, and that idea is restated in another way by the listener, the initiator of the statement will clarify, expand upon, or further explore the ideas and feelings embodied in the statement. For example:

Caller: Officer, I was robbed. I came home and all my valuables are gone.

Officer: Do you mean to say that someone came into your home while you were gone and stole your valuables?

Caller: Yes, officer. That is correct.

Officer: I see. Then your home was burglarized.

This technique is valuable in that it prevents communication breakdown between the two parties and clarifies the message being communicated.

Use the following guidelines when paraphrasing during feedback:

Restate the other person's expressed ideas and feelings in your own words.

Preface your paraphrase with a tentative introductory phrase such as:

"Are you saying...?"

"You mean that...?"

"You feel that...?"

"It seems to you that...?"

"It appears to you that...?"

Avoid any indication of disapproval or approval; refrain from blaming, expressing rejection or strong support; and avoid giving advice or persuading.

Wait for the other person's response.

Where necessary, paraphrase the other's response in order to secure the most accurate understanding possible.

To increase the effectiveness of listener feedback, consider the following guidelines:

1. Send feedback that is appropriate to the speaker, the message and the situation.

2. Be certain that the speaker understands the feedback. If there is any question, send it again to ensure proper understanding.

3. Make certain that the feedback is clear.

4. Send the feedback quickly. Delayed responses or silence may be misinterpreted as ambiguous or negative feedback.

5. Beware of sending too much feedback in too short a time. Do not overload "the system." Time your responses at appropriate intervals.

6. Delay performing any activity that might create an effect you did not intend.

7. Keep your emotional or personal feelings out of any feedback to the caller.

8. Use neutral, noncritical feedback.

9. Be sure that you understand the message before you respond.

10. Realize that initial attempts at giving more effective feedback may seem difficult at first. However, with practice, it will become easier.

Chapter 5

CRISIS INTERVENTION WITH VICTIMS

VICTIMOLOGY

While crisis theory deals primarily with the devastating effects of the emotional trauma of internal and external crisis, one other situation to be considered by the crisis intervener is the emotional aftereffects of becoming a victim. Many of the people that the criminal justice intervener comes into contact with have been victims by virtue of their crisis. Victimology is an area of crisis behavior and intervention that takes a closer look at the victim. Literature on violent crime in the past has generally focused on the criminal or the criminal act. It has only been in recent years that the third element in violent crime, the victim, has attracted professional interest. However, even these studies have dealt solely with the perspective of victim behavior, in victim-stimulated crimes. This perspective is usually called *victim-precipitated,* and it highlights the fact that victims frequently contribute to their own victimization: to their own murder by striking the first blow or hurling the first insult, to their own robberies by leaving doors unlocked and valuable possessions in plain sight, or to the theft of their automobiles by leaving doors unlocked and keys in the ignition.

Unfortunately, this tendency of crime investigators to assign responsibility for criminal acts to the victim has merely reinforced previously held and assumed similar beliefs and rationalizations held by most criminals themselves, namely, "They asked for it." The last decade has produced major improvements for protecting the rights of the accused, providing humane treatment to the convicted, and delivering services to the ex-offender. However, the plight of the victim of the crime has been ignored. While the needs of rape victims and battered women have received increased attention, what is often forgotten is the overall suffering that every crime victim endures as a result of the crime, whether it be a purse snatching or an assault. Proponents of victim services point to the disproportionate amounts of money that are expended on offenders to provide them with transportation, room and board, medical services, legal counsel, and treatment programs ranging from mental health counseling to job placement. Victims, however, must pay the bills for any similar services they might require as a result of their victimization. Moreover, it is the young and elderly, who are often poor and uneducated, who are most frequently victimized yet are least able to cope with the consequences, whether financially or emotionally.

If the offender is apprehended, the victim as a witness becomes vulnerable to further inconveniences and distress. Victims tend to perceive themselves as "pieces of evidence" within the criminal justice system. If they choose to prosecute they must be questioned, often repeatedly, and must sacrifice work days and secure transportation or child care for seemingly endless court appearances, many of which may be postponed or cancelled with no advance notice. Decisions are made with little or no explanation. Their recovered stolen property will be needed as evidence and thus may remain lost to them.

In terms of societal reactions to victims, it became apparent early in the research of the study of victims of violent crimes that society has some strange attitudes toward victims. There seemed to be a marked reluctance to accept the innocence or accidental nature of the victim's behavior prior to the crime having been committed against them and even after the crime. This reluctance was demonstrated by community responses, police behavior, family reactions to the victim, and surprisingly, by the victims themselves. This reluctance or resistance to accept or believe in the total innocence of the victims of violent crime was demonstrated in the early responses of others to the victim after the initial shock responses of the non-victim observer had dissipated. The nonvictim listener of the victim's story, whether it be police, friends, or family, is in most cases entirely unaware of the psychological trauma that is being experienced by the victim.

The purpose of this chapter is to share an understanding of the innocent or accidental nature of the victim's involvement in violent crimes perpetrated against them. It will focus on the emotional and psychological stages that the victim goes through during the course of victimization.

The following flow chart depicts the effects of victimization and the process by which the victim is assisted back to normal behavior by the person intervening (figure 5.1).

PSYCHOLOGICAL CASUALTIES: LOSS OF POWER, DIGNITY, AND SECURITY

The emotional impact of being a victim collapses the psychological world of the victim. The most prominent psychological casualty is the sense of

Figure 5.1
Victimology Flow Chart

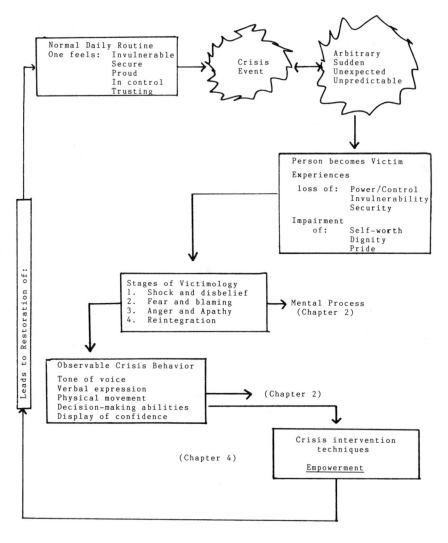

Normal Daily Routine
One feels: Invulnerable
Secure
Proud
In control
Trusting

Crisis
Event

Arbitrary
Sudden
Unexpected
Unpredictable

Person becomes Victim

Experiences

loss of: Power/Control
Invulnerability
Security

Impairment
of: Self-worth
Dignity
Pride

Stages of Victimology
1. Shock and disbelief
2. Fear and blaming
3. Anger and Apathy
4. Reintegration

Mental Process
(Chapter 2)

Observable Crisis Behavior

Tone of voice
Verbal expression
Physical movement
Decision-making abilities
Display of confidence

(Chapter 2)

Crisis intervention
techniques

Empowerment

(Chapter 4)

Leads to Restoration of:

invulnerability with which most people manage to face the risks of daily life. Also shattered are the person's sense that the world is comprehensible and has meaning, and for many years after the trauma a person's very sense of worth may be damaged. Whenever someone becomes victimized by a crime, whatever the nature, his or her very basic assumptions about self and the world are undermined. Psychological recovery requires rebuilding those assumptions. The key assumption that crumbles is invulnerability, the sense that the world is benevolent, controllable, and fair, and that so long as one acts as one should, nothing bad will happen. A catastrophe attacks these deeply held beliefs. Suddenly all the world seems bad.

This psychological trauma also includes the loss of power, the loss of dignity, and the loss of security. To individuals in their normal daily routines these three characteristics function in such a way that they give them the ability to communicate verbally, the competence to make decisions, and the ability to move about with a sense of confidence and safety. However, to the victims of crimes, the loss of these characteristics impairs their behavior to such a great extent that they are unable to function in their usual way.

Continuing research with victims of criminal violence supports the notion that the general reactions of victims are similar to the psychological responses of individuals who have experienced sudden and unexpected losses. Loss of any kind, particularly those of a sudden and unexpected nature, produces this sequence of response in individuals. It also is easily recognizable as the same phases seen in depression. This concept is of clinical value in the psychological treatment of victims. What have the victims of crimes lost? It is more than just the loss of money, valuables, or physical functioning. They have lost the feelings of individual invulnerability. They have lost their trust in a society on which they have depended to protect them from harm. Many of the victims have lost their self-respect and feel shameful when they think about their need for compliant behavior while they were with the criminal. Many of the victims also feel anger at having gained the unenviable status of suddenly becoming a victim.

Victims typically go through four major stages in reaction to their victimization. These four stages are:

1. Shock, disbelief, and denial,
2. Fright and blaming,
3. Anger and apathy,
4. Resignation, resolution, and integration.

Stage 1: Shock, Disbelief, and Denial

The first phase of the victim's reactive behavior includes shock, disbelief, and denial. Whenever one is subject to a sudden, unexpected attack of violence, there is the initial response of shock, numbness, disbelief, and then denial. The victim will freeze up, judgment and thinking may be suspended, and motor ability may be impaired. The victim may say, "I don't believe this!" or "I don't know what happened," and "I feel so numb." On the other hand, the victim may not be able to even articulate what has happened.

Denial is a psychological defense mechanism. It is an involuntary process by which the mind tries to block out the pain of a reality with which the individual cannot cope. When people are first confronted with a crime committed against them they often refuse to believe that it has occurred. Victims of an auto theft may walk all over a parking lot looking for their car, thinking that they have somehow misplaced or forgotten where they parked it, before there are ready to admit that it has been stolen. Victims of a burglary coming home to a house in disarray will sometimes firmly believe that someone is playing a joke on them. Victims of rape will report afterwards that during the crime they repeatedly said, "This can't be happening to me," and other victims of any type of crime will often say, "I still can't believe this has happened." This statement is more than just a comment in passing. Victims literally cannot comprehend what has happened to them.

A variation on the defense of denial is intellectualization. In this type of response, victims admit what has happened but do not allow an emotional reaction to occur. Such victims will be matter-of-fact and controlled in their discussion of the crime committed against them. They behave as if the experience has made no impression on them. This involuntary process is a way of coping with the event by dealing with it only at the intellectual level. They are denying the emotional impact that they have experienced and are attempting to control the situation by being rational and self-controlled while talking about it.

Victims of rape and other highly emotionally charged crimes may at times be strongly intellectual in their reactions. They usually take time to "get themselves under control" before calling the police. They will then describe the details in a flat, emotionless, and well-organized fashion. These defenses are often fragile and easily permeated by a kind word or expressions of sympathy, which will often initiate a breakdown of emotions by the victim.

Stage 2: Fright and Blaming

Once victims pass through stage 1, or if the victims' attempts at denial fail, they then become frightened and seek to place blame for what has happened. The stage of fright is usually accompanied by clinging behavior. Very frequently individuals may find themselves compulsively talking and obsessively ruminating about the event. For some individuals, in particular conforming and dependent people, there may be a prolonging of one or more stages of the victims' reactions. For example, some victims remain for months in the stage of fright, with clinging behavior as the result. Extra locks, extra precautions, and excessive suspiciousness are substituted for judgment. Victims will cling to their families, repeating the details of the crime over and over. The family may begin to feel after a while that this compulsive talking is not a good idea and will therefore encourage the victim to be silent and not relive the scene. This mistaken concept of protective silence, however, may prolong the depressive reaction.

In this stage of fright some victims report persistent, recurrent fantasies or dreams that have a similar theme. The most frequent theme is that the criminal will return and either kill them or injure them more seriously. At other times, the victim may have a fleeting but recurrent thought of killing the criminal, but this thought is completely submerged by a counterthought of "What if I fail, or I succeed and kill him? His family and his friends will try to get revenge on me in return."

Blaming means more than assuming responsibility when something goes wrong: it implies punishing the responsible party. We learn, however, to equate the two, so that to be responsible means to be blamed. We frequently believe that we will be punished after harm befalls us. To avoid punishment or scolding, many people will place complete responsibility on others when something goes wrong. The blaming process will be demonstrated in statements or questions that imply "What did you do to deserve it?" A victim of a burglary may be told, "You should have taken better care of your belongings!"

Crime victims reflect this fear of being blamed by going out of their way to blame someone else and to deny that they were anything but completely innocent victims. This desire to avoid blame and to place it somewhere leads to some predictable results. Blame is sometimes focused on particular people who are disliked by the victim or whom the victim fears. "Those people down the street," "Some guy who was hanging around here" or "Those new people who moved in" often become the target of accusations.

The police or other people who intervene in a crisis often become the target for the blame and are often blamed for the crimes committed against the victim. "This is what I pay you to prevent?" . . . "Where were you when I needed you?" or "You damned cops! I was just robbed down the block and you guys are standing here talking!" are all statements and accusations that have been expressed toward the police. This behavior is simply an example of the old maxim that the best defense is a good offense. The victim tries to avoid blame by placing it on the guardian who failed.

Other victims will blame themselves: "I shouldn't have gone out tonight" . . . "I should have known he was a rapist" or "Why did I get on that elevator, he looked suspicious!" Self-blame and self-recriminations are also part of the second stage of victimology.

Stage 3: Anger or Apathy

Anger follows from blame. Once the guilty party has been identified, it is legitimate to direct anger at him or her. However, there are many barriers to doing this. Helping the victim direct anger appropriately and to overcome these barriers is a valuable part of psychological first aid (which was covered in Chapter 4), and often also helps increase the victim's cooperation in the investigation.

What are the barriers to directing anger appropriately? One is that the selection of targets is limited and none are without repercussions, at least from the victim's helpless perspective. One obvious target, as discussed in stage 2, is the self. Anger turned against the self is manifested as depression. In depression, the self-berating and self-accusing victim has turned the anger against the self and is punishing the self with inner-directed rage.

Another target is the criminal. However, to the victim the criminal is a dangerous person toward whom it is difficult to display anger. The criminal has placed the victim in great danger and has exhibited the power to destroy the victim. The victim may fear that to display anger against the criminal is to invite even more punishment. Consequently, victims are often hesitant to voice their anger directly against the criminal. This is especially true when there has been a personal contact, as in armed robbery or rape. Rape victims are often remarkably "understanding" and protective of the rapist and hesitate to prosecute because "he is a sick man and shouldn't be punished." Such a statement may be taken as an index of the amount of fear that the victim has experienced. Instead, the victim may displace her anger at someone less threatening, who is, however, safer. This is the common defense mechanism of displacement.

Because of the barriers to expressions of anger, the victim often expresses generalized anger or focuses on a vaguely defined group or even the responding crisis intervener. What is important here is that when someone feels helpless in a hostile situation, feelings of anger and aggressiveness develop which get turned against those trying to provide assistance. Those who are helpless blame the helpers for having allowed them to be that way. Very often children who hurt themselves blame their mother for the hurt, "You should have prevented this from happening to me." Children feel that whenever unpleasant things happen it is someone's fault—this is typically a childlike response and usually directed at the mother: "Why did Mother allow this to happen to me? Is it because she doesn't like me?" People in crisis are childlike in their helpless situation and react with childlike behavior to authority figures as they did in childhood to their mothers.

Emergency personnel who understand the pressures that push the victim to express anger in this fashion can be very helpful by letting the victim ventilate and by then helping the victim direct the anger where it belongs, at the criminal. This can be very difficult to do, but it provides a good service to the victim. The crisis intervener must certainly avoid becoming defensive and engaging the victim in an agrument to prove that the anger is displaced.

Some victims have a prolonged period of anger with inner- and outer-directed rage. The victim may become angry at the criminal justice system (police, courts, etc.), the assailant, society, and at him- or herself. After these feelings of anger, the victim starts to feel that nobody cares or can do anything about the predicament.

The loss of feelings of invulnerability—the disillusionment in society's ability to protect the individual from harm—quite often intensifies the victim's feelings of resentment and anger, which will then move on to feelings of apathy. When one is apathetic he or she will appear to be absent of feeling, indifferent, and insensible. Apathy may also be a defense used to deny an extreme anxiety with which the person cannot cope. If the intervener tries to deal with the apathy by stimultaing an increased awareness of what happened, the the victim will become more apathetic. Commonly heard expressions of apathy will be: "The hell with people, who needs them anyway!" ... "You have to look out for yourself!" ... "People are animals," ... "No one gives a damn," and "The world is a jungle!" A female rape victim expressed her thoughts in the following manner:

What hurt me more was the complete indifference and lack of consideration of my feelings in my hour of need by people I know and work with. Who cares? Nobody! Nobody is going to do anything about it anyway!

Stage 4: Resignation, Resolution, and Integration

During the final stage of victimology there is a calm acceptance by victims of the misfortune that has occurred. That is, the victims resign themselves to what has happened. There then follows a resolution—the solving of the problem—whereby the victims slowly begin to reintegrate their lives in an attempt to attain their position prior to the criminal act. Victims will, during this period, gather all the parts of their lives that have been scattered because of the crisis event and bring them together to make their lives whole and solid again.

The crisis intervener plays a very important role in helping crime victims begin to recover from the psychological shock that they have experienced. Victims need help to face the facts, to place blame where it belongs, and to direct anger appropriately. They also need the information and psychological support that a crisis intervener can supply to help them develop secure expectations about the future. They need help to regain their feelings of self-respect and control over their environment.

Knowledge of these facts does not tell interveners what to do with any particular victim. However, it will encourage an understanding of victim behavior, and help to develop a framework within which to isolate behavioral goals.

If the psychological process of coming to grips with the incident is not completed, results can take the form of psychosomatic complaints such as stomach problems, headaches, or inability to work or to love. The sudden emergence of these symptoms long after the event usually catches people by surprise. Similar symptoms are commonly seen among the shell-shocked victims of war. The pattern, now called the posttraumatic stress syndrome, includes recurrent dreams of the traumatic event, the numbing of emotions, and guilt about having survived when others have not.

Some psychologists feel that the common belief that people recover from disaster after a few weeks is based on mistaking denial for recovery. Many of the symptoms do not appear until long after the victim seems to have fully recovered from the victimization, and when problems do arise—such as difficulty concentrating, depression, or sleeplessness—their causes may go unrecognized. Some people who have suffered victimization may afterward undergo a diminished sense of self-worth for 10 to 15 years, or even longer.

LONG-TERM SYMPTOMS

The normal immediate response to a severe trauma is an outcry of fear, rage, or sadness at the terrible impact on one's life. This is often followed closely by a state of dazed shock. That shock is the beginning of a psychological denial of the tragedy, a denial that seems to serve a positive purpose in allowing the person to come to grips with his or her shattered world at a rate he or she can manage. For weeks or even years after the event, denial—blocking the facts from awareness—oscillates with intrusive thoughts of the tragedy as the person slowly comes to face its full emotional truth.

If that process goes awry, a variety of more severe problems can arise. If the initial reaction of distress and fear is not relieved, the person may sink into a state of total exhaustion or the feelings may escalate into outright panic. During the longer course of recovery, people may either fall prey to extremes of denial or to being emotionally flooded by thoughts of the event. Extreme denial can take many forms, including a general numbing of emotions, serious loss of the ability to concentrate or to follow a train of thought, or an avoidance of topics even vaguely associated with the event. If the memories of the event intrude constantly, denial can take such forms as an excessive alertness to an unrealistic danger, sudden waves of uncontrollable emotion, and nightmares.

VICTIM'S RESPONSES TO SPECIFIC CRIMES

The following examples of crimes are incidents that initiate crisis behavior on the part of the victim. Because of the varying degree of stress precipitated by the different types of incidents, the intensity of the trauma will vary from incident to incident, as well as from person to person. However, even though the intensity of the traumatic experience varies, each of these incidents will trigger the full range of crisis response, thereby affecting victims' ability to communicate, their ability to make decisions, their motor abilities, and, consequently, in varying degrees, their perception of their own self-confidence.

Different types of offenses perpetrated against a victim precipitate varying degrees of psychological trauma. The degree by which the victim is affected depends on many factors. However, one determinant factor is the amount of aggressiveness perpetrated against the victim by the assailant. For example:

Assault. In the crimes of assault there is usually injury to the external self. The trauma that the assault victim experiences is far more devastating than the trauma experienced by victims of property crimes, and yet is different from the trauma experienced by the rape victim. People who are most prone to becoming victims of assault are:

1. The young, who are physically weaker and inexperienced.
2. Females, who are physically weaker.
3. The elderly: The aging human being is handicapped in many ways, including physically, and mentally.
4. The mentally deficient and other mentally disturbed; The feeble-minded, the emotionally disturbed, the drug addict, and the alcoholic all form another large group of potential and actual victims of assault.

The assault victim is often referred to as a primary victim; these are victims who may be directly assaulted and injured and who may have had property taken from them. A face-to-face contact with the assailant makes the crisis far more traumatic.

Rape and Sexual Assault. In the crimes of rape and sexual assault, part of one's self is violated through the loss of autonomy, possible injury to one's external self, and the removal or soiling of clothing. In addition, there is the possible injury to the internal self. Recent research in this area has indicated that the perpetration of this type of crime has little to do with sexual gratification; in reality, the intent is to hurt or destroy, with intense anger and power being the motivators (see chapter 7).

Homicide. In this situation, family and friends of the victim are the persons in the crisis state. Families of homicide victims experience the same stages of victimology as do victims. They are in reality the secondary victims. During the crisis phase there is an acute grief process which includes immediate reactions to the homicide, during which funeral or memorial service preparation details are made. During this period thoughts about the assailant permeate, and the police investigation interrupts family members' lives.

Losing a significant person can be a severe personal loss. Losing someone through the natural death process is already severe, but when someone is lost through a violent death such as homicide the suddenness of the event and the violent nature are much more traumatic on the family. Family members are usually preoccupied with the details of the crime, "Who did it?" . . . "How did it happen?" . . . "Where was [the victim] when it happened?" . . . and "did [the victim] suffer?"

Also, while in a natural death family and friends will take responsibility for death notifications, in a homicide this responsibility usually falls on police officers. They will be the first to break the news and will be intensely questioned about details. In addition, identifying the body places additional psychological burdens on the family. Family members will usually be confused and numb, and will suffer symptoms of shock.

Burglary. In the crime of burglary, not only is property taken, but an extension of the victim's self is violated.

Robbery. In the crime of robbery, an extension of one's self is removed from the person, and therefore a loss of autonomy is experienced by the victim.

VICTIMS OF PROPERTY CRIMES

In order to appreciate the experience of being the victim of a property crime we must be aware of the importance of the home as a symbol. In an important sense, the home is an extension of the self. Similarly, but to a lesser degree, one might also feel that one's automobile is a symbolic extension of one's self. It is not uncommon to find much unnecessary destruction and degradation at the scene of a burglary. The criminals will enter, destroy things, kill pets, and even defecate, all in an effort to exhibit power at the expense of the victim. The victims of these acts feel the loss of power and control when they return home to view this kind of devastation. Many people invest feelings of invulnerability in their homes; that is, they feel most secure and safe when they are at home. Therefore, when their security is invaded, there may be overwhelming feelings of vulnerability, loss of power and control, and loss of security and safety in what had been their haven of warmth and safety from the outside world.

Property victims, particularly burglary victims, generally conform to the stages of the victimology response pattern. The first reaction is shock and denial. This initial reaction is experienced upon the return home and the finding of a broken window or an open door. Objectively, one might expect someone coming home to this type of situation to: (1) call the police; (2) wait for their arrival; and (3) wait until the police secure the dwelling before entering. However, many burglary victims, because they are in the first stages of disbelief and shock, will enter the building immediately, not wishing to accept the fact that their home was burglarized.

The victim's next response is fright and anger. Expressions of this fear will surface with such behavior as replacing locks with expensive new mechanisms; adding window gates, guard dogs, and alarms; sleeping with the lights on; not sleeping at home; and, finally, moving to a new home. In many cases there is a fear that the intruder will return to cause further harm. Although logically and statistically this is unfounded, the fear is real and should not be scoffed at or treated lightly.

Of course, in most burglaries the criminal is not present when the victim returns home, so this fright and anger cannot be directed at the proper target. We can expect that this anger at the criminal will build up and accumulate until it is triggered by someone or something entirely uninvolved with the incident. In an attempt to develop a rational explanation for having been victimized, people will blame others who might have inadvertently "facilitated" the crime. The supposed facilitation might include such things as leaving a window open, not double-locking a door, not leaving a radio or light on, and so forth. It is virtually impossible to live in a stressful environment such as a large city and maintain a level of alertness high enough to always remember to take every precautionary step available to prevent a burglary. However, an explanation synonymous with blame must be found if one is operating under the traditional victim-precipitator concept of victimology.

It is not uncommon that blame and misplaced anger will be directed at the crisis intervener. There may be a very subtle hostility detectable in the voice of the person or evident in his or her overt actions. If the intervener accepts this as a personal criticism, the interaction will be strained and not at all beneficial for either of the parties involved.

INTERVENER MISUNDERSTANDING OF PERSONAL PROPERTY CRIMES

One situation in which the crisis intervener may have difficulty appreciating the kind of crisis a victim is experiencing occurs when the victims call in to report financial loss or personal property damage. In those types of situations in which there is no physical injury there may be a tendency by interveners to minimize the loss suffered. Consider a situation in which a woman calls to report that she returned home after a week of vacation to find her apartment burglarized. What factors are involved in the efforts of the crisis intervener to minimize this situation and the way the victim feels in reality?

From a human relations point of view an intervener has to be aware of insensitivity. This lack of feeling for the victim's plight is apt to happen for the following reasons:

1. The intervener will tend to minimize the loss incurred by the victim and to treat the matter lightly because;

a. The intervener will perceive the monetary value of the property taken as opposed to the personal value to the victim.

b. The intervener knows that there is only a very slim chance that the victim will ever have the property returned.

c. Small property losses tend to pale in significance when compared to other crimes that the intervener will frequently encounter.

2. The victim on the other hand tends to maximize the loss incurred and treat the burglary very seriously. This occurs for at least three valid reasons:

a. The monetary value of the property taken is only one aspect of the victim's plight. The property could be worth very little from the point of view of the cost of the item, but it could be priceless from a personal point of view. An item may have cherished memories attached to it that can never be replaced. It could mean and often does mean that the victim will be inconvenienced by its loss, at least temporarily. All these facts tend to raise an item's value as far as the victim is concerned.

b. The victim does not know that there is very little chance of ever getting the property back. She expects to get help and expects results and cannot understand why the intervener would treat her situation so lightly.

c. The victim has only an abstract idea of similar crimes happening to others. All the victim can think of is that, "This happened to me, and it is the worst thing that has ever happened to me."

This situation is an example of two individuals seeing the same incident from opposing points of view. The intervener cannot understand why the victim is making such an awful fuss about some small items that were taken and would really like to tell her about the auto accident that he just handled in which five people lost their lives. In the intervener's perspective, the accident is really something to be concerned about.

The victim, on the other hand, cannot understand why the intervener is treating her loss so lightly: "Doesn't he realize that one of the items taken was a precious locket that has been passed down in the family for generations?"

The result is that these misunderstandings cause difficult feelings between the intervener and the victim. The intervener may become so annoyed about the victim's emotional state that he does very little to calm or reassure her other than simply taking the required information. The victim may become so angry for the visible lack of concern that she may become embittered toward all criminal justice people in general.

The crisis intervener must then realize that if he is going to help this victim he must try to understand the situation from her perspective. He must treat the incident as seriously as the victim does. Although he realizes that there is little chance that the property will be found, he must reassure the victim that everything that could possible be done will be done on her behalf.

Crisis Intervention in Property Crimes

Restoring power to victims of property crimes is important. This restoration of power may be accomplished in many ways. A criminal justice worker has symbolic authority, which includes an aura of power to assist those who are in need. Some of this power can be returned to the victims if the intervener will do the following

1. *Ask permission.* "May I ask you some questions now?" "Do you mind if I take notes on this?"

2. *Accept credibility.* One can listen discerningly without conveying suspicion.

3. *Perception of criticism.* Realize the forces that generate hostility and do not react to implied criticism such as: "What can you people do for me now?" or "It's too late, everything's gone."

4. *Guilt Reduction.* Try to help victims realize that the negative self-evaluation they might be engaging in is unfair and nonproductive.

5. *Importance.* Make the victims feel that their cases are important. However, do not make any promises that cannot be kept. Consider all property taken as valuable. The critical point here is that I am in no way implying or suggesting that victims be falsely appeased. Saying to the victim, "Don't worry, we'll get your property back" would be a disservice to all involved. Also, to say "Forget it, you'll never see your belongings again" would be just as nonproductive. Once again, the important concern should be "What do you need now in your moment of crisis?"

SUMMARY

In this chapter the study of the victim is discussed. Victims suffer emotional, psychological, and physical trauma that is initiated by the crisis event. The victim may reach out for help while in any one of the four stages of victimology. The intervener may adjust the response mode accordingly so as to have a stabilizing effect on the victim.

During Stage 1, Shock, Disbelief, and Denial, victims are preoccupied with convincing themselves that the crisis did not occur. Therefore, they are not receptive to a logical and productive interchange. The intervener must be patient and wait for this period of preoccupation to pass.

During Stage 2, Fright and Blaming, the victims experience fear and a need to place blame. The intervener should be aware that victims may raise their voices or attempt to blame the intervener for their condition. This is not a personal issue, but is merely an expression of emotional need. Furthermore, the intervener may also expect to see a possible switch in behavior. Some victims may express clinging behavior, attempting to keep the intervener close to them, while blaming the intervener at the same time. This is not unusual behavior.

During Stage 3, Anger and Apathy, victims will reach out for help in expressing their anger. Ventilating the angry feelings should be viewed as a positive reaction, a healthy response. Sometimes a victim may suddenly refuse to talk. This may signal that the victim is experiencing apathy and is now holding emotions inside.

During Stage 4, Resignation, Resolution, and Integration, individuals resign themselves to the situation. If the crisis intervention was a positive one, the victims will resign themselves to their situation and resolve the crisis in a psychologically healthy manner.

As the medical doctor needs to examine the patient in order to render a proper diagnosis and prescribe medication for the safe return of normal bodily functions, so does the crisis intervener need to analyze behavior for effective intervention, noting the various psychological states and determining how to intervene in each stage in order to help the victim overcome the crisis.

Chapter *6*

SPECIFIC GROUPS

In the preceding chapters, crisis theory and victimology were presented in order to establish a certain conceptual framework that can be used as a focal point for discussion. We now turn to the more practical matters of crisis intervention and particular population groups that frequently come to the attention of the criminal justice crisis intervener. These may easily be neglected by interveners for various reasons. They may include the bereaved, the suicidal person, the alcoholic/drug abuser, the elderly, the mentally retarded, and the emotionally ill, and a population that have neither been treated properly nor adequately acknowledged as deserving treatment, victims of violence.

DEATH AS A CRISIS EVENT

Grief is as real as our very existence; an inevitable part of life. Virtually everyone must deal with grief at some time in his or her lifetime. This grief may follow the death of grandparents, parents, siblings, children, friends, or even pets. Some people also appear to experience grief following events in which someone has not died. These include knowledge of one's own impending death, separations, divorce, abortions, aging in loved ones, loss of children's dependence, leaving a familiar neighborhood, or giving up a life's dream. Most people are able to normally experience the grief process, but others suffer the common reaction of depression.

Death, no matter how or when it occurs, is a crisis event for those who were close to the person who died. Whether sudden or expected, the sense of loss involved creates crisis reactions in those remaining. Just the thought of human death is usually suppressed by individuals. Because of the finality of death, the fear of the unknown, the sadness of the event, and the stress provoked by both the thought and the event, people naturally tend to avoid the subject. The reminder that such thoughts evoke assurances of our finite life is the basic reason for such denial.

Nevertheless, making calls regarding death is another important aspect of the crisis intervener's job. Just about every human death that occurs in a large city except supervised deaths (i.e., those occurring in hospitals or institutions) requires some form of criminal justice involvement. Besides the necessary administrative matters, such as cards, reports, notifications, and other required duties, the intervener must be able to recognize crisis symptoms among those who witness the death and render proper service consistent with crisis intervention techniques.

Types of death have been classified into three categories: natural, accidental, and intentional. These are now briefly defined as they are related to criminal justice involvement:

1. *Natural death:* Heart attacks, old age, and chronic illnesses usually comprise the bulk of non-suspicious deaths that are handled by criminal justice agencies.
2. *Intentional death:* This area includes all homicides (justifiable and criminal) as well as suicides.
3. *Accidental death:* The range in this category is quite diverse. Traffic accidents account for the greatest number of these deaths, although fires, poisoning, and drug abuse also have their impact. More recently, the autoerotic death has gained much attention and also belongs in this category.

For the crisis intervener, the human relations aspect in each of the three categories is basically the same. Every major loss disrupts the development of self-esteem, the smooth progress of life, and the sense that events are predictable and meaningful. In each situation, the intervener will interact with a concerned party of the victim—coworkers, a close friend, a spouse, or other relative. Recovery from such losses requires that damaged self-esteem be repaired, continuity be reestablished, and a sense of meaning be restored.

Bereavement is the term used to describe the effects of a loss, by death, of a loved one. Interveners should be able to deal with expressions of bereavement by others. They should be able to interact with and offer comfort to those who are closely involved with the situation. Not only must interveners efficiently handle the situation, they must also be emotionally able to handle the call themselves. Calls regarding a person dismembered in an automobile accident or struck by a train, or regarding an infant death, all manage to emotionally sneak through the staunchest defenses. Interveners must be comfortable with the topic of death and thereby their own mortality.

Becoming too engrossed in obtaining information for reports and over-absorption in gathering information regarding the death scene are common reactions in the performance of the inexperienced crisis intervener. These responses are expressions of the defense mechanisms of denial and intellectualization already discussed in chapter 2.

In order to understand grief and its impact it is important to describe the process of normal grief. Grief is a psychological process that follows a loss. It allows one to cope in a gradual manner with an overwhelming loss so that it can be accepted as a reality. If the full impact of the loss were suddenly experienced, the person might be psychologically overwhelmed. In grief, the existence of the one who is lost is prolonged so that the person gradually may come to terms with what has happened.

Crisis Intervention in Bereavement

The process of bereavement usually takes from four to six weeks to complete and it is characterized by the emotional side effects that accompany it. The stages are similar to the stages that are found in victimization. In the first stage, the initial reaction to learning of a death is shock and disbelief: "I don't believe it. It didn't happen." During this stage the bereaved may experience an alarm reaction—anxiety, restlessness, and the physiological accompaniments of fear. This will shift in the second stage to self-blame and feelings of guilt: "Maybe there was something I could or should have done."

The bereaved tend to be irritable and angry, and may direct angry outbursts toward those who press them toward premature acceptance of the loss. Statements such as, "Well, we all die at some time" . . . "It's a blessing" . . . "Time will heal" . . . "If there's anything I can do, just call" . . . "I know just how you feel," or "Thank God, he was so ill," are likely to draw an angry outbrust from the bereaved. These standard words for consoling the bereaved, no matter how well-intentioned, can only prolong grief and agony. A nursing surpervisor who had requested crisis intervention training for her staff recalled the incident that so clearly illustrated the need for this training:

One of our patients, an elderly man, 87 years of age, had died after enduring a long illness. His two sisters who had doted on him were very distraught over his passing. In an attempt at providing comfort, one of my nurses said to them, "'Tis a blessing from God. He's better off now." The two sisters became enraged at this perceived insenstivity to their loss and filed a formal complaint against the nurse.

The anguished sisters naturally wondered why their brother had to suffer an illness for such a long time and were focused on their own loss at that moment rather than what their brother had felt.

Bereavement is often mixed with conflicting love and hate. Sometimes this conflict is expressed because of previously unsolved problems that the bereaved had with the deceased. Sometimes the intervener will hear expressions of hostility, aggression, and anger directed toward the dead person for various reasons; for not remaining alive, for leaving work unfinished, or for causing the grief. A young mother left with small children might say: "That jerk! How could he leave me at a time like this, with all of these kids to take care of!"

Emotional Side Effects

Healthy grieving has certain characteristic signs and symptoms. The bereaved will experience feelings of pain, sadness, and emptiness during these stages, as well as a feeling of helplessness. The psychological discomfort is often accompanied by waves of weeping, experiencing a feeling of tightness in the throat, or a choking accompanied by a shortness of breath and sighing. Feelings of exhaustion are common, as well as insomnia, loss of interest in the surroundings, loss of appetite, and constipation. There is usually a preoccupation with the image of the deceased, and a reliving of memories involving that person. Gradually the death is accepted and the final stage of resolution and resignation sets in. Crisis interveners can and should be skilled and instrumental in relieving the guilt immediately after death, and demonstrating compassion for the family.

Interveners must realize that rejecting attitudes may be expressed by family, friends, or anyone who had a close relationship to the deceased, and that rejection will, in turn, cause guilt and shame. Emotional expressions may include grief at loss, rage at desertion, and guilt for having failed the victim. At the same time, these members, particularly a spouse, may experience a number of reactions and feelings and may show contempt for the victim. It is not uncommon for the intervener to hear:

- "Why did she do this to me?" (rejection)

- "What am I going to do without him?" (loss)

- "If only I had been home. This wouldn't have happened." (guilt)

- "That louse, leaving me with all these kids." (anger)

- "I tried to help him. It didn't work." (sense of failure)

- "Why didn't I believe his threats?" (inadequacy)

- "It's all my fault." (guilt)

- "I hope no one finds out about this." (shame)

- "She left me. Now I'm all alone." (abandonment)

- "He couldn't have really loved me or he would have let me help." (neglect-helplessness)
- "If I had loved him the right way, I would have been able to help." (guilt)

Such statements will be intermixed with expressions of guilt and grief. The intervener may be required to continually reassure the involved persons that the suicide was not their fault, that they did all that they could for the deceased. The bereaved person will need assistance in accepting these feelings. Encourage ventilation of anger and even give the person permission to have such feelings. Help the bereaved explore their meanings. It is not necessary for interveners to respond to all of these feelings, but they should be aware of their existence and be sensitive to them when they are expressed. This will allow responsibilities to be completed more efficiently and avoid any unnecessary confrontations.

Normal grieving, like resolving crises and the final stages of death, requires acceptance. Interveners can help in the grieving process by understanding the stages and relaying this information to those who are grieving. Normal grieving entails:

1. Dealing with the memory loss of the deceased.
2. Openly expressing pain, sorrow, hostility, and guilt. The person must be able to mourn openly by weeping and expressing feelings of guilt or anger.
3. Understanding that the intense feelings associated with loss are a normal part of grieving. Feelings of going crazy, guilt, and hostility, when worked through with a caring person, gradually subside.
4. Eventual resumption of normal activities and social relationships without the lost person. Once the memories and feelings associated with the loss are worked through, new patterns of social interaction develop.

Successful intervention with the bereaved means:

1. Listening actively and with concern; being nonjudgmental, uncritical and comforting;
2. Encouraging the open expression of feelings;
3. Helping the person gain an understanding of the crisis, thus curtailing self-blame; and
4. Helping the individual gradually accept reality.

CRISIS INTERVENTION IN CRIB DEATH

Of the many death situations criminal justice personnel may respond to, none is more traumatic or baffling than that of "crib death." Sudden Infant Death Syndromoe (SIDS) describes a mysterious and frightening disease that annually claims the lives of between 10,000 and 20,000 babies in the

United States who are between two weeks and twelve months of age. They seem to be healthy, normal babies; then suddenly, inexplicably, they die. SIDS strikes without warning, without previous illness, without any sound or struggle, and always while the infant is asleep. It strikes seemingly normal babies and is neither predictable nor preventable. Since the child dies within minutes, it is unlikely that even the presence of a physician at the precise moment of occurrence could prevent the fatality. It almost invariably happens at home, in the middle of the night, and is discovered upon the parents' awakening in the morning.

The uncertainty connected with this type of death makes it especially difficult for parents to accept. They are completely unprepared for the possibility that their new baby might die, and very often blame themselves. Bereaved parents experience severe psychological reactions to the death of their infants. They are usually convinced that they did or did not do something that caused the death:

"Maybe I should have been a better parent."

"Was it something I fed the baby?"

"Maybe I was sleeping too soundly and didn't hear the baby gagging."

"Did I hurt the baby unknowingly?"

"Did the baby suffocate because of the pillow I placed in the crib?"

"I had too many blankets on the baby. It's my fault."

"I must have crushed him when I turned over in the bed."

When one adds to this self-blame the questioning, interrogative approach of the responding police officers, and the queries of acquaintances, strangers, and relatives, one begins to understand the trauma that the parents suffer. Suspicious neighbors, concerned relatives, and inquiring police officers oftentimes blame the parents as well. In 1969, the Second International Conference on Causes of Sudden Death in Infants defined SIDS as "the sudden death of any infant or young child, which is unexpected by history, and in which a thorough postmortem examination fails to demonstrate an adequate cause for death." According to this definition the cause of death can only be established at autopsy. Nonetheless, in a small town in South Carolina in 1972, a baby died of SIDS while being cared for by his father. Not knowing that a healthy infant can die suddenly for no known cause, and taking the facial discoloration caused by SIDS to be a sign of foul play, the police arrested the father for murder. He was not released from jail until after the child's funeral, when analysis of the autopsy findings confirmed that the infant had died of SIDS. A SIDS victim may have a small amount of blood-tinged fluid in his nose and mouth, and bruise-like marks on the body where blood settled after death. Some officers may mistake these signs as the signs of physical child abuse when they are really the normal and routine signs of death in a SIDS victim.

Criminal justice and emergency medical personnel, faced with a dead infant and no history of antecedent illness, may unintentionally imply suspicion of neglect or infanticide. Considering the statistics on infant death, there is some natural ambiguity regarding criminal justice intervention. During one month in early 1987, 7 babies were found dead and abandoned in the streets of New York City. It is estimated that 200 may die this way each year in the United States. In New York State in 1986, 42 percent of children killed were infants less than one year old; in 78 percent of the cases, the mothers were the culprits. Therefore, it is not always clear whether the death of an infant is natural or infanticide. SIDS has been considered by critics as the medical discipline's method of explaining many unexplainable infant deaths.

At one time prior to the recognition of SIDS as a cause of infant deaths parents automatically came under suspicion. Not only did they have to contend with the loss of their child but also had to suffer the humiliation of police questioning. In recent years, although SIDS parents have been treated more compassionately, there has been an increasing negligence of proper investigation by police and social service agencies. It is assumed that the majority of infant deaths are SIDS, thus requiring little intervention. It seems to some that the pendulum has swung too far in the opposite direction. Nevertheless, in investigating infant deaths it is important to remember that, until the autopsy and other investigations reveal otherwise, the parents are to be treated with respect and consideration for their loss.

Causes of Crib Death

Historically these deaths have been blamed on smothering due to a pillow or blanket, or even the careless movements of the infant's mother while sleeping with the child. However, research has since demonstrated that smothering is rarely the cause of crib death. The actual cause of death is still unknown. Some researchers have noted that SIDS victims have mild colds at the time of death. Respiratory failure or weakening of the breathing responses has been noted as one possible cause. Another theory, proposed by Alfred Steinschneider, argues that SIDS infants have poorly developed brain mechanisms for coping with an occurrence of apnea. Apnea is a sleeping disorder associated with difficulty in breathing during the night. Steinschneider points out that autopsies of SIDS victims often reveal the pathological signs of long-term hypoventilation (the inadquate intake of air). This hypoventilation leads to underdeveloped body organs and body size.

Other researchers report that crib deaths are due to infant botulism, low levels of biotin in the livers of infants, abnormality of the infant blood's ability to carry oxygen, and alcohol abuse by the mother during pregnancy.

Psychologist Lewis P. Lipsitt, director of the Child Study Center at Brown University, has suggested that these infants die because they do not make the normal transition from reflexive to voluntary control of body mechanisms. This usually occurs between two and four months of age, the most dangerous time for SIDS. As a result these infants do not cry, move their heads, or take other steps to take in oxygen when air is blocked. Since babies have a built-in defensive reflex that protects them from breathing blockages, why is it that some babies do fail to use this reflex? Lipsitt discovered that there were some commonalities among the SIDS group that were not found in the control group of babies examined. He discovered that the victims were usually of lower birth weight, and the mothers of SIDS victims were more likely to be smokers, ill, less educated, and lower socioeconomic status, and living in more crowded conditions. It also appeared that nutritional and health factors associated with smoking, poverty, and illness may have a direct bearing on crib death.

What Can Be Done?

Parents and caregivers of infants can be especially careful in handling babies. Although botulism in infants may be due to spores already in the child's intenstine at birth, there are also external sources that may produce spores. Researchers have pinpointed honey as possible source of enough toxin to harm an infant. Physicians have been notified that honey should not be recommended for infants younger than six months. Raw agricultural products can be another source of spores, so all vegetables and fruits must be well cooked before being fed to an infant. All unclean objects should be kept out of an infant's mouth. Researchers have found botulism spores in the dust of a vacuum cleaner used in the home of an infant botulism victim. Parents should be also advised not to place their fingers in the infant's mouth, or kiss the infant on the mouth. Sometimes parents place their fingers on the infant's lips in order to determine if the child is hungry. Since all infants have a sucking reflex, this is not an accurate indicator of hunger, and is certainly another way to transmit diseases to infants.

Also, as indicated by the research of Lipsitt, infants who do not show strong rage reflexes (covering their mouth with a cloth and temporarily blocking air should produce a rage reflex) are at a higher risk of crib death than infants who cry or struggle in response. Parents may wish to have their pediatrician test any infant younger than one or two months of age in order to determine if they are at higher risk. Several programs have shown that babies can learn improved life-saving breathing skills. Lipsitt has begun a program at Brown University that uses the principle of operant conditioning to teach babies. The experimenter plays a sort of peakaboo game with the baby by placing a gauze pad lightly over the baby's nose and mouth. If the baby moves his head or cries, he is rewarded by having a nipple placed in his mouth for a few seconds. This functions as a reward for taking proper action and reinforces the behavior.

Those factors associated with SIDS are:

Mother
Ill;
Less educated;
Of lower socioeconomic status;
Living in crowded conditions;
Under age 20;
O, B, or AB blood type;
Smoker.

Pregnancy
Mother had urinary tract infection;
Pregnancy was less than eight months;
Mother had anemia (not enough iron)

As shown, nutritional and health factors which may be associated with smoking, poverty, and illness have a direct bearing on the SIDS death. As for the infant:

Infant
Female infant, first-born;
Male infant, later-born;
Lower birth weight (under 5 1/2 lbs).

Situations
Death more likely in winter;
Death least likely in summer;
Infant is 2 to 4 months;
Infant has a cold, with stuffy nose;
Infant was bottle-fed.

Immediate Intervention

Police officers responding to the scene of a crib death may find many different responses on the part of the parents or caretakers. Parents may be dazed and glassy-eyed, tearless or hysterically crying, or stunned. They may appear vague and confused, giving inconsistent stories. They may be hysterical, incoherent, and unable to speak clearly about what happened. The strongest emotion of the victim's caretakers is guilt. Crisis interveners should be skilled and instrumental in relieving the guilt immediately after death, and demonstrating compassion for the family.

Death, no matter how or when it occurs, is a crisis event for those who were close to the victim. Whether sudden as in crib death or expected, the sense of loss involved creates crisis reactions for those remaining. The stages in SIDS bereavement are similar to the stages of victimology and bereavement (see earlier in chapter). Recall that statements such as "Well, the baby must have been ill!" or "You shouldn't put so many covers on a small baby!" or "It was God's will!" are likely to draw an angry outburst from the parents. During the immediate stages of crisis the anguish of the bereaved family may be relieved by proper crisis intervention. Some guidelines to keep in mind are:

- If the signs of SIDS are present in the baby, explain to the family briefly that this may be the Sudden Infant Death Syndrome or "crib death."
- Assure the parents that they could not have prevented the death.
- Assure them that they are not to blame.
- Explain that only the required autopsy can determine whether SIDS was the cause of death.
- Conduct the questioning in a patient, sympathetic manner, as an interview and not as an interrogation.
- Make referrals to local SIDS helping agencies or other groups that assist in grief counseling.

Facing the death of a child is extremely difficult for all concerned, and can break through even the staunchest of defenses. However, calls regarding death are another part of the police officer's job. A calm, empathetic, compassionate officer can aid in supporting distraught parents through a most difficult time in their lives. In summary:

- Allow the parents to ventilate, and do not interrupt their narration.
- Maintain eye contact and be polite.
- Try not to rush the parents through the paperwork because of your own uncomfortable feelings. Monitor your feelings.
- Convey to the parents that you are there to help them.
- Keep them informed of what will be happening.
- Above all, de-emphasize blame. The parents are suffering enough with their own guilty feelings.

Well-developed crisis intervention skills are important, but also important is an in-depth understanding of specific types of crises, what causes them, and how people tend to respond to them. Such insights are necessary in order to effectively handle the various kinds of situations that confront the field of criminal justice.

SUICIDE: CRISIS INTERVENTION

Suicide is one of the most difficult problems confronting persons in the criminal justice system. It is rare that any person working with people in the area of criminal justice can escape coming into contact at some time in his or her career with the need to evaluate and intervene in a suicidal situation. Suicide ranks 11th as the cause of death in the United States. Before this year is out, at least 30,000 Americans will have died by their own hand. About 200,000 others will have attempted suicide. Criminal justice crisis interveners, especially those working on hotlines, are the front line defense against suicide. The suicidal person is usually caught in the midst of a severe crisis. Suicide is now almost the only direct psychiatric cause of death and usually, although not always, can be avoided. The prevention comes from first suspecting that there may be a risk, and then assessing this risk and arranging adequate change in the mode of communication accordingly.

For the crisis intervener, calls from those persons contemplating suicide are perhaps the most frightening and challenging of all calls received, and at the same time present many complex questions:

- What state of mind drives people to the point that life is not longer worth living?
- What is the intervener's role in preventing suicide?
- How does the intervener recognize suicidal tendencies in the depressed caller?
- How does the intervener interact with the caller contemplating suicide?

What the questions really mean is:

- Does the intervener have the necessary insight to recognize the potential suicide?
- Can the intervener successfully interact with the suicidal caller in such a way as to play a major role in the prevention of that caller's carrying out his or her plans?

Ideally, the role of the crisis intervener is to prevent the suicide from occurring. Although interveners may respond to thousands of other types of calls during each year, they may fail to recognize their own potential for preventing suicides. Unless the person actually manifests psychotic or bizarre tendencies, the call may not be recognized as a possible suicide call. The intervener should realize that it is not only the obvious "jumper on the bridge" who is desperate and wants to die. Potential suicidal calls are received from less obvious, but equally as intent persons.

It is wise of crisis interveners to become acquainted with attitudes and facts about suicide as well as assessment, techniques, and procedures for handling suicidal calls. Studies have shown that most people who attempt suicide seek help prior to their suicide. One of the features characterizing suicidal persons is ambivalence. For this reason they will reach out for help, not knowing whether they really want to die or whether they would prefer to live. A situation may involve someone who is angry at his or her mate and who ingests a lethal dose of barbiturates and then call someone for rescue before losing consciousness. Although most people have a stronger wish to live than to die the strength of the two imposing impulses will vary. It is this ambivalence, however, that makes suicide prevention a possibility.

This significant point illustrates the fact that from a primary-prevention standpoint it might be possible to reduce suicides by alerting crisis interveners to this high-risk population. The knowledge acquired about suicide will help improve skill in dealing with these calls, and, hopefully, will increase the probability that a call from a person contemplating suicide will be successfully thwarted. In addition, knowledge about suicide and its causes may tend to reduce the distress and anxiety in dealing with a problem that usually causes discomfort for everyone involved. Three areas that relate to these goals will be covered:

1. A description of the persons and methods involved.

2. The reasons individuals attempt suicide.

3. The actions that a crisis intervener can take in various suicide situations.

Each of these will be treated separately, and each will have its unique contribution toward improving the intervener's effectiveness and ability to make an accurate assessment. The goal is to provide a service that will accomplish prevention and be performed in a professional, understanding manner. Specifically, the goal is to provide guidance and support for those persons involved, enabling them to get through the critical period so that they can adequately adjust to and deal with their present problems and cope with future ones without resorting to self-destructive behavior. This can be accomplished through proper intervention on the part of the crisis intervener.

The intervener may at this point be thinking: "How can I detect these tendencies, I'm no psychiatrist!" However, in fact, as was mentioned previously, most people overtly threaten suicide before they actually kill themselves. Rarely will someone commit suicide without giving some prior indication of his intent. Thus, the crisis intervener equipped with some basic understanding of the psychology of suicide should be able to identify certain cues that might indicate suicidal behavior. From this point, questioning might reveal a past history involving suicide attempts. Then, the intervener will be in a position to make a proper diagnosis and proceed with the correct method.

Social Variables in Suicide Attempts

The average suicide victim does not exist. Self-destruction is a problem of the young, the mature, and the aged of both sexes in all walks of life. However, the literature on suicidal behavior includes information regarding age, sex, and other soical variables.

Age/Sex/Lifestyle

Lethality increases with age. For men, the suicide rate rises progressively until age 85; for women, until age 65.

Attempted suicide is associated with a higher risk for males, although women attempt suicide three times as frequently as men.

Men commit suicide four times more frequently than women, but there are more attempts by females than males.

One in every four suicide victims is black; the majority are white.

The suicide rate for people between 15 and 24 years of age has increased from 5.1 per 100,000 in 1961 to 12.8 per 100,000 in 1981; the rate for people between 75 and 84 years has taken a downward course from 26 percent in 1961 to 22 percent in 1961.

Suicide rates are higher among those who are single; within the married population, among those who are childless.

Children less than 10 years of age may commit suicide.

Recovering depressed and schizophrenic patients have a high rate. According to one research study, as many as 90 percent of suicide victims have been diagnosed with a psychiatric disorder. Forty to 80 percent have affective disorder, most commonly depression, followed by alcoholism, schizophrenia, and antisocial and borderline personalities.

Prior suicidal attempts increase the risk of a subsequent try.

Loss of a loved one increases attempts.

Presence of a chronic illness or terminal disease, recent major surgery or childbirth, and alcoholism and drug abuse all increase the risk of suicide.

Other Social Variables

Groups with a warm, nuturing influence have low suicidal rates. Such groups as the Irish, Italians, and Norwegians have been identified in this way.

Communities with a reputation for cold and uncaring behavior, such as skid rows, the homeless, and disorganized areas have high rates.

Those communities demanding strong, independent styles of living have a high potential. Countries like the United States, Russia, Japan, and Germany, where a high emphasis is placed on an individual's performance, have been cited.

People in professions that require an extraordinary amount of concern and nurturance to others have high suicidal rates.

Societies with governmental problems, period of social unrest, or a pessimistic outlook have high rates.

How the subject of suicide is tolerated is a factor. The influence of the Catholic Church in the low suicide rate of countries such as Italy, Spain, and Ireland supports this view. In Pennsylvania, the Amish who have been living by a strict moral code of suicide as moral sin for 300 years, have had only 26 suicides in the past century.

Personal religious values play an important part in an individual's decision about his life and his death.

Anger as a Motive

Each person has feelings that need to be satisfied (e.g., love, affection, dependency). In order to satisfy these needs, the person reaches out to others and develops and sustains relationships with these others. If a conflict develops in a relationship between two people in which affection or dependency played a major role, suicidal thoughts may develop.

It is important to remember that suicide is not a solitary act occurring in a vacuum. The suicidal person operates in a family or a social setting that influences and sometimes causes him or her to consider suicide. For years the prevailing feelings were that an attempted suicide was an unsuccessful try to end one's life. On the contrary, a number of studies indicate that while a suicide is generally a final solution to one's problems, the attempt is usually aimed at improving life. Many suicide attempts are made by people who in their own minds have little intention of actually dying but rather are attempting to force a change in an intolerable or overwhelming situation. For example:

- A wife who feels that her marriage is undesirable because of her husband's insensitivity to her needs may attempt suicide as a way of overcoming the communication block that exists between them. Other potential victims might be:
- A well-established businessman in his forties who is angry with his wife and feels she is emotionally and physically rejecting him.
- A young girl recently jilted or a wife facing a divorce she does not want. Both are filled with intense anger and overwhelming feelings of rejection and worthlessness.
- A teenager may feel angry with his father for giving more attention to his brothers and sisters. He may not be able to express the angry, aggressive feelings toward the father because of respect, and will instead turn them inward on himself.

These attempts are ways of communicating some message to another person to change their behavior, rather than kill oneself. It may be an attempt to make a spouse, a parent, or a lover change his or her actions in some way. It may be an angry effort to strike back at someone or to persuade him or her not to take an unwanted action, such as a divorce, a separation, or other change.

Other Motives for Suicide

Besides anger at significant others that is turned inward, there are other motives for suicide attempts. One of these may be a fear of being punished for a real or imagined wrong that has been committed. For example:

- A respected business person being arrested on a morals charge.
- A student faced with final examinations and fearful of failing and disappointing his or her family.
- An older person suffering from an incurable or serious illness.
- A widow or widower who feels lost, a burden, or not needed by others.

Many times the person will mention the presence of a severe, recent, or chronic medical problem. The presence of medical difficulties, such as cancer or a severe heart problem, increases the risk of the person carrying out a suicidal act. The other problem that is often mentioned is a recent loss. The loss can be due to any one of a number of events: death of a loved one or close family member, loss of a job or other financial setback, or rejection by a partner through a divorce, separation, or quarrel. The presence of any of these or other losses increases the risk of a successful suicide.

A typical suicide attempt may be made by any person of any age group who is motivated into an act of self-destruction by a variety of factors.

Some statements that the intervener may hear are:

"My family would be better off without me."

"Things just haven't been going right."

"I just can't sleep anymore. I can't eat. I don't want to work anymore. I'm just not interested in anything."

"I gave away all of my jewelry yesterday."

"I've been so unhappy lately. I have no energy for anything."

"A voice inside my head is telling me to take 150 pills. Should I listen to the voice?"

Generally, the danger of suicide is present when a person perceives his or her life situation as overwhelming, hopeless, or unsolvable, or when suffering seems unbearable. Thoughts of suicide may occur in many persons, but the common factor is depression. Probably everyone at one or several points in their lives has been depressed. However, approximately 60 percent of people who attempt suicide have some signs of being depressed prior to the act.

Assessment of Suicide Behavior

A major problem of interveners is how to identify the person who is a serious suicidal risk. A first consideration is to listen very carefully to what the person says about the attempt and the nature of the intent. The person may report that he has been feeling "sad." He may say that he has been "feeling blue" or "down in the dumps." He may be crying or may indicate that he has been crying frequently lately. The individual's speech will be soft and slowed down. He may indicate a loss of interest and motivation to do certain things (e.g., work, household chores, recreation, etc.). His conversation will center around his feelings of inadequacy, hopelessness, failure, unworthiness, and guilt. He may report inability to sleep, loss of appetite, and "feeling tired all the time."

Any recent change in social conditions should be noted; these may include a new home, loss of job or relationship, death of a loved one, disappointment in love, an accident, some occupational setback, or feelings of guilt concerning failure.

With the mentally disturbed, because of severe disturbances of motivation and behavior, it may be impossible to determine their reasons for attempting suicide. In schizophrenic persons a suicidal episode may be produced by delusions or may be the result of hallucinatory instructions; the person responds without insight and therefore has no capacity to control the impulse. Quite often it is difficult to obtain adequate explanations as to what has happened, in which case it may well be part of a general and motivational abnormality. In addition, it has been noted that schizophrenics on medication for long periods sometimes develop typical depressive symptoms, which may lead to suicidal acts. These examples are not meant to suggest that each attempt can be identified with a specific motive. The mixture of feelings involved is nearly always complicated.

Methods of Suicide

The choice of suicide method is influence by sex differences. While women may choose nonviolent means, men usually choose more violent ones such as the use of firearms, jumping from high places, cutting or piercing vital organs, hanging themselves, or throwing themselves in front of vehicles.

Those persons whose personalities are the type that deal with problems orally—for example, alcoholics and drug abusers—are very likely to make suicidal attempts usually by increasing their intake or adding other substances, which is an extension of their familiar means of relieving distress. In addition, impaired self-control while under the influence of alcohol or drugs may be another important factor. Whatever the reasons, alcoholics form a large group with a high risk of death by suicide. Drug-dependent persons may become disturbed or depressed and make a suicidal attempt, but they sometimes kill themselves without suicidal intent as a result of increasing their dose of drugs or as a result of abnormal behavior.

Alcohol is frequently taken together with an overdose of other drugs, which may cause potentiation (one drug combined with another chemical, thus intensifying the strength). Statistics indicate that excessive drinking and attempts at self-destruction are sometimes related. Add alcohol to the despair and low self-esteen that a chronic alcoholic may feel, and the stage will be set for a suicidal encounter. It has been stated already that excessive consumption of alcohol suppresses human inhibitions and weakens self-control. Inasmuch as the impulse to engage in self-endangering or reckless behavior may be one of the factors kept in check by normal inhibitions and personal controls, it should come as no surprise that the absence of inhibition and control may lead to dangerously suicidal actions.

Adolescents

In the past decade, the suicide rate among adolescents has jumped an astounding 50 percent, to the point where every 90 minutes, a young person ends his or her life. Between 1950 and 1979, the suicide rate for those in the 15 to 24 age range tripled, and while the pace has leveled off, the number of deaths remains extraordinarily high. About 5,000 adolescents successfully achieve their own destruction each year, and authorities estimate that another 400,000 attempt suicide but fail.

Adolescents quite often reach a point of crisis after a phase of increasing rebellion, perhaps against intolerant parents, perhaps hoping that in the resulting emotional upheaval of a suicide attempt, attitudes will be reappraised, with a possible improvement in their relationship with their family. Troubled youngsters are highly susceptible to the power of suggestion, and the news of one suicide in the community usually triggers a copy-cat type of response in other youths. Youngsters commit suicide for many reasons: trouble with family, school, boyfriend or girlfriend, money, peer pressure, drugs, alcohol, and sex problems. Others see suicide as a symptom of much more basic problems in America's social fabric. Family dynamics, shifting value systems, increased personal freedom and responsibility, and the complex demands of our society on adolescents are all said to contribute to suicidal behavior.

In a study of 200 teen-age suicides, "psychological autopsies" were obtained and compared with the findings of an equal number of teen-agers who were considered normal. Attempting to identify risk factors that separate those who committed or attempted suicide from the normal group, the preliminary results indicated:

- More than half (54 percent) of the adolescents sought help from a health professional prior to their deaths;
- Thirty-two percent previously had attempted suicide;
- Two-thirds had exhibited either antisocial behavior or were involved with drugs or alcohol. Eighty percent were diagnosed with either depression or antisocial behavior.

• Family history reports revealed that more than half of all teens lived with only one parent; 44 percent of the families interviewed have a history of depression and 32 percent had a history of suicidal behavior.

Warning Signs

There are early warnings of the onset of depression which may lead to suicide. These include:

• Changes in personal habits for the worse—dirty clothes and messy living conditions,
• Loss of interest in once pleasurable activities such as sports, movies, and so on,
• Decline in school achievement,
• Increase in sadness, moroseness, depression,
• Loss of appetite,
• Use of alcohol, marijuana, crack, cocaine, or other drugs,
• Increased crying,
• Talk of death—sometimes in a joking fashion,
• Sudden withdrawal from social scene, friends, and family,
• Not willing to talk, and sitting around doing nothing.

Accidental Suicide—The Autoerotic Death

The recent wave of self-inflicted deaths among teenagers that struck the Westchester area in New York and certain areas in New Jersey has raised much concern about the reasons why adolescents would take their own lives. In a small but significant number of adolescent deaths, victims typically seemed happy and well-adjusted, leading perplexed families, friends, and classmates to wonder what could have suddenly gone wrong. In these cases, accidental autoerotic death or sexual asphyxia is reported as being the cause. Forensic and psychiatric scientists have become increasingly concerned about the increase in this practice. A four-year study of adolescent deaths in Massachusetts resulting from such activities (Hazelwood, Dietz, Burgess, 1983) documents 150 deaths, 132 of which resulted directly from the excessive application of an asphyxial mechanism used for the purpose of enhancing sexual excitement. The types of sexual asphyxia involved in this study included hanging and strangulation, suffocation, airway obstruction, anesthetic agents, and chest compression. The authors estimate that 500 to 1,000 such deaths occur each year in the United States and add that most are misdiagnosed as suicide or homicide or covered up by the family because of the social stigma that surrounds a sexually motivated death. Although autoerotic asphyxiation is well known to readers of erotic material and practitioners of sexual bondage, its occurrence is virtually unknown to the general public. It is therefore a shocking discovery to families, physicians, and professional counselors.

A review of erotic literature indicates that this sexual practice was been described in explicit detail as long ago as 1891. An old English poem describes the hanging of a man for raping a little girl, who had an erection and ejaculation upon death. In novels (*The Mandrake*, A. Starch, 1917), plays (*Waiting for Godot*, Samuel Beckett, 1954), writings of Marquis de Sade (*Justine*, 1965), movies (*In the Realm of the Senses*, 1977), and, more recently, in the magazine *Playboy*, references are made to sexual asphyxia and in some cases details are given on its practice.

Indications that will pinpoint the scene of an accidental sexual asphyxiation may include the following;

1. An adolescent or young male. Out of 132 autoerotic deaths in the Massachusetts study, 127 were male and 5 were female. In addition, the behavior begins in adolescence as a solitary act and continues on into adulthood. At this point the "buddy system" may become part of the practice and when used renders this a less lethal practice.

2. The absence of a suicide note.

3. Partial or complete nudity, and/or wearing female lingerie.

4. The presence of ropes, belts, or other binding material so arranged that the victim could have tightened and released them.

5. Evidence of masturbation.

6. A towel or cloth around the neck to prevent burns and marks.

7. The presence of pornographic literature.

8. Presence of binding of the body and/or genitals with ropes, chains, leather, and in some cases vacuum cleaner hoses.

9. The victim is found suspended by the neck, either in a standing, sitting, or lying down position, and generally behind a closed door.

10. The presence of a knife or other sharp object that could be used to cut the rope or belt at the last possible moment.

Persons who practice autoerotic repetitive hangings are a very diverse group, with no apparent common denominator. According to Dr. Robert Litman (1966), in contrast to a fairly normal group of children who use this technique for sexual enhancement, the adults that he studied tended to be very lonely and depressed people. Other experts state, however, that many of the practitioners were readers of erotica who were happily married men and were in no way deprived of sex or companionship. In the following situation, as reported by an emergency medical services aide, it was just this type of person. The aide described the scene in this way:

It was Saturday morning and we received a call to an office building that had been already closed for the weekend. It seems a concerned young wife had called the police because her husband had not returned home after work on Friday night. Fearing the worst, the woman met police officers at the building where her husband maintained an accounting practice. When the superintendent was located and appeared on the scene to open the office door, the police officers found an unusual sight. The accountant was seated at his desk, dressed in female underwear, with a belt tightened around his neck and tied to the leg of his desk. He apparently had been dead since the night before. On the desk in front of him was a copy of some porn magazine. It was the first time that I had ever seen an autoerotic death, and it was the same with the responding police officers.

Talking about Suicide Plans

Most suicidal persons are willing to talk about their suicidal thoughts or intents, since most if not all who are suicidal continue the struggle over whether they should live or die right up until their last moments. While the intervener may be reluctant to ask about suicide, persons are never hurt by direct, respectful questioning. They are usually responsive to the crisis intervener. Questions covering the possible suicidal act can be asked in a matter-of-fact manner.

An effective way of inquiring about intentions is to say, "Often when people feel the way you feel, and have gone through some of the things you have gone through, they think about taking their life. Have you been thinking about this?" Approaching the subject in this way indicates an understanding on the part of the intervener and will open communication more readily to the subject. On the other hand, the insensitive intervener may be heard to say, "Wow, if I had so many problems, I'd think of jumping off the bridge too!" This type of statement could only make the suicidal person defensive and uncooperative.

If the person states that he or she has not thought about suicide, the intervener should accept this unless there is a reason not to. However, if the person states that he or she is considering suicide, it is very important to ask certain follow-up questions. These may include:

- "How long have you been feeling this way?"
- "Have you thought about how you would end your life?"
- "Have you made plans?"
- "Have you acquired the means?"
- "When do you plan to do this?"
- "Where do you plan to do this?"

These questions do not invade privacy (as the person is often quite willing to share this information) and are important information for the intervener to have. Contrary to common belief, talking about suicidal feelings does not intensify the suicidal behavior, but to the contrary will help break down the barriers of anxiety and conspiracy that have been built up both by the disturbed person and those close around him or her. Hope is the chief product offered. The feeling produced in the person in crisis will be that of having found someone who cares. If the person responds by saying that he or she has feelings of "being better off dead," with no specific plans made as to the carrying out this statement, there is no need to pursue this type of questioning. This person is not as highly suicidal as the person who gives specific information and may be just reaching out for a reassuring word or someone to talk to.

An inquiry may be made as to previous attempts at suicide. The absence of any previous attempts is a positive indication; the presence of previous efforts is a negative indication. The crisis intervener evaluates all aspects, makes a decision, and continues on with a definite course of action with the suicidal person.

Developing a Language That Is Supportive of the Suicidal Caller

Initial Contact

The telephone used in crisis is gaining acceptance as an intervention method. Suicide crisis centers have had to rely on the telephone as a tool to help talk people out of the suicide act. Criminal justice crisis interveners are also reached out for via telephone by those contemplating suicide. In responding to these calls, the crisis intervener must immediately indicate an interest in the person's situation. He or she must make immediate efforts to establish the caller's name, address, and telephone number in case the line is disconnected. Maintaining communication with the caller is critical. The caller must be reassured from the start that you want to help. Most callers are reluctant to reveal identifying information at the start. In these cases, the intervener may direct his or her efforts at establishing rapport with the caller and attempt to get the location after the caller has gained trust.

From the onset it is very important that the intervener project a certain attitude to the caller. This attitude can be best described as one of concern and caring. The intervener's first verbal contact should be to introduce him- or herself by name. Often it is helpful to give your full name, such as, "I'm Barbara Peters." This allows the caller to respond on a more personal and informal basis by choosing to use his or her first name. The intervener may ask the caller by what name he or she prefers to be called. Most callers will respond with just a first name in order to protect their identity. This does not present a problem but rather will allow for a more personal communication relationship to develop, which should be the intervener's goal.

Avoid any sudden aggressive comments or display of impatience, and refrain from using abusive language. These reflect hostility and a lack of understanding, and may be just the impetus the caller needs to follow through on his or her plans. When a person is threatening to jump from a high place and talks about taking 200 pills, the intervener should be cautious and thoughtful about what is being said. Every effort should be made to engage the caller in conversation. Once the intervener has established trust with the caller by speaking calmly and nonjudgmentally, and has been able to communicate a nonthreatening position, he or she will usually receive positive responses to questions, and can then move on to problem areas that are more emotionally charged.

Vocalization

This term refers to the volume, speed, and pacing of speech. It is generally a good idea to speak to callers in a soft and slow voice, while allowing a few seconds to lapse between questions. People who are upset tend to speak loudly and quickly. The intervener's soft, slow voice will lead them to speak in a similar fashion. People who hear themselves speaking in this manner are likely to be better able to control their own emotions than people who hear themselves talking loudly and quickly. Pacing questions slowly gives an impression of patience and concern. The rapid firing of questions leads to an impression of impatience and adds a note of interrogation, which can lead the caller to feel blame.

Self-Disclosure

Following this initial interaction, the intervener can begin to establish rapport and find a common ground. This is very important for building trust, and can be accomplished with the techniques of self-disclosure. People tend to be more open with those who are open with them. We tend to be more disclosing about our own thoughts, feelings, and backgrounds when others first reveal such information to us. For example, the intervener can very easily find a common ground with the caller concerning the following topics:

Age group,
Ethnic group,
Similarities in family settings; number of children, brothers, or sisters,
Troublesome parents, teachers, and so on,
Background life experiences,
Schools attended,
Other interests: sports, movies, and so forth, or
Area that the caller lives in.

If the intervener offers information concerning himself and his own life, the caller will begin to gain trust in him. For example:

"You know, we're the same age."

"I'm Irish, too."

"Yes, my parents have gotten older and are more dependent on me now also."

"My friend went to the same school you did."

"My aunt lives in Brooklyn. She lives in Sheepshead Bay. Which section do you live in?"

"I understand. My wife walked out on me last year. It was a difficult time for me also."

Communicating with the caller through conversation about various topics is an effective deterrent to most suicide callers. Talking distracts the person, as he more or less has to pay attention. It also allows time for him to consider his actions and for help to arrive. Try to give hope to the caller while at the same time respecting his predicament. Moralizing over the telephone to someone you do not know and cannot see is seldom effective. Inquire about friends, relatives, or neighbors. Attempt to establish if there is anyone he can trust and has confidence in. Loved ones, family members, and friends may be in a position to give emergency assistance. Offer to contact them with the caller's permission. However, do not attempt to pass off the caller to someone else, as this may be interpreted as disinterest and a form of rejection. The understanding and interest you display toward the caller and the speed in which you react can all be instrumental in preventing the distressed and disturbed person from ending his life.

Active Listening

When another person is talking, we may simply be present or we may communicate that we are interested in hearing what is being said. The latter process is called active listening. Some of the main features of active listening are as follows:

Clarification. We clarify when we repeat to the speaker something he has just said but in our own words, or ask a question about what was just said. Using this procedure serves to show the caller that we have been listening and paying attention, and also encourages him to go on and provide further details. It also serves to indicate to the caller that what he is saying is important to the intervener. It is best to clarify when the person has finished a complete segment rather than to interrupt repeatedly to ask about details.

Shared feelings. Whereas clarification stresses repeating back some facts to the caller, this procedure focuses on expressing to the caller an understanding of his main feelings. Some interveners are rightfully taught to be impartial. Unfortunately, as noted previously, this is often translated as being impersonal. When dealing with callers contemplating suicide, a personal expression of concern and shared feelings, such as "I'm sorry this has happened to you," can be very comforting to the caller. Rather than try to conceal the emotions, the intervener will convey to the caller that they are present. To reflect the caller's feelings accurately, the intervener must pay attention both to what the caller is saying and to how he is saying it. The suicidal caller might know his feelings are being shared with an intervener who says, "Everything seems dark to you right now; there doesn't seem to be hope anywhere."

Personalized statements. Crisis interveners do not differ from other persons in large organizations in their tendency to make impersonal statements such as, "It's probably a good idea for you to see a psychiatrist." When dealing with potential suicides, it is far more effective to personalize statements by prefacing them with, "I feel" or "I think." This conveys personal concern and involvement with the caller.

Stating the obvious. Persons contemplating suicide are usually confused and thinking slowly. In many respects, their emotional level has reverted to that of children in that things are not clear to them. Therefore, the intervener can reassure the caller with what may seem to be obvious statements. These are, for example: "I am here to help you," "I want to help you," or "I can see that this has been an upsetting experience for you." These types of reassurances may seem condescending, but are in reality very important messages for the caller to hear.

Responding nondirectively. This technique is used when one wants to help the other person in a conversation to continue talking. It is especially effective in situations where the topic is sensitive and you want to give the other person control over what may be said. Responding nondirectively allows the other party to cover a topic in psychologically satisfying sequence and to feel that he has made the decision about the hows and the whats of the discussion. Responding nondirectively is grounded in the theory of positive reinforcement. People like to talk to those who support them, or at least to those who do not deny or reject them. If you react or respond in a supportive manner to something the other person has said, he will feel that his comments have been reinforced.

Theme Identification

In the majority of suicide calls, one or two major themes will be present: either a feeling of hopelessness and helplessness, or a feeling of anger and disgust. The latter feeling may be prompted by wanting to get back at someone the caller feels may have hurt him.

Once the general theme becomes obvious, the intervener can respond appropriately. In the call where the person is feeling hopeless or helpless, the intervener can provide hope by mentioning the other people he has helped in similar situations who have handled their problems with the proper help. He can also indicate that there are specially trained people (psychologists, psychiatrists, social workers, etc.) who are concerned about people, as he is, and who can also help.

If the call appears to be one that reflects mostly anger and disgust, the responses should be different. In these situations, the suicide attempts may be a way of getting back at or hurting another individual. The person contemplating suicide may be justified in his rage toward these other persons. The response of the intervener in these situations is twofold: (1) recognizing the caller's anger so as to legitimize it and allow ventilation (i.e., "You're really feeling very angry and upset at him,") and (2) offering the possibility of more effective alternatives than suicide for dealing with such feelings. Because one feels depressed and overwhelmed with one's problems, one may tend to have a narrow focus. Most suicidal people will say that they have tried all the other options open to them. However, upon questioning, the intervener will discover that only a few solutions have been thought of and tried. Simply providing the opportunity to discuss the problem or difficulty with an individual who is trained and objective will often produce new, more realistic solutions.

Which particular emotion is being demonstrated will depend partly on the person calling and partly on the motive for attempting suicide (loss of a loved one, family fight, shame, intoxication, drug addiction). However, regardless of whether the person involved is highly aggressive, angry, confused, dazed, depressed, or hysterical, it is the intervener's responsibility to first gain the caller's trust and confidence in order to appropriately help that person.

An effective crisis intervener is a flexible intervener. The intervener must be especially flexible in dealing with the suicide call. The type of questions asked and the areas of discussion must be varied, depending on the circumstances and the attitudes of the person calling. A single approach is not suitable for all circumstances; instead, the intervener varies his behavior, depending on the caller and the nature of the call. In order to be flexible, one must know a variety of approaches well and develop the knowledge of which one to apply at which time.

The caller will be most likely to continue conversation with the intervener if he is shown in a variety of ways that the intervener understands him. These include the methods described earlier; active listening, clarification, shared feelings, personalized statements and stating the obvious. As a general rule, it is usually a good practice to begin asking questions in those areas that are not as emotionally charged, and slowly work toward the person's more troubling concerns. Remember, what may appear to be insignificant to you may be overwhelming to the caller. If you indicate that you feel his problems are minor issues, you will lose your opportunity to understand what really is occurring in the situation.

Professional/Nonprofessional Resources

In speaking with the suicidal person it is important to keep in mind the need to assess his or her strengths and weaknesses. Most often they will present alarming serious negative feelings which may be offset by some positive features. If the person is willing to speak with you in the first place, responds to questions, and accepts suggestions and directions, the potential for a positive outcome is good. An important hopeful sign is the improvement in mood and thinking that can be seen within the course of one conversation. It indicates the caller's ability and willingness to respond to proffered help. On the other hand, if there is an evaluation of high suicide potential that appears out of control there is a need for immediate hospitalization.

Most calls received have a low suicidal risk and can be handled satisfactorily by simply providing sympathetic and understanding listening, counseling, and advice. In these cases, family or close friends may be contacted with the caller's permission to provide help in bringing the situation under control. They may also be used to gain cooperation in the referral process by giving information concerning professional agencies and eliciting promises to provide assistance for the person in need. The type of referral depends on the evaluation of the situation. It may involve either a nonprofessional or a professional resource or both. Someone with a suicidal problem that is not immediately serious but who presents emotional disturbances may be referred to a psychiatric clinic, private therapist, or family agency. A resource book of community agencies is helpful to keep available. The suicide call is a cry for help in dealing with life's problems and professional referral is necessary.

In approximately 10 percent of suicidal cases there is a higher suicidal potential that requires more active participation. These cases usually require immediate hospitalization. The goal at this point is to gather as much information as possible to identify the person and to provide him with immediate medical attention.

In summary, the resources available in suicidal situations will be of two types, nonprofessional and professional. Any one or combination of these resources should be considered and utilized. They are:

Family. The family may be one of the most valuable of resources available in a time of crisis. Family members may be called in to handle situations requiring support. The acceptance of the family as a unit implies that the intervener understands the effects of one member's crisis on the family as a group. Crisis situations may be turning points that determine a change in the course of a person's life; it is important to realize that in a short period of time, all kinds of decisions have to be made, as well as changes in the psychological orientation and functioning of families. Family members can be helpful by providing support during times of crisis. People should be encouraged to discuss problems and situations with their family members. If there is a need for someone to be with the person during the crisis, the family should be called on and apprised of the situation. However, always consult with the person prior to calling on the family. Encourage the reluctant person to believe that the family can provide help. Involve the family in accepting responsibility during the crisis and for attaining help during the referral process.

Friends. Close friends can be used in the same way that family members are used. Friends may be able to stay with the person during difficult times, and can be helpful in talking things out. The support that friends can provide should not be ignored.

Family doctor. The person that has a good relationship with his doctor should be encouraged to call on him or her for help. Doctors often serve as supportive authority figures in times of medical as well as emotional difficulties. Doctors can also provide needed assistance with medication and hospitalization.

Clergy. Encourage the person to rely on his pastor, priest, or rabbi for emotional support.

Employer. If the situation involves conflict or problems with employment, the person should be encouraged to discuss the problems with his employer.

Emergency rooms. Most city or private hospitals have psychiatric emergency rooms within their regular emergency rooms. These are available for 24-hour emergency treatment or hospitalization.

Psychiatric hospitals. Most large communities also contain psychiatric hospitals that can be used in emergency situation. Generally, these kinds of referrals involve persons so disturbed that they present a hazard to themselves or others, and/or are so disoriented that they can no longer exercise proper judgment or direction of their lives.

Bluffing the Caller

A frequently heard comment among crisis interveners is that the suicide caller is "only trying to get attention." This type of thinking only supports impersonal feelings about suicide and may, therefore, cause the intervener to ignore suicide callers or even to ridicule them. Some mental health and criminal justice professions are under the impression that would-be suicides derive a great deal of satisfaction from getting others upset. They feel that the best approach is to show them that suicide will accomplish none of their goals. One psychiatric center instructs telephone operators to request the would-be suicide's name and address. The caller would think that it was needed to send emergency help; however, the operators were instructed to state that it was needed so that they would know where to send the hearse. These kinds of statements only reinforce to the caller that no one really cares, despite what the professionals at this particular center would think.

Don't belittle the caller's actions or minimize his or her attempts. Under no circumstances should the intervener attempt to bluff the caller with mistaken ploys such as:

- "Go ahead, kill yourself. No one cares!"
- "Hey pal! If you want to end it all, go ahead. Why are you bothering to call me?"
- "I know what you're up to. You just want attention. Nobody cares if you kill yourself. Go ahead!"
- "Listen. If you really want to kill yourself you'd do it. You wouldn't call me. So stop putting me on!"
- "If you're going to jump out of the window, better take your keys. It's late and you wouldn't want to disturb anyone when you want to get back in!"
- "Boy, will your wife be relieved. Now she can really screw around!"
- "Well if you're going to kill yourself, will you do it after 12:00 midnight. Do it on the next guy's shift!"

Approaches such as these often signal to the caller to carry out his or her intentions, as the intervener is seen as giving approval to such actions. This all too often ends in needless tragedy.

Actually, there is some element of truth to the statement that the attempted suicide is a bid for attention. It is an attempt to call attention to the person's problem or state of mind. It is a cry for help. If it is not answered, another perhaps more serious attempt will follow. Any indication that someone is considering suicide is a cry for help and a call to action. The concern of the intervener here is in developing language and responding in a supportive manner to the potential suicide victim. Helpful tactics include:

Be supportive,

Be empathetic,

Achieve rapport immediately,

Open lines of communication,

Ask questions: What do you think is going on? How do you see this situation?

Talk calmly,

Don't be judgmental, and

Don't bluff the caller.

By asking the caller questions, the intervener can accomplish many things. He can keep the conversation flowing at a steady pace, and this indicates to the caller that he is interested. He is also gaining information about the person, which just naturally flows out in conversation, and gaining insight into the person's problem. The caller, on the other hand, is getting an opportunity to ventilate some of his feelings, which helps to reduce the stress of the situation. Also, the caller will feel that the intervener is concerned and will tend to cooperate with whatever the intervener says.

As the caller is talking about his difficulties and problems, the intervener should be alert and responsive. The intervener should be gently probing with questions so that he can gain as much factual data as possible in order to evaluate the person's actual intentions. In addition, by gaining the caller's trust, the intervener will gain cooperation to the point that the caller may offer his location so that help can be sent to him.

In order to trace calls in which the caller is reluctant to disclose location, the average time needed is approximately 45 minutes. This time may vary in different locations. Most interveners who have handled these types of calls report that it is an extremely rewarding experience to be able to talk a caller contemplating suicide out of acting on his or her impulses. They state that it is also rewarding to be able to hold on to a caller until help arrives. According to those who have had this experience there is nothing like the feeling of speaking to the responding police officer who has arrived at the caller's home to provide assistance. The personal experiences of one crisis intervener testifies to this fact:

I received a call from a woman who said that she was about to commit suicide. She planned to jump in the path of a subway train. Her boyfriend had deserted her, she said, and she didn't want to live any longer. This was despite the fact that she had three young children. I talked to her for a long time. Having children also and having been deserted myself, it was easy to relate to her situation. I talked to her for more than one hour while the call was being traced. Finally, help got to her and the suicide was averted. I felt like I had done something extraordinary for a fellow human being. It was a nice feeling that has sustained me in times when I have hated this job.

In short, these seven steps should be followed when talking to suicide-prone persons:

1. *Show understanding.* By your words and your tone of voice you can make it clear to the caller that you accurately understand what the person is feeling and how strongly he is feeling it. Do attempt to understand the person's view.

2. *Do create rapport with the caller.* The intervener may indicate legitimate agreements between himself and the caller in as many areas as possible. Some examples of this might be agreement on the difficulties of raising a family, the hurt involved in a loss, the problems of not having enough money, and personal likes and dislikes in such areas of interest such as food, movies, sports, and so on. This helps to develop the relationship and allow the caller to feel that the intervener can understand him since they have some similarities in their backgrounds.

3. *Don't be judgmental.* Criticizing, judging, and giving advice is rarely helpful to the person contemplating suicide. It only increases his or her feelings of failure and inadequacy and heightens the suicidal intent.

4. *Don't call the person's bluff.* Attempts to shock the caller back to reality by minimizing his attempts and calling his bluff never help the caller.

5. *Keep the conversation flowing.* Respond nondirectively so that the caller will continue talking.

6. *Don't be afraid to share feelings*. Being impersonal only turns people off. Personal expressions of concern are necessary in these situations.

7. *Be flexible*. Vary your approach according to the caller and the nature of the call.

Summary on Suicide

Suicide and suicide attempts are always tragic and unsettling situations. The increase of the incidence of suicide in our society is of serious concern to the mental health profession, social scientists, and the general public. Suicide, unlike other deaths, is avoidable in many situations. Crisis interveners are the front-line defense in these situations. This chapter has examined some of the attitudes and facts about suicide behavior, and has presented a detailed assessment of suicidal behavior in terms of nature of intent, effect on the person, social matrix, and techniques for communication. Confronting and dealing with the suicidal person is uncomfortable. However, the knowledge that you have helped a person back to life is rewarding.

It is through a connection to another human, whether a volunteer at a hotline, a 911 operator, or a desk sergeant working the graveyard shift, that persons in distress can begin to find ways out of their agony. Small bridges can be built so that they may find a way out of their isolation. Hope, gained through this connection, can change someone's outlook and make things look bright once again. Hope is within the criminal justice intervener's power to give.

THE ELDERLY

The behavior of the elderly may be considered to be similar to alcohol/drug abusers in that the elderly sometimes suffer from loss of memory, slurred speech, and loss of the ability to connect logic to reason. In this section, the problems faced by the elderly will be addressed so that the crisis intervener can gain a better understanding of these issues and ease the way for more effective crisis intervention strategies.

With advancing age, the acuity of the senses declines in some individuals. People over the age of 65 are apt to have problems seeing in the dark, which often prevents them from driving at night. Those who ignore these signs of diminishing eyesight may become involved in serious auto accidents. Hearing problems are more common than visual ones, with older persons having special difficulty following conversations. Even when they can understand what is being said to them, they may hear the words but not know their definitions. In terms of taste, older persons often complain that their food does not taste as good as it used to. This seems to be caused by a loss of sensitivity in taste and smell. In addition, the vestibular senses, which help to maintain posture and balance, often deteriorate, which may cause dizziness and serious falls.

Some older persons have difficulty with their memory. They often lose the ability to recall the immediate past but may have vivid recall of events from their childhood. This is often the result of brain damage—senility that is thought to be brought on by hardening of the arteries in the brain. Other types of memory loss can follow emotionally or physically painful experiences.

An older person may also suffer from a form of paralysis that impairs ability to shape their lips properly in order to form words properly. This can be a particular problem when communicating over the phone as there may be some difficulty attaining the location of an elderly caller in distress. An older person who has isolated him- or herself because of fear may not be familiar with some of the more modern terms for his or her surroundings. He or she may, however, remember a location of a building that has been torn down years prior.

Older persons may have difficulty getting along with people, and may become childlike in their habits, quarrelsome, and may hoard strange objects. They may also have a tendency to wander and become forgetful. They may leave their house, walk a short distance, and forget where they were going or where they are. They may not remember what they ate for breakfast, yet be able to vividly describe events in their youth. Their speech may become rambling and incoherent, and they may tell convincing lies to compensate for their inability to remember recent events. In some instances, they may even fail to recognize relatives.

Alzheimer's disease causes the bulk of all cases of physical and mental deterioration that are known as senility. Early symptoms include signs of forgetfulness, confusion, irritability, incontinence, and sometimes a complete inability to speak or care for oneself. Some people continue to function on some levels, even playing tennis, gardening, and maintaining personal relationships, while losing their ability for other more complex projects.

All too often symptoms of senility are not accurately diagnosed and not treated because such symptoms are expected in old age. Many instances of confusion, memory loss, and similar symptoms do respond to proper treatment that may seem all too obvious. For example, some of these states can arise from overmedication, as when several drugs interact with each other; depression, resulting from poor health, surgery, or the death of a spouse; underlying disease, such as alcoholism (common in the elderly), malnutrition or low thyroid function; and difficulty in adjusting to social change such as moving to a new home.

Elderly persons may come to the attention of criminal justice crisis interveners for many different reasons. They may be lost, hurt, involved in an accident, victims of burglary or robbery, victims of the growing problem of elder abuse by their children, victims of a rape or mugging, or even the perpetrator of a crime, most probably shoplifting. Although we know from statistics that at least half of all reported murders, violent street crimes, and thefts are committed by persons under 26 years of age, we also do know that there has been a change in the age composition of population in the United States. Because age is related to the commission of certain crimes, a change in this age composition alters the frequency of these crimes. The U.S. population is now growing older, which means there is a higher proportion of older persons than ever before. This demographic shift signals the potential for more crimes committed by older persons. The committing of crimes by the elderly may be considered a crisis because the act is typically an indication of some other problem, such as an illness or side effects of medication.

Many individuals tend to become depressed about "feeling old" as they age. In addition, the elderly encounter a succession of life changes, stressors, and status changes as they age. With retirement, the difficulty of living on a fixed and inadequate income becomes apparent. Among the elderly, nearly 30 percent have an annual income of less that $3,200. Relatives, mates, and friends may die, causing an increase in social isolation that may cause depression. With depression there often come thoughts of suicide among the elderly. Suicide rates are higher in older adults than for the general population. Some supporters of the right-to-suicide movement believe that elderly people have the right to end their lives if their continued existence would result in psychological or physical deterioration. They feel that these individuals should be allowed the choice of dying in a dignified manner, particularly if they suffer from a terminal illness. This raises moral, ethical, and legal concerns, and is a difficult question to resolve. Nevertheless, criminal justice crisis interveners have been trained to preserve life, and they have a legal obligation to do so.

Elder Abuse

According to some recent reports, estimates of neglected or abused elderly people range from a half million to 2.5 million cases. Most abuse victims are over 70 years of age, and most are women. Only 43 states require that hospital personnel and others, such as senior citizen center staffers, report suspected cases of elder abuse to government agencies. Many of the laws protecting dependent adults focus on mandatory reporting and consider that charges against abusers are already covered by assault and battery statutes. Because of the ways these laws are written, much of their enforcement rests on welfare departments or state agencies on aging. These organizations follow up on reports of abuse and neglect. After the social agency has investigated, reports may be filed with police departments for action.

However, as with the laxity in the reporting of child abuse, most cases of elder abuse go unreported. Interpretations of what constitutes neglect or abuse of the elderly can be confusing to crisis interveners. The categories lack precise definition since neglect, for example, may be purposeful or come from ignorance. Can someone be charged with neglect for not providing adequate nourishment, or allowing a bedridden elder to develop painful bedsores? What about for locking an older person out of the house, or allowing him or her to wander around outside on a swelteringly hot summer afternoon? Likewise, definitions of abuse can cause confusion. Abuse can mean shoves, punches, kicks, sexual offenses, and beatings. It can also mean financial exploitation, theft, menacing, or gaining compliance by using the threat of institutionalization.

As with abused children, the abused older person is generally afraid to tell others about the abuse. While children fear being taken away from their family, older persons fear the nursing home. To compound the problem, detecting abuse is difficult because of the need to protect the family. Bruises and broken bones in the elderly can easily be accounted for by a fall caused by a loss of balance or by bumping into the furniture in a dark room.

The Abusers

Because people are generally reluctant to have their own relatives arrested, or are dependent on or terrified of their tormentors, law enforcement agencies have difficulty providing information on the extent of abuse. Most studies reveal, however, that elder abuse occurs most often in middle-class settings, as children pressured by the demands of their own growing families and economic stressers become further burdened by aging parents. The physical limitations of the older person may be difficult for already oppressed children to cope with. When children take aging parents into their homes, personal adjustments have to be made. In addition, adjustments in attention and allowances of resources may cause conflict. Unresolved conflicts and shifting roles where the child now becomes the caretaker may cause persistent stress.

Some other studies claim that most harm to older persons occurs in families in which violence, mental illness, or addiction already exists. Patterns of family interaction in which abuse has played a major role during the children's lifetime lead to elder abuse. Some abusers, having suffered real or perceived mistreatment by parents earlier in life, may now have revenge on the vulnerable parent. One or more of the above situations may act as the precipitator of the violent abuse of the elderly. It may be discovered by the purposeful reporting by a concerned family member, neighbor, or physician, or may be uncovered quite by accident while the crisis intervener is responding to another kind of call.

THE MENTALLY RETARDED

Mentally retarded persons are childlike in that their intellectual development was arrested during the developmental stages. Therefore, their intellectual functioning is subaverage. This results in some degree of social inadequacy or impairment in one or more aspects of maturation, such as learning, social adjustment, and general adaptation to achievement.

Basically, mental retardation means an intelligence quotient (IQ) score below 75 or 80 on valid, repeated administrations of an individual intelligence test. However, there are several levels of retardation. Mildly retarded individuals have an IQ range of 50 to 70, which indicates a mental age of 7 to 11 years after reaching adulthood. They are considered educable and capable of achieving social and vocational skills as well as basic academic skills.

Moderately retarded individuals have an IQ range of 30 to 50, indicating a mental age of 3 to 7 years at adulthood. They are considered trainable and have the capability to communicate orally, to care for themselves physically, and to become economically productive in sheltered environments. They can participate in simple recreation and travel alone in familiar places. Severely retarded deficients have an IQ below 30, indicating a mental age of 3 years or below. They are capable of performing daily routines and repetitive physical activities under close supervision in a protective environment. They generally require continuing directions and may even need nursing care. It is not my premise in giving this information on retardation that crisis interveners will thereby be trained as mental health therapists. However, the role of the crisis intervener in recognizing and handling the mental retardate needing assistance is one of importance. The need for help in this area is understandable when one realizes that the mental age of the person ranges between 3 and 11 years of age. Therefore, the intervener must remember to handle this person with simple, step-by-step directions and guidance.

Common Situations Involving the Mentally Retarded

Missing person cases are common situations that the intervener will encounter with children, the elderly, and the mentally retarded. Often these persons wander away from their caretakers and are then reported as missing. They may aimlessly wander the streets until they realize that they are lost, and then ask for help. Retarded adults are just as likely to become lost as retarded children. This is not to imply that retarded persons cannot learn their way to different places or even to travel by themselves. Retarded persons can travel to familiar places in unfamiliar locations but may not be able to reason how to find their way.

Some retarded persons realize their differences and try to compensate for them by acting bold and tough on the streets. They can also be easily influenced by others to act unlawfully and to get into situations in which they can be injured. Some people will deliberately exploit a retardate or a child and instigage them into doing something they would not ordinarily think of doing themselves. In addition, it is not uncommon for retarded persons, because they are vulnerable, to be cheated or forcibly robbed of their money.

Another area of exploitation is that of sexual abuse. Because of their vulnerability, the mentally retarded are easy targets for sexual molestation. These cases will usually be observed by someone or uncovered through the child's expression of symptoms. Consider the following scenarios:

A 10-year-old mentally retarded girl was seen by neighbors being led into a teenage boy's house. When the police arrived, they caught the young man attempting to have sexual intercourse with the child. In another case, an 8-year-old mentally retarded boy kept complaining to his mother of nausea, stomachaches, and anal pain. Upon medical examination, physicians observed evidence of anal penetration. After much coaxing and questioning the boy revealed that he was being sodomized on a regular basis by a neighborhood boy.

In concluding this section on the impaired person requiring crisis intervention, some practical suggestions are summarized:

1. Take time to consider whether a person fits into this unique group.
2. Never rush these calls or make assumptions. Talk to the person, ask questions, and find out all you can.
3. Tell the person that you are there to help. Soothe him or her with your calm demeanor, your manner, your voice, your understanding, and your patience.
4. Keep assuring him or her that he or she will be taken care of.
5. Avoid the sound of excitement in your voice. Do not abuse people with words or threats. Besides being discourteous and unprofessional, such behavior will only make the job of gathering information more difficult and longer.
6. Speak slowly and distinctly. Do not let the person in crisis set the pace. Practice asking questions, gathering information, and giving directions and instructions in a simple, step-by-step, slowly paced manner.
7. Use words and language that are exhaustive in meaning. This means words that have only one meaning and cannot be misunderstood.
8. Ignore verbal abuse. Be aware that some persons that fit within this category will frequently be abusive.
9. Do not deceive. Lying to a confused and frightened person may only strengthen his or her belief that no one really cares. Never resort to lies in order to gain cooperation from the caller.

Chapter 7

VICTIMS OF VIOLENCE

SEX CRIMES

The face-to-face violent sexual encounter is one of the most dreaded aspects of violence. The offenses that are contained within this category of crimes are those that cause most people to fear victimization the most. In most instances, having all of one's valuables taken through a burglary may not be nearly as traumatic as having to confront a rapist in a face-to-face encounter. The two incidents are qualitatively different. The rape is feared by the urban dweller most because it impinges on privacy in a most personal way. The individual who walks down a street carries with him his "egocentric territory," and an infringement on this personal space is analogous to trespassing on his property.

Sex crimes are an important problem area for the criminal justice professional. The crimes cover a wide variety of sexual behavior. Nonviolent sexual behaviors rarely come into contact with the criminal justice system. These would include the victimless crimes of masturbation, voyeurism (observing nude bodies or couples engaged in intercourse), fetishism (extremely strong sexual attraction for a particular nongenital part of the anatomy such as hair, feet, or fingers), and homosexuality between consenting adults. The types of sex crimes that do come to the attention of law enforcement personnel might include prostitution, fornication, statutory rape (seduction of a female under the age of consent), exhibitionism (displaying the genitals), scoptophilia (peeking Tom), bestiality (sex with animals), necrophilia (sex with corpses), coprolalia (using obscene language as with obscene telephone calls), and frotteurism (rubbing the genitals up against someone). The crimes that come under the heading of sex crimes and that would cause both physical as well as psychological harm to the victim, requiring crisis intervention, would include rape (an act of intercourse accomplished by a male with a female through the use of force or threat of force), sadism (using violence as a source of sexual gratification), pedophilia (sex with children), and incest (sex within the family).

Crisis interveners are in a key position to help victims of violent and nonviolent face-to-face sexual contacts because of their close association with facilities to which victims come for help. There are several considerations to be given to this type of criminal offense.

First, given the fear of the general public, it is wise for the intervener to be able to distinguish between the types of and frequency of actual physical contact. The intervener may then be able to grasp more fully the interaction that has taken place between the offender and the victim.

Second, the crisis intervener should also be aware that face-to-face contact between victim and offender is also qualitatively different depending on the situation. For example, a bank teller may be robbed in a face-to-face contact, but loses no personal belongings. This contact would be qualitatively different, however, if the teller were injured during the robbery, in which case the physiological and psychological consequences would be far more devastating.

RAPE

Rape is defined as sex or attempted sex without a victim's consent. Its legal definition is: "The carnal knowledge of a female forcibly and against her will." Rape is a crime of violence and hostility rather than a crime of sex. According to Federal Bureau of Investigation statistics, approximately 90,434 cases of rape were reported in the United States in 1986. Between 1977 and 1986, the rate increased by 42 percent, making rape the most rapidly growing major crime in the United States. Furthermore, it is estimated that up to 50 percent of rapes go unreported, making the number committed actually far greater. Only about 16 percent of reported cases result in a conviction for this crime. Another 4 percent of those charged with rape have the charges reduced and are convicted of a lesser offense. Up to one-third of rapists are known by their victims. The rape rate for nonwhites is one-third higher than for whites, a phenomenon that may be related to socioeconomic factors and patterns of reporting.

According to current national estimates, one woman in four and one man in eight is victimized sexually; by the age of 18, one in six women will be raped. Infants, children, and elderly people of socioeconomic, marital, educational, and ethnic groups may be attacked. Although most victims are young women in their teens or twenties, there is no typical victim. Victims as young as 2 months and as old as 73 have been reported. Rape crisis centers have reported a rise in the number of calls they are getting from men who have been raped by other men. The victims are both gay and straight, as are the rapists.

Rapists, too, come from all levels of society; most of them are actively involved in relationships with consenting sexual partners. Rape is always a symptom of some psychological dysfunction. However, in one survey, the following statements about rape were presented as either true or false:

1. Women who get raped while hitchhiking get what they deserve.
2. If a girl engages in necking or petting and she lets things get out of hand, it is her own fault if her partner forces sex on her.
3. Many women have an unconscious wish to be raped and may unconsciously set up a situation in which they are likely to be attacked.
4. A woman who is stuck-up and thinks she is too good to talk to men on the street deserves to be taught a lesson.

Unfortunately, over half the general population that was polled believed that these statements are true. These kinds of statements are called sex myths because they are usually believed by a high percentage of rapists. People are more likely to believe rape myths if they accept the stereotypical sex roles of men and women, approve of the use of interpersonal violence, and distrust the opposite sex. Rape myths are difficult to change, as they are associated with other pervasive attitudes about sex roles and the use of interpersonal violence.

Types of Rapists

Based on interviews with rapists and their victims, researchers have posited that although genital sex is a part of the rape, it is not the prime factor. Instead, sex becomes the vehicle by which the rapist expresses power and anger. Based on these findings, the following kinds of rapists were delineated: the anger rapist, the power rapist, the sadistic rapist, and the acquaintance rapist.

In the anger rape, the intent of the act is primarily aggression, rage, and resentment. The anger rapist carries out an impulsive, savage act with uncontrolled physical violence. Far more physical force is employed by the offender than would be necessary to overpower the victim. The attack is usually of short duration, accompanied with abusive language and brutal physical treatment such as punching, choking, kicking and beating, resulting in broken bones and bruises. The rapist's satisfaction is met by the expression of hostility that accompanies the rape.

The power rapist is the one who commits 70 percent of the rapes. His acts are carried out not to physically hurt, but to possess, humiliate, and degrade the victim. These rapes are usually premeditated and are preceded by fantasies about the rapist's strength, competence, and masculine desirability. These assailants often carry weapons that are used to threaten the victim and gain submission through intimidation, rather than to harm. There is actually no wish to harm the victim, as usually this type of rapist only uses whatever force is necessary to overpower or subdue the victim. Generally the victim is not physically brutalized.

The sadistic rapist makes up fewer than 5 percent of the rapists. These men are the most dangerous because physical force is eroticized and expressed as such. The victims chosen by the sadistic rapists are often regarded as promiscuous by them, and are subjugated by torture, bondage, and often murder.

The acquaintance rapist is more often motivated by the sex act itself rather than by hostility or aggression. There are often social situations in which the victim may go to the rapist's apartment, which he perceives as a signal of sexual availability.

Types of Attacks

In a study of rape victims, a report on how the assailant approached the victim noted that the type of attack was an important determinant to the victim's later recovery. Three main styles were identified: the blitz, the confidence attack, and the gang rape. It appears that victims are set up in two ways: They are either singled out for a sudden surprise attack or they are deliberately deceived and betrayed.

The Blitz Attack

The blitz attack, as the name implies, occurs suddenly and without prior interaction. Victims may be returning home from a day of work as they usually do every day and suddenly become a victim; they may be out for a late-afternoon jog in the park, on their way home from a movie, alone asleep in their bedroom or working in their workshop on a project and suddenly, unpredictably, their entire life is changed. For the victim there is no logical explanation for the incident. The perpetrator is suddenly there, forcibly attacking, taking what he wants and leaving.

The Confidence Attack/Date Rape–Acquaintance Rape

Date or acquaintance rape is defined as being physically forced by a dating partner, boyfriend, neighbor, or family friend to have sexual intercourse. More subtle than the blitz, in this situation the assailant gains access to his victim under false pretenses. Typically there is some form of interaction prior to the attack. Often it may be a short relationship, and sometimes it is a long relationship that suddenly becomes violent. In either situation, the perpetrator encourages the victim to trust him and then deceives and betrays this trust. This type of rape is the one that is least reported. Because the rape was not perpetrated by a strange man who leaped out of the bushes or a dark alley wielding a gun or knife, it rarely is considered to be a rape. Here are two examples:

Mary had recently moved to a new city and met John at a single's party, where they danced and stayed together for the evening. John asked her out, and during a romantic, pleasant dinner insisted on doing something afterwards. Mary wanted to dance but John wanted her to go to his place to talk. Mary felt that he was an ideal gentleman, sensitive and romantic, and saw no harm in spending more time with him. She felt more secure at her own apartment so she suggested that they go there after dinner. As soon as they got into the house, instead of talking he lunged for her, tearing off all her clothes, pinning her down, and brutally raping her. Mary became frightened, and tried to soothe him and get him out of the door. However, she lost control, becoming more and more passive during the encounter. She later related that she did whatever she had to to get him out of her home.

Joe plans to meet his friend Steve at a bar after work for a few drinks. When he gets there Steve is accompanied by another man, whom he introduces as Harry. After a few hours of drinking, Harry invites them both back to his place, but Steve decides to go home instead. After a few drinks in Harry's apartment, Joe blacks out. In the morning when he awakens, he feels discomfort and pain in his anal area. Suspecting the worst, he goes to the hospital emergency room.

Gang Rape

A gang rape refers to the sexual assault of a victim by two or more offenders. An alarming number of gang rapes involving fraternities on college campuses are being reported nationwide. The incidents typically occur during sorority and fraternity parties. Studies of jail rape indicate that gang rapes are the usual means of attack. The rape of a woman in Big Dan's tavern in Bedford, Massachusetts, in 1983 is also an example of a gang rape. According to newspaper reports:

A 21-year-old woman who went into a blue-collar bar to buy a pack of cigarettes was pinned down and raped repeatedly on a pool table by six men while other patrons cheered. Police said the rape occurred when the woman entered the bar to buy cigarettes and stopped to have a drink with a friend. When she tried to leave, a man grabbed her and dragged her to a pool table, where she was stripped, beaten, and raped repeatedly. Police described the barroom scene as a cheering frenzy. "She cried for help, she asked for help, she begged for help—but nobody helped her," police said. Three hours later the woman finally broke free and ran out of the tavern. She flagged down a car, and the driver took her to a telephone.

Psychologists speak of the homosexual dynamics that are a part of this type of rape. According to these theories, there often appears to be a subtle, unconscious desire for the group of males to have sex with each other, and instead they use the female victim as a vehicle for achieving this. Each of the men feels the need to prove his masculinity to the other group members (to deny any homosexuality), and performs with the intent of impressing his friends. Consequently, the sex becomes more forceful and degrading, more brutal and sadistic.

Either of these types of attacks are used on rape victims. A woman may be suddenly attacked while jogging through a park, raped after a date with someone she has been dating for months, or even be forced by a man to whom she has been married for years. A male may spend the evening drinking with a new buddy and suddenly be beaten and sodomized by him. A student feeling safe on a school campus grounds might suddenly be raped or set up for a gang rape by other students.

Rape Trauma

The psychological trauma that is experienced by rape victims is perhaps the most serious of all cases of victimization short of homicide. It is a highly traumatic event. Rape victims experience physical, emotional, and behavioral reactions to this life-threatening event. Rape is a crime in which the physical damage may be not as significant as the mental harm inflicted. Rape constitutes a violation of not only the physical person and his or her personal space but also basic beliefs about one's environment (safety, security, predictability), other people (trust and respect) and about the self (competence, self-confidence, self-esteem, and ability to protect oneself). This trauma may leave the victim in a state of disorientation. Consequently, the behavior displayed by the victim may appear to be bizarre and counterproductive in overcoming the traumatic experience. Although this may appear to be the case, the behavior really represents a desperate attempt to overcome the trauma.

In rape situations where the victim suffers minimal physical trauma, the psychological consequences are far greater. The victim tends to have much guilt and to blame him- or herself for having cooperated out of fear: "People are accusatory because I didn't fight him off," . . . "I feel guilty, as if I should have done something," . . . "There was nothing I could have done!" In the case of a male victim this may even be more traumatic, "Why wasn't I able to defend myself?" . . . "This wouldn't have happened if I had been in better shape." A woman may worry that her clothes were too suggestive ("Maybe I shouldn't have worn black, black is a seductive color" . . . "Maybe I shouldn't wear my hair long." . . . or that she acted too flirtatious, or that by going out late at night she was "asking for it." A male may worry that he is too effeminate looking, or too short, or maybe that his hair is too long. When a friend or acquaintance rapes, the victim again tends to blame him- or herself, thinking "I used such poor judgment. What does this say about my judgment of people?"... "What does this say about my behavior?" This guilt often accompanies the power rape and the acquaintance rape. Victims experience psychological distress, physical problems, phobic reactions, and sexual dysfunction.

There is general agreement that during the first days and months after a rape, the victim's life is seriously disrupted. There may be a variety of physical symptoms such as urinary tract infection, vaginal infection, or psychological trauma itself. If there was anal penetration, rectal bleeding and pain are usually reported. Victims also complain of stomach pains, poor appetite, and nausea. In terms of physical trauma there may be general soreness and bruising about the throat, neck, breasts, thighs, and arms. There are usually tension headaches and exhaustion, as well as sleep disturbances.

The psychological symptoms that have been reported by victims include nightmares, difficulty in sleeping, fear, general anxiety, decline in work or school performance, angry acting-out behavior, and sexually focused behavior. Many of these symptoms decrease with time. However, a one-year follow-up of rape victims found that 50 percent of the victims reported problems of depression and fear of such things as darkness, being alone, and being in enclosed places. Many reported that they had difficulty functioning in social situations, at work, at school, or in the home. They were also unable to resume sexual activity for at least six months after the rape, and had continuing sexual problems. Their enjoyment of sexual activity was also negatively affected.

Medical Examination in the Emergency Room

For female victims, pelvic examination is essential following sexual assault to allow treatment of injuries, tests for venereal disease, prophylaxis, prevention of pregnancy, and collection of evidence. The medical check-up following a rape will include a physical and internal examination by a gynecologist. During the examination, the gynecologist will collect specimens to include within a specially designed evidence-collection kit called the Vitullo Kit. All evidence should be collected within hours of the attack since sperm and semen will not survive after 72 hours. Even victims who decide not to press charges should be encouraged to seek medical treatment. The sexual offense evidence collected for the Vitullo Kit will include slides, cotton swabs, fingernail scrapings, head and pubic hair samplings (obtained by combing both head hair and pubic hair), semen-stained underwear, soiled clothing, and other items. Blood tests, pregnancy test, pap smear, and sperm smears should be taken. Each item of evidence collected (hair, dried fluid, sperm) is marked with the victim's name and other identifying information. These are placed in sealed envelopes labeled with date, time, place, physician's name, nature of sample, name and shield number of police officer, and name of nursing witness. Prophylactic antibiotic treatment and pregnancy prevention drugs will be given if the physician and victim agree to their need. This procedure involves prescribing 25 to 50 mg. of diethylstilbesterol a day for five days to protect against pregnancy and 4.8 million units of agueous procaine penicillin intramuscularly to protect against venereal disease. The victim will be given an appointment to return to the hospital clinic to be retested two weeks later for venereal disease and for the results of blood tests taken. A follow-up pregnancy test may be recommended. Notes of findings including physical bruises and injuries should be entered on the record; these will be useful for possible future legal proceedings.

Role Amplification of Hospital Staff

Many rape victims complain of a hostile and indifferent attitude toward them in the hospital emergency room on the part of staff. The nature of the hospital emergency room physical setting as it is structured is one of a non-private order. The victim is made to endure lengthy, embarassing waits in sometimes congested emergency-room waiting areas. In that setting, the victim continues to feel vulnerable and unprotected. Doctors, because they deal with so many patients, have a tendency not to give the kind of personalized attention needed in rape cases. Doctors have been heard shouting for the nurse to "Bring in the rape case," or to ask in a loud voice "Where is the rape case?" This type of negative attention is an invasion of privacy and causes the rape victim to feel as if the entire emergency room is watching and whispering. In particular, when dealing with adolescents and children it is not uncommon to hear medical staff inquire about prior sexual behavior. This prying is usually justified by the staff as necessary information gathering. It is not. Biased staff have been heard making judgments about the victim and in a knowing way saying to each other, "First she screws around with her boyfriend, then she screams rape!" or in the case of a male rape, snickering about homosexuality and disbelief about the man's ability to defend himself.

In addition, the victim's dignity and privacy are not protected by hospital personnel. Every effort should be made to accommodate the patient's need for privacy, including the desire to be examined by a woman physician. This also means the minimization of the number of persons involved in the medical examination. There have been times in which there have been too many people in the room while the victim was being examined. One gynecologist, one nurse, and one crisis counselor are enough. All other participants are excessive and an imposition on the victim's already diminished privacy.

In addition to these problems there is the problem of role amplification on the part of medical staff. While most physicians and nurses know the roles that they are supposed to play in attending to the medical needs of rape victims, some do not. Many feel that it is within their rights as medical staff to inquire as to the details of the rape itself. Often, when pressing for details they will ask the victim questions beginning with the word "Why?"

For example, "Why didn't you try to jump out of the car window?" ... "Why did you go out so late?" ... "Why didn't you run?" ... "Why didn't you try to get the knife out of his hand?" Once the question "why" is asked, the problem of role amplification begins. It is at this point that the medical staff develops an inflative and negative expansion of their role. The asking of the question "why?" satisfies the questioner's need for a motive. Furthermore, this particular question has an air of interrogation about it. Is it really necessary for medical staff to ask the question "why?" To press an already pressured rape victim for an answer to this unnecessary prying question only serves to satisfy the personal needs of the person asking and has nothing to do with the medical care needed. Therefore, it is entirely inappropriate. Instead of attending to the medical needs of the victim, the medical staff focus on their own biases and fears and begin to make moral judgments about the victim. Those physicians and nurses who were confronted with the prying nature of their questions have tended to righteously retort with "Well, what if I have to go to court? I have to know all of the details of the case!" A simple explanation to them, stating that as physicians they will be questioned concerning medical details and not as investigative detectives, is usually enough to deter further questions.

Community Sanctions

While rape has long been a private problem because of the social stigma attached to the act, in recent years it has been recognized as a societal problem. However, the other dynamic of victimization has been the community reaction to the crime. While elements such as seductiveness, poor judgment, improper conduct or manner of dress, or just being at the wrong place at the wrong time of day or night do not justify the offense of rape, neither does a victim's previous consent, particularly important in acquaintance or date rapes, confer such rights. Nonetheless, these variables come into play when a female reports the rape to authorities. In many cases the first community group a rape victim contacts is the police. The police officer's attitude toward the crime of rape, its offenders, and victims may be strongly affected by the myths surrounding rapes, as well as the officer's own sociocultural background, values, and morals (as discussed in chapter 3). As a result of faulty myths and stereotypes, many sex crime detectives feel that only one-third of rapes reported are "real rapes." Those considered real rapes tend to be those that are committed by strangers and are accompanied by much physical trauma such as bruising and broken bones (indicating that the victim put up a struggle). The remaining two-thirds are felt to be erroneous and reported for various false reasons including retaliation against a boyfriend; inability of the victim to account for time taken for personal use; a sexual encounter that needs to be explained because of guilt, pregnancy or fear of pregnancy; and the sudden presence of venereal disease.

There seems to be a need for social institutions to rationalize and explain the criminal behavior that has taken place within the community. The experience of becoming a victim of a violent crime is tragic enough; however, when we add to this experience the paradoxical attitude of society and the institutions that are usually mandated to help, the situation becomes compounded. Communities have strange attitudes that block sympathetic responses to a victim's situation. One of the attitudes is the primitive fear of contamination if one associates with the unlucky victim. The result of this primitive response of fear is to isolate or exclude the victim.

This type of exclusion is particularly seen in the community responses toward the rape victim. There is a general attitude that most if not all rape victims "asked for it." This attitude persists even in situations where the woman was terrorized, had tried to get away, and was physically injured. If she was not physically injured ("She hardly had a scratch on her!"), there are suspicions about why she did not resist. The presumption goes that since the victim did not resist, she must have enjoyed it. As a result, the victim experiences isolation, exclusion, and notoriety. There are whispering campaigns questioning the innocence of the victim. If she is young and single, she can be subjected to annoying behavior from the men in the community without the usual protective interference of other individuals. Some rape victims who experienced this exclusion and notoriety have had to move from the neighborhood. That the victim feels isolated, helpless, and alone in a world perceived as being hostile produces profound adaptive and defensive patterns, which form the core of the secondary psychological trauma experienced by many rape victims.

Another response is that of seeming indifference to the victim's plight. This is the most common complaint of victims of violent crimes. The manner in which rape victims are managed reflects an attitude of contempt on the part of the predominantly male police force, hospital personnel, and lawyers. The attitutde is perceived as caused by male assumptions that women enjoy being raped. The attitude of seeming indifference of the community, as well as of the police, may also be due to the fact that by the time the victim is seen, the criminal act is in the past and the criminal is gone. There is nothing active that the listener can do, and the victim's expression of distress is experienced by the listener as an implied demand that something be done. Also implied is criticism that the listener failed to protect the victim from the tragic experience.

The court process is another area that perpetuates victimization. Any rape case that comes to the attention of the criminal justice agencies will be investigated. There will be questioning, interrogation, interviews, and visits to police stations to view mug shots. If the case goes to court, the impersonal attitude of the court and the participants is perceived by the victim as uncaring. Rape is possibly the only crime in which the jury may be advised to examine the testimony of the complainant with caution. The victim can and usually is questioned about her prior sexual experience and general sexual morality, while the accused rapist will not be asked any questions about his past. This may lead to an acquittal situation since the jury will not be apprised of any prior sex crimes committed. Jurors tend to be less sympathetic to victims who are unwed mothers or who are sexually active. Also, juries do not believe a woman can be raped unless she has been beaten first. They tend to discount the testimony of women who smoked marijuana, took other drugs, frequented bars, or kept late hours. If a man was well-groomed, married or had a girl friend, jurors tend to have difficulty seeing him as a rapist. The victim most likely to be taken seriously is married and assaulted in her own home while the door is locked.

Reactions of the Victim's Family

One of the immediate reactions of most parents is revenge, or the desire to do something physically about the assault. Overwhelming feelings of helplessness trigger this wish for action, which is usually directed against the assailant. Members of families will often describe feelings of outrage, anger, and aggression against the assailant. The father of a young girl who had been raped screamed: "I'm going to get that kid. I know where they hang out. I'll just go there and win over their confidence. I know just how to talk to them. Then I'll find out who did it and and then I'll have my revenge!" Other parents may refuse to allow the victim to return to school because of shame and guilt. Many fathers and brothers experience feelings of helplessness at not being able to protect their child or sister. One brother gave his sister a gun to protect herself. He also loaded one for himself and stayed with her, hoping that the rapist would return so that he could "Blow his brains out!"

Husbands and boyfriends also share much of the suffering. Some men have become enraged, feeling a loss of manliness because they were powerless to prevent the attack: "If I were with her, it would not have happened," or "I was brought up to protect my woman and I couldn't." Some feel shame that "their woman" has been sexually violated. They may feel as if they had been raped also. Others disappear because they cannot handle the emotions that arise. Often the spouses of rape victims take on some of the anger that they feel their spouse is not expressing. Some rape victims are so happy to be alive, to have survived the trauma, that the anger is not acknowledged or expressed. Misinterpreting the lack of surface anger as a sort of pleasure, the spouse will doubt what really happened. These husbands may experience periods of anxiety, guilt, and depression, and either are suspicious in quiet or ask too many questions concerning details of the rape: "Did you know the rapist?" ... "What did he look like?" ... "What did he say?" ... "What did he do?" ... "Did you like it?" ... "Was he better than me?" The shock of a rape can destroy any relationship. Some husbands, reluctant to believe the innocence of their own wives, will press for premature resumption of their sexual relationship. If refused, they then tend to assume that she enjoyed the rape. As one enraged husband said, "Sure, now that you had him, you don't want me!" Although these spouses may be physically present, their emotional support is often lacking. Due to their wives' and their own suspicions, they tend to blame their wives for what has happened and become accusatory and unsympathetic, instead of supportive, understanding, and helpful. This suspicion derives from the reluctance to believe the total innocence of the victim, and so occasionally the rape victim will subsequently experience separation and divorce.

Sometimes, since the assailant is not around to answer questions, the community assesses the victim's behavior in order to explain why the crime occurred. People will do this to psychologically protect themselves by trying to distinguish the victim's behavior from their own. They may be heard saying:

"Well, what was she doing out so late?"
"She should have known he was bad!"
"Just look at the way she dresses!"
"Well, you know what happens when you have one drink too many!"
"She shouldn't have been hanging around the schoolyard. Why didn't she come home directly after school?"

This type of questioning of behavior continues on in the investigation of the crime. There seems to be a human need inherent in questioning techniques that tend to perpetuate the continued victimization of victims:

"Didn't you know this neighborhood is dangerous to walk in after dark?"
"Couldn't you have avoided that street?"
"Didn't you have the door locked?"
"Weren't you suspicious of that man in the elevator?"
"Why did you take the chain off the door, if you didn't know who you were talking to?"
"Why didn't you scream?"
"Did you look before you opened the door?"

All the above are examples of questions and comments that victimize. In general, the theme is an aggressive questioning of the victim. These questions take the form of "Didn't you know," "Couldn't you tell?" and "Why, why, why, did it happen?" These types of questions wrongly imply that the victim's injuries could have been prevented or avoided by being careful, or dressing differently, or taking a different route home after work.

The community's first response to victims stems from a basic need for all individuals to find a rational explanation for violent crimes, particularly those that are brutal. Exposure to senseless, irrational, brutal behavior makes everyone feel vulnerable and helpless. If it can happen to this person, then it can happen to anyone, at any time and any place. It is relieving to establish, even if wrongly, that the victim did something or neglected to do something that plausibly contributed to the crime. It makes others feel less helpless, less vulnerable, and more safe, all at the expense of the victim. These comments and questions that attempt to determine the rationality of the crime are always directed toward the available one, the victim, in the absence and nonaccessibility of the criminal.

Male Victims

Males not only are frequently victims of sexual molestation but are even more likely than females to hide their victimization and be overlooked as victims by criminal justice agencies as well as other social institutions. Male victims of rape are less likely than female victims to report the assault because of the overwhelming social stigma attached to the act. According to National Crime Survey statistics it is estimated that in 1985, 12,300 males were raped. In another confidential questionnaire study of male college students, 20 percent had been victims of "at least one act of criminally forced sodomy" and another 10 percent of violent attempted sodomy "while on campus or in surrounding community." None of these acts were reported to school or criminal justice authorities. Male rape is commonly thought of as something that rarely occurs outside prison walls, yet statistics prove this to be yet another myth associated with rape.

Studies of jail rape indicate that victims tend to be younger, smaller, underweight, and jailed for less serious offenses than their abusers. Gang rapes were the usual means of attack, and many victims were intimidated into submission through threats of mass rape or other violence such as being forcibly held down and raped. Those prisoners most vulnerable were those who were first-timers, not streetwise, not gang-affiliated, and not accustomed to violence. Prison rapes typically involve a weak victim and a group of aggressive rapists who dominate the victim through their collective strength. Those judges who are aware of this problem are reluctant to sentence young offenders to a jail term, knowing that they would immediately be subject to rape by the violent inmates.

Whether in jail or outside, male victims are more frequently gang-raped and are often abused more violently than female victims. Other research findings are:

- Victims and assailants are usually heterosexual;
- Rape of males as with females is a crime of violence and an assertion of power rather than of sex;
- Victims tend to be young, usually teenagers;

- Victims tend to be beaten severely during the assault;

- Male victims are far more likely to be gang-raped and to have been forced into multiple types of sexual acts than females; and

- Approximately 40 percent of the abusers were themselves sexually abused as children.

Male Rape Trauma Syndrome

Men experience similar victimization reactions to rape as do women, both physical and psychological, short-term and long-term. There are two specific major concerns of male victims. First is a questioning of their subsequent masculinity. Many male victims feel that the rape will cause them to become homosexuals ("Have I lost my manhood?"). Second, since there are social expectations concerning the ability of men to be able to defend themselves, they experience more intense feelings of helplessness and loss of control.

Reporting the Rape

Despite the high rape statistics, only 1 in 10 rapes is reported to law enforcement authorities. It is one of the most underreported of all crimes because of victims' fears of their assailants and their embarassment over the incident. Rape is an extremely controversial, humiliating act, during which the victim suffers pain and embarassment long after the crime is over. The dilemma of whether to report a rape is faced by thousands of rape victims. For many, the answer is not to report the incident. Although regrettable, the response is understandable. Police, prosecutors, and medical examiners have been accused by many rape victims of insensitive and unsympathetic behavior. Since force and intent must be proven before an act of sexual relations is considered a rape, a common courtroom defense for a rapist is to claim that he was encouraged or seduced by the victim. Many victims find that they are on trial, and their character and behavior become the subject of humiliating scrutiny. This process in itself becomes more humiliating than the actual crime. Social service agencies are often ill-equipped to deal with the rape victim's special needs.

Therefore, a pattern emerges; the lack of support from the community and family and the low priority given rape cases by police and prosecutors alienate victims and discourage many from reporting assaults. Those victims who persevere to the trial stage find themselves "put on trial," as defense attorneys grill them about their own sexual histories. It is not surprising that actual rapes far exceed the number reported to the police, nor is it any wonder that many women who do report later refuse to prosecute.

The irony of the situation is that when rape victims, police, prosecutors, and the general community cannot work together effectively, they unwittingly perpetuate the pattern. The result is that rapists remain free to victimize others, again and again.

Crisis Intervention

The research findings presented above suggest that the treatment of rape victims requires dealing with both short- and long-term effects, some of which persist for years after the rape. In dealing with the immediate after effects of rape, however, crisis counseling should have as its goal the return of the victim to the previous level of functioning as quickly as possible. The stages of victimology must be kept in mind. The crisis intervener should be aware of the following:

Stage 1. Shock and disbelief in this case may remain for a couple of weeks or even longer. The shock and disbelief of having been violated to the degree that accompanies rape is far more devastating than in simple assault or burglaries; therefore, it may take the victim several days to become angry enough to move to stage 2, or to even get up enough nerve to report the incident. In reviewing the details and expressing her feelings the victim may be heard saying "Why me?" . . . "I can't believe this happened to me." She may try to deny the entire experience and block memories of the assault because of shock. Furthermore, a person who is raped may even remain in the presence of the attacker for a day or two because of the clinging effect, which is part of the next stage.

Stage 2. Fright and blaming in cases of rape account for the emotional reactions that a victim suffers. The victim may suffer from frequent flashbacks of the attack, causing general sleeplessness and nightmares or screaming during sleep. She may fear physical injury, mutilation, or death in reaction to the threat of being killed during the rape. She may be fearful to go out of doors or to stay indoors, to remain alone, or to interact with people, including her own family. Frequently, the victim will change her telephone number to an unlisted number and change the locks on doors and windows. The victim may do this as a precautionary measure in reaction to the fear that the assailant knows where she is and will return to inflict further harm, or the woman may develop rape-related fears of her neighborhood, of men who resemble the rapist, or of everyone she encounters. Panic attacks can occur if the victim is exposed to a stimulus associated with the rape. If the rapist threatened revenge if she reported the rape to the police, she may be especially suspicious or paranoid. In terms of blame the victim may be placing blame on herself by thinking, "I should have stayed home," . . . "I should have fought back," or "I shouldn't have worn that short skirt."

Stage 3. Anger and apathy may be exhibited by the general discharge of anger at the assailant, her predicament, and the people who are trying to provide assistance. Victims may be heard expressing anger at criminal justice personnel as criticism for not being there to help her: "I've just been raped, and you guys are just sitting on your butts taking all of this casually!" or "Listen mister, I already gave you that information. What are you stupid or something?" Apathy may be expressed by the victim's feelings that no one is going to help: "You aren't going to do anything to find the rapist anyway. Why bother with this information?"

Stage 4. Resignation, resolution, and integration make up the last stage of the immediate crisis. At this point the rape victim may find herself making rules to follow: "From now on I will never wear a skirt on a date" . . . "If I'd worn jeans, I would have had time to run away" . . . "From now on I will never go to a man's apartment" or "I will never talk to a stranger again." The victim acknowledges what has happened and accepts this as fact. Plans are then made for getting on with the business of life.

Referrals

Sexual assault victims require additional treatment and assistance and should be referred to their local rape counseling service via written instructions and telephone numbers. While assessing victims for referral, crisis interveners should notify them that there are agencies that provide ongoing assistance. Interveners should familiarize themselves with community resources and maintain a list of helping agencies and the services they provide, including the name of the agency, address, name of contact person, hours of operation, and whether there is a fee for service. Hotline crisis phones are among the first alternatives offered. They provide people with a constant link to a sympathetic listener. They are available in many cities, and some provide follow-up counseling and advocacy services. These programs will provide long-term treatment rather than short-term crisis intervention and provide services needed for victims that may need help in straightening out sexual issues, dealing with their friends and relatives, or sorting out confusion about their lives. If the intervener has been professional and sincere in his or her efforts, the victim will be more likely to follow-up on his or her advice.

Guidelines for Intervention

1. All suggestion of force, aggressiveness, or pressure must be avoided. This kind of behavior resembles the rapist's actions. If the intervener hopes to gain confidence, he or she should be nonjudgmental and patient. Place the victim at ease and create an atmosphere that will allow the person to relate his or her story.

2. Interview the victim in a private, quiet spot.

3. Be nonjudgmental and sensitive. The message should be: "I'm willing to help you get through this crisis. I'm willing to work with you."

4. Allow the victim to ventilate.

5. Expect clinging behavior.

6. Expect fear of hospitalization and medical treatment.

7. Be tactful and supportive of family members.

8. Expect long periods of silence during interviews.

9. Confront your own embarrassment concerning sexual details. Avoid passing these on to the victim. If the victim stammers or indicates discomfort concerning sexual details, encouragement can be given by stating: "I know this is difficult to talk about. Take your time." Sometimes victims are embarrassed to discuss unusual sexual behavior on the part of the assailant. Important information can be gathered by stating: "I know that rapists sometimes force women to do other things besides sexual intercourse. If he made you to anything else, be sure to mention it to the doctor who will be examining you." This statement acknowledges that unusual acts are not uncommon in rapes and opens the door for the victim to discuss them.

10. Maintain respectful eye contact and body distance.

11. Consider the victim's fearful state. Avoid touching.

12. Make referrals to local victim hotlines or victim service agencies for follow-up counseling and advocacy services.

Victims of sexual assault will have confidence and trust in criminal justice interveners who display sympathetic and supportive attitudes as well as skillful interview techniques. As a result, valuable information which might otherwise have been withheld because of fear or anger will be provided for the investigation. Initial contacts with victims provide the basis for future contacts. The success of subsequent interviews, investigation, and prosecution may be dependent on the initial impressions that the intervener has made. Initial contact with the victim provides the basis for future contacts in that impressions made by the victim of the intervener and the criminal justice system will determine how cooperative the victim will be with subsequent interviews. This, of course, will reflect on the success of further investigation and prosecution of the case.

THE CHILD VICTIM

Although child abuse has been a social problem in America since the nation's inception, only in the past 30 years has there been any movement toward confronting it. Historically, it has been the parents' absolute right to do whatever they wanted with their child (sell, use as chattel, brand, cripple, destroy, or have sexual intercourse with). The child was considered to be the sole property of the parents. Despite the development of child-protection laws, children are still victimized. In New York City alone, in 1986 there were 41,000 reports of child abuse and neglect involving nearly 70,000 children. Many of these reports involve sex crimes which came to the attention of criminal justice professionals. Recent statistics suggest that as many as one child in four becomes the victim of sexual abuse by the time he or she reaches the age of 18. Both boys and girls are the victims of abuse, and children may be abused at any age from infancy to adolescence. Intervening with these children invariably means intervening in one of childhood's most traumatic crises. These crises are particularly apparent when intervening in situations involving sexual exploitation of children. Proper intervention at this point will not only reduce the potential of future trauma to the child but also establish a base for furthering the investigation. It is unfortunate that more than 90 percent of all child abusers do not go forward to prosecution, and are instead released to further abuse their victims and other children. In some of these cases, the decision not to prosecute is based on concerns about the impact of the court process on the child. However, in many other cases the child just refuses to cooperate because he or she is fearful of and intimidated by social service and criminal justice investigators. A knowledge of and understanding of child developmental issues will assist the criminal justice intervener in establishing a working relationship to meet the victim's needs in light of the intervener's own legal responsibilities. Children are generally reliable witnesses if handled sensitively and with a consideration for their limitations.

Developmental Differences

Up until this point we have been mainly discussing crisis intervention with adults. Although many of the concepts discussed can be applied to children, it is important to remember that children cope with crisis situations in different ways than adults. Contrary to the theories of some psychologists, children are not miniature adults who experience crisis in smaller doses than adults. Besides physical size and chronological age, children differ in other aspects, including:

Life experience. Lacking life experience places children in the position of not realizing that the crisis situation will pass or somehow be resolved. Children only experience their vulnerability and their helplessness. Since their self-concept and identity are undeveloped (see Erickson's stages in chapter 2) they cannot rely on the inner strengths that an adult may use to cope. Consequently, they lose whatever developing sense of self they have achieved, and whatever sense of trust, initiative, or industry they have developed.

Cognitive abilities. Children do not have the ability to think problems through as do adults. As adults, it is usually possible for us to attack and solve a personal problem as we do any other kind of problem—such as in mathematics or science—by asking clear questions, assembling evidence, judging the possible consequences, and trying to verify in practice what we have concluded from the evidence. Children are not able to do this complex kind of thinking. Furthermore, the way children think about moral issues depends on their level of intellectual development.

Cognitive and Moral Development

Children develop in stages, during which they acquire capacities for new functions and understanding. Stage theory has been used to explain psychosexual as well as psychosocial developmental gains (Freud and Erikson). In terms of intellectual development, the most influential explanation of modern times was put forward by the Swiss biologist and psychologist Jean Piaget (1932), who formulated a theory to explain the various levels of cognitive development, or the ability to think and acquire knowledge. Piaget presumes an ever-increasing ability to acquire knowledge that proceeds in an orderly sequence (see table 7.1).

As for moral development, it was Lawrence Kohlberg (1964, 1968) who developed his six stages of moral reasoning based on Jean Piaget's theory. Defining "moral development" as the development of an individual's sense of justice, Kohlberg concentrated on how people think about morality. To test his theory, he devised a set of moral dilemmas ("Should a man who cannot afford the medicine his dying wife needs steal it?" ... "Should a doctor 'mercy-kill' a fatally ill person suffering terrible pain?") and a system for scoring people's answers to these dilemmas. He maintains that while children begin to think about issues of right and wrong at an early age, they cannot attain moral reasoning until adolescence, and that some people never reach this level.

A combination of the two theories applied to child development would result in the following schema:

During Piaget's first stage, the Sensorimotor Period (Birth to 2 years) the infant learns through its senses and its motor behaviors rather than using thought in the way that adults do. This is a time of learning through action, as babies learn to go from responding primarily through reflexes to organizing their activities in relation to their environment. The ability to reason morally is undeveloped at this stage.

During the Preoperational Stage (2 to 7 years) children make a qualitative leap forward thanks to their new ability to use symbols such as language to represent people, places, and objects. They can now use language and numbers, imitate actions that they do not see at the moment, and think about objects not directly in front of them. There are, however, major limitations in thought. Children at this stage generally fail to take all the aspects of a situation into account, and instead focus on one aspect, ignoring others that are just as important. They also do not understand that actions can be reversed to restore an original state. Furthermore, they are egocentric, that is, they have difficulty considering another person's point of view and view

Table 7.1
Developmental Stages

Ages	Psychosexual (Freud)	Psychosocial (Erikson)	Cognitive (Piaget)	Moral (Kohlberg)
0-18 mo.	Oral	Basic trust vs. mistrust	Sensori- motor	
18 mo. - 3 yrs.	Anal	Autonomy vs. doubt/shame		
3-5 yrs.	Phallic	initiative vs. guilt	preopera- tional	premoral
6-11 yrs.	Latency	Industry vs. inferiority	Concrete operational	Role/ conform
12-17 yrs.	Genital	Identity vs. role confusion	Formal operational	Moral principle
Young adult		Intimacy vs. isolation		
Maturity		Generativity vs. stagnation		
Old age		Ego integrity vs. despair		

* Freud and Erikson's theories are discussed in chapter 2.

life as if everyone were seeing things as they do. They see themselves as the cause of all significant events. For example, abused children may feel that they caused the abuse ("If I hadn't been bad, Mommy wouldn't have beat me" . . . "If I hadn't been in bed that man wouldn't have done what he did to me"). In terms of Kohlberg's stages of moral development, their emphasis is on external controls that are followed in order to avoid punishment. To avoid punishment, children obey the rules of adults who stand in a power position over them through age, authority, or some other way) "What would happen to me if I didn't do what he says?" . . . "I have to obey him, he's my father!") Children are also vulnerable to misrepresentation of moral standards. If a trusted adult tells them to do something, it is "O.K. to do it." As one child victim said, "She's my mother. If she told me to do it, it must be all right to do it!"

During Piaget's stage of Concrete operations (7 to 11 years), children make a qualitative leap as they shed their egocentrism and begin to use new concepts. They can classify things into categories, deal with numbers, take all aspects of a situation into account, and understand reversibility. They are much better at putting themselves into another's place, which has implications for their understanding of other people and for making moral judgments. Children now want to please and help others. They want to be considered "good" by the people whose opinions count. They are concerned with showing respect for higher authority and maintaining good relations with it by doing what they feel is the right thing. ("I was brought up to respect my parents. This means I should do what they want, and please them!" . . . "He told me that a good little girl would do what he says.")

Piaget's stage of Formal Operations (12 years and older) is the forerunner of the ability to think abstractly. Children in this stage can approach a problem that is not physically present, work out a hypothesis, and systematically go about testing it. Their emphasis is on possibility rather than reality. In terms of moral development, for the first time the child acknowledges the possibility of conflict between two socially accepted standards, and tries to decide between them ("I know this is wrong, but if I tell, everyone will know that my uncle is a pervert"). The control of conduct is now internal, both in the standards observed and in the reasoning about right and wrong. Children begin to think morally as individuals regardless of the opinions of others. They act in accordance with internalized standards, knowing that they would condemn themselves if they did not ("I can't live with this any longer. I have to tell!" . . . "I don't have to live with this anymore"). It is at this stage of intellectual and moral development that decisions are made either to tell a higher authority or take actions into their own hands. Adolescents may choose to take either a fight or flight approach at this time. They may report the abuse to a parent, trusted relative, schoolteacher, or criminal justice representative (fight); or take flight through self-abusive behavior such as drugs, alcohol, runaway behavior, or prostitution. Some may take the situation into their own hands and arrange for the murder of the abuser or murder him themselves (fight). Several recent cases illustrate this point.

Albany, New York: A 17-year-old girl shot her father 11 times with a 22-caliber rifle, striking him in the back and head when he attempted to force her into her home. The estranged father had visitation rights, but couldn't enter the house where his wife and daughter lived. At the trial, the defense demonstrated that the father had sexually abused his daughter and that she was fearful of a sexual assault on the night of the shooting.

Santa Ana, California: An 18-year-old boy killed his legal guardian after suffering years of sexual abuse. The guardian sexually abused him four to five times a week after adopting him at age 13. The boy finally resisted a sexual advance, and, in a rage, shot the guardian in his sleep.

Hauppauge, Long Island, New York: A 16-year-old female paid a schoolmate $400 to kill her father in order to end an incestuous relationship. The teenage girl feared that her father was also about to begin abusing her 10-year-old sister.

Moral development depends on cognitive development largely because children cannot judge the morality of another person's actions until they can put themselves in the place of all the people who would be affected by those acts. Until they have abandoned egocentrism they cannot weigh the effects of their own behavior, let alone anyone else's.

Unrealistic Expectations of Children

The major individual cause of concern that a crisis intervener will encounter with sexually abused children is disbelief. Many professionals are inclined not to believe a child's story of sexual molestation. The usual justification is that children have a vivid fantasy life and make up stories. In addition, there are questions about how a child could be sexually abused and not tell anyone about it for so many years (cases of long-standing abuse). Surely they would tell someone; "Didn't they know it was wrong?" Standard explanations have been that the child was: (1) fearful of the abuser, (2) afraid that the revelation will break up his or her home, and/or that Mom and Dad would get in trouble (cases of incest), and (3) ashamed and embarrassed. However, in consideration of the theories of Piaget and Kohlberg, children are also not capable of thinking about, understanding, and moralizing about what has happened to them. Children experience difficulty with concepts of sexual abuse and assaults. They often lack the verbal skills and creative fantasy ability that help adults cope with crisis. This deficiency hampers their adjustment to crisis events. The inadequate solutions that they will develop are clung to with tenacity. While adults will seek out friends where they can ventilate and who will give them advice, comfort, support, and a clearer perspective of what has happened to them, children do not.

Furthermore, since children rely on external controls (parents or adults) to avoid punishment, they will tend to obey the rules ("I'd better do what he says or else!"). They also, as we have seen, want to please others, and they have respect for higher authority. It is therefore not only relatively easy to intimidate children into submission but also to gain compliance by manipulation of these needs. Most cases of long-term child molestation are exposed when the child decides that he or she will not comply any longer. This usually happens at the beginning of adolescence. According to Kohlberg and Piaget, the child is then capable of abstract and logical thinking, and has at the same time developed internal control of his or her own conduct. It is therefore logical that the child will expose and/or terminate the behavior at this point in development.

Patterns of Child Sexual Abuse

The sexual abuse of children can be categorized into three different types:

1. *The brief isolated incident* may happen only once to the child. The abuser may be a stranger or an acquaintance. The child may be walking to school and be touched in the genital area by a stranger, or a man may expose his genitals to the child. A child may be raped by an acquaintance or stranger. Both boys and girls may be involved in brief incidents of sexual abuse.

2. In *incest*, the sexual abuser is a member of the child's immediate family, usually a father, stepfather, or older brother. The abuse usually begins gradually and usually occurs more often as time goes by. The victim is most often female, and the incest will continue until it is exposed or until the child reaches adolescence and is effective in putting a stop to it. Not quite so prevalent, but being seen increasingly, is the male victim and female perpetrator. (While cases of stepfather-stepdaughter incest, mother's boyfriend–daughter, or foster father–foster daughter sexual contact are commonly reported, opposite types of contact such as stepmother–stepson are rarely documented.) The victims in these circumstances, although not always the female molester's own children, are nearly always a child (or children) with whom she lives—stepchild, foster child, or the son or daughter of her boyfriend or lover. Sometimes the victim may be a child who is visiting his father and may be sexually abused by the father's girlfriend. One mother reported such an incident in this way:

For the two years of my separation from his father, I have been allowing liberal visitation rights. During this time my ex-husband had been regularly dating one particular woman and was planning to marry. Consequently he spent a great deal of time with her while taking care of my son. Lately, my son has been behaving strangely. He has been trying to put his hands inside of my pants telling me that he wants to touch my "coolie" and that I will like it. His playmates' mothers have refused to let him play with their children because he forces them to undress and then pins the kids down to the floor. He shows an unusual preoccupation with genital play, and loves to expose himself to other kids. This kind of behavior got him thrown out of two nursery schools. He always has been hyperactive and aggressive, but this is too much. I consulted two psychologists about his behavior, and they told me that children tend to make up stories, they have vivid imaginations and advised me to ignore him. Meanwhile, my son tells me that some strange things have been happening at his father's house.

When this child was brought to the emergency room for examination he refused to talk to a female crisis counselor. A male was then asked to try. Using the anatomically correct dolls, he said to the child, "O.K. John, man-to-man now, tell me what happened!" John had identified the two adult dolls as his father and his father's girlfriend, and the young female doll as his cousin and the male doll as himself. What happened next was shocking to even this experienced counselor, himself the father of two children. He reported later that he watched as John in an excited franzy ripped off all of the dolls' clothing and threw them all around the office, saying that this was what they usually did after they all jumped into bed together. He then described the various sexual combinations that he participated in with these bed partners, in particular sex acts performed with his father's girlfriend. They included every possible sexual behavior imaginable, including oral-genital, mutual masturbation, anal penetration, spankings, and attempts at sexual intercourse. Physical examination of the child revealed no evident trauma; however, charges were pressed against the father and his girlfriend resulting in the decision that the father not be allowed to visit his son unless accompanied by another adult.

3. *Long-term relationships*, as opposed to incest situations, involve persons other than relatives. The abuser may be a neighbor, teacher, family friend, coach, Big Brother or Sister, or camp counselor. One child reported to his parents that the boy scout leader told him, "You have such cute buns. I can't wait to get my hands on them!" As with incest, the abuse begins gradually as the abuser gains compliance and continues until it is exposed or ended by the child. The victim may be male or female.

Behavioral Indicators

The most obvious problem for crisis interveners is to be cognizant of what determines sexual abuse. There seems to be wide disagreement with the idea that diagnosis is the field of medicine and mental health. Although diagnosis will be made by qualified medical personnel typically in emergency rooms it is important to interact with other professionals and understand their definitions of the situation so that effective intervention and referral can be coordinated. Essentially intervention should be a team effort; and nowhere is this more valuable than in the early recognition and subsequent early treatment of the sexual assault victim. There seems to be a general reluctance among criminal justice professionals to work with social workers, and vice versa (see chapter 1). Nevertheless, consultation with child protection workers, medical personnel, and social workers can encourage greater cooperation and result in more cases being brought for prosecution:

Behavioral indicators of sexual abuse may include:

- Regressive behavior. Children who have been sexually abused may withdraw into fantasy worlds and/or exhibit infantile behavior (sucking their thumbs, curled in fetal position). Sometimes these children may be mistakenly diagnosed as autistic or mentally retarded.
- Bed-wetting, nightmares, fear of going to bed, or other sleep disturbances. Fear of certain persons, baby-sitters, or neighbors.

- Delinquent, aggressive, or rebellious behavior. Unable to cope directly with the source of their anxiety, children will displace their anger, hurt, and resentment outwardly onto their peers and their environment.

- Sexual promiscuity, drugs, prostitution, and runaway behavior. For preteens especially, these four variables are often responses to sexual exploitation.

- Excessively seductive or sophisticated behavior. Some parents get a clue about sexual abuse of their child when the child exhibits unusual sexual behavior (kissing with open mouth and tongue insertion, performing strip tease dances, attempting to pin down and fondle other children).

- Bruises, pain, or bleeding in the genital area, which may cause difficulty in walking or sitting.

- The presence of a vaginal or penile discharge and genital or mouth sores, which may be indicative of veneral disease.

- Child openly reports sexual assault by caretaker, sibling, or other person. Sometimes the abuse may be discovered by accident. As one mother recounts:

My 4 year old son had been a friendly, outgoing, huggy kind of boy who loved going to nursery school, but suddenly that all changed. His behavior drastically changed. He'd yell at people, kick them, spit on others, and bite them. He didn't want to sleep alone, waking up in the middle of the night screaming. He began to wet his bed. Becoming concerned I brought him to his doctor for an examination. During the examination the nurse routinely took the boy's temperature rectally. My son said, "This is what my teacher does at school. Her takes my temperature every day at school. Her takes my clothes off."

The mother contacted the director of the school as well as child protective services. Prosecutors interviewed the child and his classmates and arrested the day-care teacher, who was charged with 163 counts of sexually abusing, assaulting, and molesting 31 children in her class.

Crisis Intervention with Child Victims

Preliminary Considerations

The purpose of the initial contact with a child is to gather information regarding the report and to make a determination concerning the child's safety. There are several issues that must be taken into consideration to prior intervention. Relevant information should be obtained from parents, guardians, and/or child welfare counselors, social workers, and physicians. From this information professionals should assess three factors: The first is the child's general developmental level. For example, age, grade in school, and intellectual capabilities (able to read, write, count, tell time) will determine the ability to evaluate what has happened. Second, are there any physical problems (autism, mental retardation, disabilities)? Finally, categorize the type of sexual assault. The kind of assault and the degree of violence will have an impact on the child's emotional state and determine the response to questions. Also to be taken into consideration is the relationship of the child to the assailant. Understandably, family members and assailants who have threatened retaliation will be protected by the child.

Intervention

Truthfulness. Remember that children seldom lie about acts of sexual exploitation. It is important that the child feel that you believe what he or she is telling you. On the other hand, the intervener should never lie to the child or the parents. Be honest about your role in the situation.

The setting. Initial contact with a child may take place in a variety of settings such as the child's home, medical facility, school, or child care facility. Bear in mind that the more comfortable the child is, the less anxious he or she will be. Some investigators suggest the most comfortable place is the child's home; however, this is a poor choice where there is suspicion of molestation having occurred there. Taking the child for a walk or to the playground may facilitate free, open conversation.

Privacy. Respect the child's privacy. Do not allow anyone to be present or overhear what is being discussed unless they need to know. Keep the child's short attention span in mind. Try to avoid interruptions.

Gaining rapport. Interveners should introduce themselves and their purpose for meeting with the child. Upon introduction it is a good idea to offer to shake hands. Children have many feelings about what has happened, and one of these is feeling unclean. Shaking the child's hand assures him or her in a nonverbal way that he or she is accepted by you.

Using eye level is another important variable when speaking to children. An effective method for gaining rapport with children quickly is to come down to their physical level. Adult height and bulk can intimidate children. You need to squat or kneel down, talk directly to children, look kindly and intently into their eyes, reach out and take gentle hold of their arms or shoulders, or sit down with them to talk.

Assess the child's level of development and find a common ground. Establishing rapport and forming a common bond are very important for building trust. Some topics for discussion may include family composition ("I have two brothers too"), favorite foods ("Do you like pizza?"), favorite television shows ("Do you ever watch 'The Smurfs'?"), movies, games, pets, and so on.

Playing games. Be prepared to participate in any play activity appropriate to the child's developmental level. Most facilities have games, paper, crayons and coloring books, or little toys that the child will want to play with. One burly detective stated after interviewing a child, "Sure I got the details, but it was only after forty-five minutes of playing with cars and trucks with him under the desk!" Many therapists use a draw-a-picture method for eliciting what has happened to a child who is reluctant to discuss the details. Crayons, color markers, and pencils could be used to draw the scene, or as an expression of feelings. This could be a starting point that will prompt further discussion of the actual details of the crime. Children will usually be quite willing to talk about the details that they have drawn on paper.

Another technique used by therapists is role-playing. Although the role playing is a game, it is also a way in which the child can reenact events. The advantage of this method is that it helps to relieve the guilt that the child bears about the event by describing it through objective items (dolls, toys, puppets). Verbalizing about the incident through the mouth of another is called guilt transfer. Responsibility for the incident is then placed onto the object that is used in the role-play and taken off the child.

Terminology. Use language appropriate to the child's level. Be alert to signs of incomprehension, confusion, blankness, or embarassment. Children will not understand words like penetration, ejaculation, withdraw, or fornication, and may not know words like penis, vagina, and breasts. Let the child be the guide in using familiar terms. Also become familiar with words that children will use to describe parts of the body (i.e., thing, pee pee, weiner, volvo, pishy, buds, private, toushy, ding-dong).

Likewise, children may not be able to pinpoint at what time (hour, day, or month) the abuse occurred, but may be able to establish that it happened in the morning before school or after school, what they were watching on television, and whether it was snowing out or during holiday recesses.

Anatomically Correct Dolls

The child should be encouraged to talk; however, he or she may be embarassed to discuss sexual details. If the child is reticent or withdrawn, the use of anatomically correct dolls may be helpful in helping the child express him- or herself. The use of these dolls as a visual and sensory aid will assist the child in describing the event. Anatomically correct dolls usually come in a set of four: adult female, adult male, child female, and child male. They are realistically designed to be anatomically realistic. They all have realistically depicted body parts relative to the intended age of the doll. The adult female doll has breasts with nipples, pubic hair, belly button, and vaginal and anal openings as well as oral and ear openings. The adult male doll has all the body openings including a fully developed penis and testicles as well as pubic hair and chest hair. The child dolls have all the body openings and depictions of appropriately developed sex organs. The dolls allow the victim to "show and tell" graphically what occurred through demonstration and verbalization.

Questioning Techniques

Behavior. Avoid aggressiveness and any suggestion of force or pressure. This behavior will be experienced as overbearing and persistent by the child, encouraging noncooperation in return.

Reluctance. Expect reluctance on the part of children to cooperate with an investigation.

Support the child's decision to tell. Make it clear that telling you what happened is the right thing to do and that you will protect the child from future harm. Tell the child that he or she is "safe" now.

Guilt. Explain to the child that he or she has done no wrong. The child will assume the guilt and responsibility for the incident and generally feels to blame for what has happened. Even though they could not have prevented the sexual incident, children will often feel that they are at fault. The intervener must convey understanding and reassurance that the child has done nothing wrong.

Challenges. Avoid challenging questions that begin with "Why?" Examples include "Why didn't you tell your mommy sooner?" . . . "Why did you let it happen?" . . . "Why did you go into the house?" . . . "Why didn't you tell?" Instead, offer positive statements such as: "I know you couldn't help it" . . . "It wasn't your fault" . . . "It's not wrong to tell me what happened" . . . "You're not to blame"; or supportive statements such as "I understand, you're really upset."

Be nonjudgmental. Such comments as "That must have hurt." . . . "That made you mad, didn't it?" . . . "Your father must be some animal to do this to you!" or "You should have ran away from there." are to be avoided. Avoid accusing or criticizing comments about the offender. Remember, many children will have strong emotional ties to the offender and will defend him or her.

Phrasing questions. The way questions are asked is extremely important in this type of interview. It is wise to ask direct, simple questions, as open-ended as appropriate for the child's level of comprehension and ability. Also, ask questions in a manner that does not imply blame or active participation on the part of the child. For example, questions such as: "What did you do with the man?" . . . "Where did you touch him?" . . . "Did you touch his penis?" . . . "Did you put his penis in your mouth?" or "Did you take off all of your clothes?" can imply active participation on the part of the child. These kinds of questions also reinforce guilt, making it more difficult for the child to respond. Instead, consider these alternatives: "What did the man do to you?" . . . "Did he ever touch you? Where?" . . . "Where did he put his fingers?" . . . "Did he put his penis in your mouth?" . . . "Did he make you take off your clothes?" and "Did he make you touch him? Where?" These place the blame on the abuser.

Allow the child to ask questions. Pause every once in a while to allow the child to think of and ask questions.

Provide information. Do not allow the child to have unreal expectations of what you are going to do or what is going to happen. Keep the lines of communication open. If the child is older and able to use the telephone, emphasize to the child that he or she can call you as needed for support, information or reassurance.

Taking these guidelines into consideration when intervening with a child victim of sexual abuse will ensure that the child's emotional needs have been met and protected. At the same time, the needs of the investigator to meet the goals of the investigation will be accomplished. Children react in the same ways to sexual assault as rape victims. In addition to the physical injury, the psychological effects can be devastating. The major determinants of how a child ultimately copes with the trauma of sexual abuse are: (1) developmental stage, (2) the specific circumstances of the abuse, and (3) the reactions of surrounding adults to the disclosure. Although there is no way of changing the first two determinants, conscientious crisis interveners can influence the third factor. If they offer a sense of security to the child and reassurance that he or she is not to be blamed and is believed, the psychological trauma can be reduced.

SUMMARY ON VIOLENT SEXUAL ENCOUNTERS

The main objective of this section on sex crimes is (1) to increase the criminal justice intervener's knowledge and awareness of the nature of the problems of sexual assault, as well as his or her personal reaction to it in order to better meet the victim's needs in light of his or her own legal duties; (2) to gain control of the situation, especially concerning knowledge of hospital procedures concerning treatment of rape and sexual assault victims, and to provide factual information about the need for and the procedure of the physical examination at the hospital emergency room; (3) to increase awareness of one's feelings and attitudes about the crime, the offenders, and the victims of rape; (4) to provide information about the physical and emotional trauma experienced by the victim, including typical reactions and resulting needs; and (5) to develop interviewing skills and intervention techniques based on this knowledge so that he or she may provide assistance to the victim while carrying out his or her legal responsibilities.

CRISIS INTERVENTION IN HOSTILE SITUATIONS

While in the majority of criminal justice situations intervention is desirable and necessary, there are some situations of crisis in which intervention is not desired by one or more of the participants. Crisis intervention in hostile situations is not a new experience for most criminal justice personnel, yet it is a troublesome one. Criminal justice workers are in a vulnerable position because of their one-to-one relationship with their clients, and because of cultural expectations that they are one of the caretakers of society and will assume responsibility. In addition, some of the esteem traditionally accorded them has been dissipated because of the general level of hostility that has risen over the past decade. This reflects general societal changes that are expressed by anger against authority figures. How can the intervener remain an effective "caretaker" when the person he or she is mandated to help is hostile? How can the hostility be used to the advantage of the crisis intervener?

The almost universal reactive response to anger is to become angry in return. A vicious cycle then begins, with each person becoming more and more angry as a result of the other's hostile expressions. Placed within its proper perspective, the hostility can be considered an extention of crisis intervention, as simply another complication that the crisis intervener should be able to negotiate. In a one-to-one situation, this might be easily accomplished. However, there are other, more complicated hostile situations that are not quite so manageable. Probably the most common hostile situation that the criminal justice intervener will become involved in is domestic violence. It is one situation where the intervener must be ready and able to help the disputants while at the same time ensuring his or her own emotional and physical safety. The possibility of a hostile attack and the likelihood of sustaining injury are high in this type of dispute. Physical violence occurs between family members more often than between any other category of individuals. One is more likely to be murdered by a member of one's own family, especially by a spouse, than by any other category of person. Domestic violence, which includes physical assault, sexual abuse, psychological abuse, and verbal harassment, is most often perpetrated against females. It occurs in all socioeconomic, ethnic, racial, and age groups, but is more visible in the lower socioeconomic groups because of their contact with social agencies and institutions.

Basic Problems

The ineffectiveness of the criminal justice system to adequately protect and assist those involved with domestic violence has been documented in many places. Police, prosecutors, and judges find domestic violence to be a difficult, time-consuming, and frustrating problem to handle. Some criminal justice professionals become indifferent and angry when they consistently see complainants discontinue prosecution proceedings and return to the abusive relationships. Failing to understand the reasons for returning, they inevitably make generalizations concerning all domestic violence incidents no matter what the extent of abuse, and hesitate to become involved.

The police. It was generally believed that responding to a domestic violence call was dangerous work. According to statistics compiled by law enforcement agencies as recently as 1985, up to 23 percent of officer deaths occurred during domestic disturbances, and more police officers are injured while responding to ordinary family disputes than other more "dangerous" situations. Contrary to these findings, new studies report that while there is some risk in answering family violence calls, other police assignments are indeed far more dangerous. One new study placed the correct figure at less than 6 percent of officer deaths. This study said the former erroneous statistic stemmed from the assumption that the "disturbance" category of F.B.I. statistics included only domestic problems, but that the category actually includes disturbances ranging from bar fights to gang brawls. The report pointed out that from 1972 to 1984, only 69 officers died in responding to domestic disturbances, compared to the 210 officers who were killed when responding to robbery reports, in spite of the fact that police handle 4 to 10 times as many domestic disturbances as robbery calls.

The police officer dreads this type of call more than any other because of the volatile and uncertain nature surrounding domestic conflict. The police officer is usually the first outsider to arrive on the scene of a domestic disturbance. There is a special challenge for the officer, because the call for assistance is made when the condition is acute and when violence is occurring or imminent. The symbols of authority, the badge and the uniform, may provoke rather than reassure those involved in domestic violence. Although intervention in disputes is an important function of police work, the officer's intervention may be seen variously as an intrusion, a source of annoyance, and a frustration (the Persecutor); a possible ally of the opposition (the Rescuer); or simply a new problem for both parties to deal with (the Victim). The violence, a coping device for frustration, is already in play when the officer arrives and may simply continue with an additional participant, the officer, being assigned one of the above roles.

The courts. If the situation moves to the courts, police, prosecutors, and judges become frustrated and angry at those who first file charges, vehemently pressing for an arrest, and later drop them. Police arrest proceedings, the prosecutor's preparation, and court assignments entail much time and energy spent in bringing the abuser to court. It is frustrating to learn after all this work that the victim decides to discontinue prosecution, tearfully stating, "I've reconsidered." . . . "I want to drop the charges." . . . "He really loves me, he didn't mean to hurt me." . . . "I love her, how can I live without her?" and "If he goes to jail, who will pay the bills?"

REASONS FOR FAMILY VIOLENCE

There are seven major reasons why families today are so often embroiled in conflict and violence:

Alcohol and drug abuse. The one major factor that has been found to be strongly associated with family violence is substance abuse. This is not to say that it is by itself a direct cause of domestic violence, but alcohol and other drugs do reduce the controls necessary to avoid violence in stressful situations. The substance abuser may ingest prior to the attack, permitting emotions such as anger or jealousy to surface, or may ingest afterwards to forget the abusive behavior.

Sex role socialization. In our society males are socialized to be aggressive, domineering, and to feel superior to females. These values are reflected by males' use of violence, aggression, and force in their relationships with females. The abuser often blames the female for the violence, insisting that if she would only stop doing things to anger him, he would stop beating her. Others argue that they beat women because they "need" it, or because it is a demonstration of their love for them. Still others feel that "You have to hit her once in awhile, to show her who's boss." Some women, on the other hand, are socialized to be passive and submissive in their relationships with men: "He's my man, I have to do what he says."

Isolation. Some families establish patterns of isolation, becoming dependent on each other to provide all their physical, emotional, and social needs.

Financial problems. Inadequate income may result in strain and conflict within the family, leading to violence.

Medical problems. Some families, instead of pulling together during a medical emergency, will pull apart.

Unemployment. Frustration over being fired or inability to find a job will often trigger violence.

Abusive upbringing. The more violence a child experiences while growing up, the greater likelihood that this child will become a violent, abusive adult.

In addition to the above reasons there is one more. There are some couples who have a chronic, habitual pattern of unhealthy interaction. They are just very adept at game playing. Some couples and even families characteristically communicate through the playing of painful games, usually involving trivial matters such as meals or the way an ashtray is placed on the coffee table. Police are expected to mediate in these conflicts as well as enforce the law. In the majority of cases, an objective authority is sought. Third-party understanding and skill may be even more necessary in conflicts between intimates than among people who are less close and, hence, less likely to be as intensely hostile.

Caution must be used in approaching these types of disputes. More than likely, the disputants will not be ready to listen to the underlying causes of their problems and are merely looking for a new player in their game. For example, perhaps the most common game the intervener can get involved in regarding family disputes is a game similar to being in a courtroom. Three players are required for this game, two of which will have the game in progress when the third player is called in to be set up as a judge. The two will then

Figure 7.1
Playing the Game of Courtroom

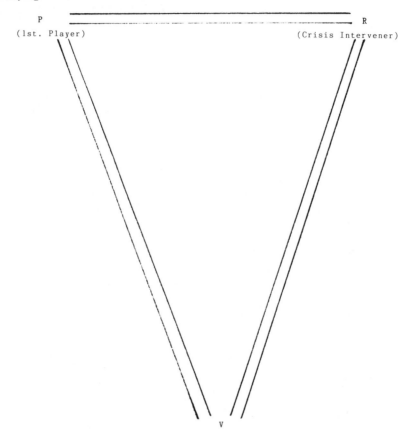

recite their grievances one by one to the intervener. They will then expect the third player to play judge and present a judgment (figure 7.1). The only loser in this game is the intervener, who gets involved by rendering a judgment about who is right and who is wrong. By doing so the rules will shift, with the intervener becoming "the Persecutor" and one of the players becoming a Victim (figure 7.2). This will then provoke the remaining disputant, who has become the Rescuer, to come to the aid of the Victim, and against the crisis intervener, who then becomes the Victim.

Types of Domestic Violence

Many disagreements between couples result in violent fights in which one or the other strikes or in some way physically abuses the other. However,

Figure 7.2
Switching Roles in the Game of Courtroom

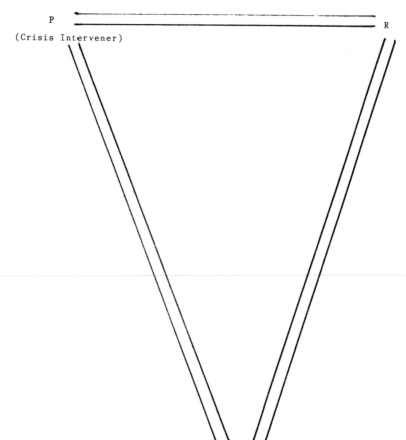

there are disagreements in which there is just hollering and screaming; general, verbal harassment going on without physical abuse. Then there is the domestic situation in which one partner is consistently physically abused, usually the female. There are several types of domestic violence, which must be recognized and addressed differently.

Verbal dispute. In this type of domestic dispute, there is usually some kind of disagreement between the members of a couple, which may result in verbal screaming and arguing and perhaps one or two objects being thrown. One partner may throw the object in the direction of the other with the intention of frightening him or her, or the object may be thrown as an expression of intense anger, in order to release some of the tension that is building. This type of dispute may result in some physical damage which is usually directed at one's self: for example, punching a wall and hurting one's hand, throwing a dish against the wall, or ramming one's own head into a sharp edge causing lacerations to the scalp.

Physical dispute. In this type of domestic dispute, there is intention to do harm to the other party. Physical violence may involve slaps, punches, or blows with a wooden plank, a machete, fists, feet, wooden clothes poles, broken bottles, canes, belts, knives, vases, or hammers. For victims of physical abuse, any one of these abuses may result in bruised and swollen eyes; body wounds; gashes on the head or arms; missing teeth; deep scratches across the arms, legs, or face; or fractures of the nose, ribs, arms, fingers, jaws or skull. Victims have been thrown down flights of stairs, dragged through rooms by their hair, thrown up against steel gates, thrown out of windows, burned, bitten, and robbed of their money, jewelry, and food stamps. One man became so enraged that his girlfriend had purchased new shoes that he beat her repeatedly in her left eye with the heel of one of them. It took the surgeon hours to sew back all the minute muscles surrounding her eye, which she may eventually lose anyway.

Battered spouses. The isolated verbal and physical dispute is a quite different phenomenon from the battered spouse situation. The battered spouse syndrome may involve physical, pyschological, and sexual abuse, and may involve either females or males as the victim. Some researchers estimate that although approximately 50 percent of women will be abused at some point in their lives, the figure is only about 20 to 30 percent for men. During the first six months of 1985, the New York City Police Department report of domestic violence offenses indicated that within the category of aggravated assault, wife victimized by husband, the total was 654 reported complaints for the period January to June 1985, and for husband victimized by wife the total reported was a little more than half as many, 333 complaints. Despite the fact that men may be more reluctant to seek medical or criminal justice attention, they nonetheless are also battered by their wives and/or girlfriends.

Battering involves severe, deliberate, and repeated physical injury incorporating psychological terror tactics. Such tactics may include public humiliation, denial of food or funds, constant threats to safety, or denial of sleep, and may be compared to terrorism on a micro level. We have global terrorism on a macro level and terrorism on a micro level—one person terrorizing a small group. This can happen in either a small family or within a society.

Consider the following incident in which an estranged husband waited until the order of protection against him ran out and then visited his former residence and terrorized his wife, her sister, and his children:

The wife reported that she was watching television when she heard a noise outside her home followed by the doorbell ringing. She looked outside and saw a van parked on the street and her husband at the door. As she opened the door, he pushed himself inside followed by his friend who handed him a pipe and a hammer. Suspecting the worst she ran to the telephone. Since there was no dial tone (the wires had been cut on the outside), she ran across to a neighbor to telephone police. When she returned the two men were at the china closet smashing dishes and crystal. Two children ages 3 and 6 were screaming hysterically. When the women protested they were pushed to the floor and threatened with knives. Four other men appeared and asked "What do you want to do next?" They ripped the basement door off, disconnected the alarm, and proceeded to the boiler room. The men destroyed the motor to the furnace and the hot water tank. They returned to the upper floor, smashing glass tables, mirrors on the wall, the dining room table, the china closet, lamps, and the television. While this was going on, one of the men was watching for the appearance of the radio car. Before leaving, they threatened to return to set the house on fire while the inhabitants were sleeping. Despite numerous calls from neighbors, a radio car appeared two hours later. The woman was informed that since her husband was still part owner of the house, he could "invite his friends over and wreck the whole house if he wanted." Is this not terrorism?

It is useful to distinguish between those disputes that are primarily verbal; those disputes that erupt into mild physical violence such as pushing, shoving, and the throwing of objects; those disputes that involve severe physical violence; and those disputes that involve battering. Distinction is important not only for the sake of clarity, but also for determining the course of action. It will generally fall into three categories: mediation, referral, or arrest. Mediation is applicable when assessment of the situation through information and observation establishes that advice and limited counseling will suffice. Referral can be made to organizations that can handle more complex issues on a long-term, ongoing basis. While mediation and referral may be appropriate for a verbal dispute, arrest is indicated upon complaint or evidence of a criminal offense.

Why does she stay? Why does he stay? It is estimated that every year in the United States, 3 to 4 million women are battered: both physically and psychologically abused by their husbands, ex-husbands, boyfriends, or lovers. A smaller number of men will be battered by their wives, girlfriends, or lovers. Nonetheless, most of these partners will continue to stay in their abusive relationships. There are a variety of reasons why they stay. Consider the following:

Lack of funds	"How will I feed the kids?"
Fear of retaliation	"He told me he would kill me if I left!"
Children	"My kids need a father in the house, I'm going back."
	"The kids need their mother. I can't press charges."
Religion	"My religion forbids me to get a divorce."
Helplessness	"I've been to the courts. They did nothing to help us."
	"They told me to go home and forgive and forget."

Home	"This is me and my children's home. Where will I wind up?"
	"It's my home just as much as it is hers."
Love	"He really loves me when he's sober."
	"He beats me because he loves me."
Guilt	"It's all my fault. I shouldn't have gone out shopping."
	"I didn't have dinner ready and that irritated him."
	"I shouldn't have gone out drinking after work."
Embarrassment	"I don't want my parents to find out. They didn't want me to marry him."
	"I'm bringing disgrace upon my family."
	"What if my friends find out that my old lady beat me up?"
Illness	"I have cancer, who else would want me?"
	"I have a drinking problem. What other woman would take this?"
Loyalty	"He's my husband, through thick and through thin."
	"She's my wife. I'll stick it out."
Low self-esteem	"I should be prettier."
	"It's my fault; I'm not smart enough for him. I brought it on myself."
Change	"He'll change. I know it. Someday he'll stop beating me."

The cycle of violence reinforces the belief in change because often right after the battering, the male repents and the couple enter a honeymoon phase. The man will usually lavish love and attention and expensive gifts on his victim in a contrite effort to make up. He will offer apologies and will promise never to abuse her again. Eventually, the frustration builds up and violence erupts, beginning the cycle once more.

Crisis Intervention

The primary goal of crisis intervention in a dispute is to reduce the general level of hostility and maintain an adequate safety level for all participants. Once this is accomplished, the precipitating cause of the dispute can be identified and mediated. During the crisis period, criminal justice professionals can provide crisis intervention and support for the non-offending parent and child victims of domestic violence. The non-offending parent and the children will need each other for support as well as follow-through on either referral to social agencies or prosecution of the offender.

Techniques of crisis intervention as presented in chapter 4 will be briefly reviewed here as they might apply in domestic violence incidents.

Information gathering. Establishing a quick rapport with the combatants while gathering information will help toward resolution. The rapport can be encouraged by treating them with respect; being honest, trustworthy, and empathetic; and by listening intently to what they have to say. A calm and in-control intervener can serve as a good role model for the disputants, and can decrease the chances of escalating a dispute already in progress.

Identification. Crisis intervention includes identifying the issues and making an evaluation of the situation. Once these have been identified, keep focused on the details. The goal here is to understand as much as possible, including the reactions of the disputants. Is this a violent, physical dispute or a verbal dispute? Is it a battering situation? Are there children involved? Are they safe? Does anyone need medical intervention? Allow for ventilation, but not physical contact or assault.

Intervention. At this point the intervener makes plans for crisis intervention. Most professionals who are involved with conflict management agree that the most lasting and effective solutions are those that the disputants themselves come up with. The intervener's goal is to help the disputants solve their own crisis, not solve it for them. In dealing with a marital dispute, for example, the intervener may first separately and then together encourage and help them to arrive at their own solution. Assistance can then be given through a give-and-take dialogue so that they can come to an agreement on their own. The important point here is that the couple arrive at a solution themselves, with the intervener serving in the role of peacekeeper and helpful mediator.

Investigation–Questioning Techniques

After determining the cause of the dispute and allowing time for the disputants to recapture their sense of dignity, questions may be asked. Use tact and sensitity in obtaining information. Request rather than demand answers. Do not become personal. Use caution in the type of questions asked in a dispute. Be alert for sudden, violent reactions as some questions as well as comments can increase the emotional level of either party. Questions such as: "So how come you're cheating on him?" . . . "Can't we handle this like adults?" . . . "Why don't you lay off the sauce?" or "Why don't you keep the house clean for him, he works hard for you!" suggest preaching or moralizing and place the intervener in a superior position, inhibiting communication. For example, if the female is complaining about the male's late hours, the question, "What time does he come home?" places the intervener in the role of judge. Once hooked in this role, the couple will keep reinforcing the intervener's behavior by referring to him for "judgments" and evaluations of each other's behavior and lectures about how to act. Since there are no "right" answers to this type of question, any solutions that the intervener arrives at will only be reflections of his or her own values and attitudes. Appropriate responses may include paraphrasing complaints and labeling feelings, as discussed in the prior chapters on communication and crisis intervention.

Other types of confrontative questions place blame and put people on the defensive. Some questions may include: "What did you do to provoke him?" ... "Do you realize he will lose his job if he gets arrested?" ... "Why did you make him hit you?" and "Why do you want to make trouble. Think of what he'll do when he gets out!" Especially patronizing is, "Why don't you kiss and make up?"

Personal Biases

The seed of the crisis intervener's perception of a domestic violence situation transcends departmental policies concerning proper handling of disputes or extensive training. It is deeper than any arbitration, mediation, negotiation, conflict management, or dispute training in which an intervener may participate. It is important to realize that to every domestic dispute, the intervener comes along fully equipped, a sort of "package deal." He or she carries along one's own personal perceptions, biases, cultural expectations, sex role stereotypes, prejudices, distortions, and attitudes concerning couples, relationships, and marriage that they have experienced and developed throughout their lifetimes. These barriers to communication, as discussed in chapter 3, need to be identified in order to be objectively isolated and changed. The conscientious intervener will recognize these personal biases for what they are, realize their impact on effective intervention, and work toward changing them before they interfere with effective intervention (figure 7.3).

Dealing with Anger

Responding to anger in a reactive or natural mode will be neither helpful to the situation nor conducive to the continuation of the interaction and resolution of the problem. Therefore, a differentiation should be made between a natural response and a learned response to anger. Crisis interveners need to give learned responses that will preserve a positive relationship and help the combatants to dissipate their anger. The almost universal reactive response to anger is to become angry in return: "How dare you!" ... "I'm not letting you insult me, buddy!" ... "You think that I'm just going to sit here and take this from you!" ... "You have to be put in your place!" A verbal attack is considered an insult by the person attacked, but should really be considered an expression of anger by the attacker. If this is not realized, a vicious cycle begins, with each party becoming more and more angry as a result of the other's hostile expressions.

When a crisis intervener is unjustifiably verbally attacked he or she will feel blameless. It is natural to believe that a grateful victim should not become hostile. The intervener may feel, for example: "After all, I'm there to help them." ... "What did I do to him?" ... "These people shouldn't

Figure 7.3
Impact of Intervener's Personal Biases and Past Experiences on Domestic Violence Incidents

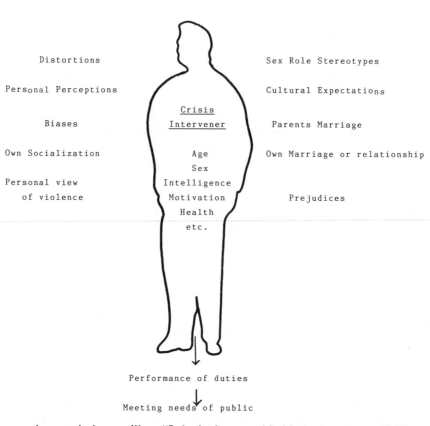

Variables within the Individual Subject

Distortions

Personal Perceptions

Biases

Own Socialization

Personal view
of violence

Crisis
Intervener

Age
Sex
Intelligence
Motivation
Health
etc.

Sex Role Stereotypes

Cultural Expectations

Parents Marriage

Own Marriage or relationship

Prejudices

Performance of duties

Meeting needs of public

question my judgment!" or "I don't deserve this kind of treatment!" The result is to reject both the attack and the victims. From the victim's point of view, the attack is justified, merely an expression of anger.

Handling this anger can be puzzling, draining, and distressing because of the anger feelings that are often stirred up. Many people are not taught in childhood how to deal with anger as a fact of life. They learned that anger was "bad," and were made to feel guilty for expressing it. It is easier to deal with others' anger if this notion is done away with. The goal is not to repress or destroy angry feelings—in others or ourselves—but to accept the feelings and help channel and direct them constructively.

To respond effectively, it is useful to understand what triggered the outburst. Anger may be:

- A defense needed to avoid painful feelings;
- Associated with failure and low self-esteem;
- Associated with isolation;
- Related to anxiety about situations out of one's control;
- An expression of sadness or depression; or
- Associated with feelings of dependency.

Anger must also be differentiated from aggression. Anger is a temporary emotional state caused by frustration. It will not subside unless it is expressed. Aggression is an attempt to harm someone or destroy property.

In dealing with the angry, hostile person, the goal should be to protect and teach, not to punish. Crisis interveners may show the angry person that they accept their hostile feelings, while suggesting some other way to express them. Interveners may say, for example, "I accept your angry feelings." or "Let me tell you how I handle my anger." In this way the angry feelings are being recognized, clarified, and accepted, and an acceptable way of coping may be introduced. Suggestions may include physical exercise, relaxation exercises, deep breathing, taking a walk, going to a movie, and so on. It is also therapeutic for victims to realize that they have been understood, for them to gain some insight into the real feelings that were expressed. Be aware of the powerful influence that appropriate behavior on the part of the intervener can serve.

The interaction will be different if the intervener feels guilty. In this situation, nonverbal messages will be picked up by the victim, who will then become suspicious. When people feel guilty, the response is to become defensive. Often this defensiveness is based on an attempt at self-justification, but the attacker makes the assumption that if the intervener is defensive, there must be another reason. Victims may assume that they are receiving substandard treatment. It is important to remain in the caretaker's role rather than a defensive role.

The intervener, in the caretaker's role, must be able to listen, to understand, and to respond calmly and reasonably. The result is a safe environment in which both parties can communicate their anger freely without fear of recrimination. The goal is to reduce or dissipate the hostility, and not to prove that anyone was right or wrong in expressing the anger. It is helpful for the arguing couple to view the intervener as a fellow human being, but one who can maintain an emotional balance and remain neutral in the disagreement. If the intervener becomes emotional, then reason decreases, professionalism is lost, and the likelihood of physical injury increases.

Referral

Referrals are an important part of crisis intervention in domestic disputes. A referral will be made based on a condition that the intervener can not handle because of lack of time and resources. Explosive domestic crises are not the occasion for profound attempts at psychotherapy. Additional ongoing assistance is available at many social service agencies. The crisis intervener will determine which agency best suits the needs of the incident, and discuss the services of that agency with the couple. Some persons may be referred to a domestic violence hotline. The hotline may provide:

Crisis intervention, usually on a 24-hour-a-day, 7-days-a-week basis.

Medical information, for those persons who may have suffered physical abuse and are reluctant to seek medical treatment.

Legal information, about orders of protection from Family Court and Criminal Court, eligibility for court-appointed attorneys, and the most current legislation concerning victims of domestic violence.

Social services information, especially regarding emergency funds and welfare advocacy.

Shelters, which provide safety, food, and supportive services for women and their children. The first shelter for battered women opened in a private home in California in 1964. There are now approximately 800 in the United States. It is estimated that these shelters provide only a quarter million beds annually for the several million women and children who need them. All of them have waiting lists, which leaves approximately 80 percent of those who need assistance without help.

Safe homes, a network of safe homes and apartments that will house women and children for a short period of time.

Counseling programs, providing counseling and support groups for women who have been abused.

Alcohol abuse counseling, for those persons who also have problems with alcohol abuse.

Advocacy programs, which provide advocates to help people through the social service and criminal justice systems.

Batterers' programs, providing services for men who batter. This program is designed to teach men to curb their abusive behavior with women. It operates on the principal that violence is a learned behavior and can be changed. The 10 weekly support sessions are educational counseling sessions and are modeled after the program used by Alcoholics Anonymous. Men discuss and explore better ways of dealing with anger and frustration. Awareness of nonviolent communication methods is offered. Most members are referred by criminal and family courts, some are referred by clergy or social service agencies, and some volunteer. After the required 10 group sessions, those participants who would like to can continue in an ongoing group.

Encourage the disputants to follow through on counseling, medical care, or shelter. The following information will assist them in making the initial telephone call and an appointment:

• The name, address, and telephone number of the agency;
• The agency's hours of operation;

- The name of a contact person; and
- A brochure or pamphlet describing the agency's services.

Summary on Domestic Violence

Many situations in which the intervener will become involved are manageable with little difficulty. In essence, the domestic dispute is the epitome of crisis situations that will test the intervener's ability to "take charge." Some quarreling couples welcome the arrival of an intervener because it ends the fight without either having to carry out threats that no one wants to carry out—neither side has its bluff called. The experienced intervener senses this and plays the role expected—arbiter, keeper of the peace, source of ultimate authority. However, if the participants are hostile or the bystanders unsympathetic, or if danger is sensed, then the situation will be handled differently.

Psychologists have speculated that the experience of violence in childhood begets violence in adulthood. The victims of domestic violence are not only the battered spouses, but the children of these couples. These children are generally battered along with their parent and consequently perform poorly in school, have low self-esteem, tend toward the use of violence to resolve their conflicts, and may be emotionally disturbed. Furthermore, some parents who are themselves abused misdirect their anger through the defense mechanisms of displacement and scapegoating and abuse their children. These forgotten victims may grow up to be tomorrow's abusers. Research demonstrates that children who grow up in violent homes are likely to become victims or abusers in their adult relationships.

Chapter *8*

CRISIS INTERVENER CRISES

INTERVENER BURNOUT

While the crisis situation presents an opportunity for the crisis intervener to take charge at a time when people have temporarily lost control, there may be situations in which crisis interveners themselves may temporarily lose control and need someone to take charge. One approach to these kinds of situations makes use of the concept of burnout, which has been recently under study at major medical institutions. Burnout refers to a syndrome of emotional exhaustion and cynicism that frequently occurs among individuals who do "people work"—who spend considerable time in close encounters with others under conditions of crisis, chronic tension, and stress. Crisis interveners who constantly work with these kinds of conditions may sometimes find that contacts with others are charged with feelings of anger, embarrasment, frustration, fear, guilt, or despair. They may also find that the need to maintain a tough, in-control outer shell for one's own protection tends to become dissolved when it is combined with sensitivity toward persons in crisis. It is at these times that professionals need to examine their own lives for the sake of their own mental health and the assurance of continued quality of involvement with others.

Up until this point, we have been dealing primarily with the effects of a crisis on the victim and the correct manner in which the intervener will handle these occurrences. However, an added factor that could affect the outcome of many calls for assistance requires identification at this time. This is the emotional impact of the crisis on the intervener him- or herself. Crisis behavior can further be understood in terms of the effect on the recipients of the communication. For example, the crisis communication may arouse in the intervener feelings of sympathy and compassion as well as anxiety, anger, hostility, or frustration. Interveners who are aware of this recipient communication can anticipate and counteract these reactions in themselves. They must be prepared to effectively and productively deal with the emotional aspects of the crisis scene, both for themselves and for the persons in need.

People working with critical situations can often be heard saying, "I know the job is difficult, but it's such rewarding work!" Their chief reward comes from the knowledge that they are assisting others through a difficult time. Consequently, they will be very hard on themselves, questioning their actions and double checking every decision they make in order to avoid the guilt that comes with making a wrong move. Over a period of time, however, persons working in these constantly stressful situations may begin to distrust and maybe even dislike the persons in crisis, and to wish that they would take charge of their own problems. One crisis counselor, overwhelmed with the seemingly constant flow of battered women coming into the emergency room and requiring attention, stormed into her office in intense frustration and anger, screaming, "If just one more battered woman comes to me for help after letting some guy beat her up, I'm going to smack her upside her head myself!"

This angry, detached, and even callous response is in part a protective device: It reduces the amount of emotional involvement and consequent personal stress that the counselor will experience, much in the same way that the defense mechanism of denial works for the crisis victim, who has no choice but to emotionally detach and shield him- or herself with his or her protective emotional armor and withdraw. However, at the same time it seriously impairs the quality of the service that the counselor is there to provide, and, as a by-product, feelings of guilt emerge because one knows what one should be doing but is helpless to become involved because of the emotional pain.

The Body's Reaction to Stress

In addition to negative feelings about the crisis victim, many people-helpers may begin to feel negative about themselves. Psychological burnout may also be accompanied by physical exhaustion, vulnerability to disease, or psychosomatic symptions such as ulcers, back tension, headaches. Doctor Hans Selye, of the University of Montreal, is the world's leading authority on stress. In his book *The Stress of Life*, Selye (1956) outlines his concept of the general adaptation syndrome. There are three reactions by the body, which together constitute the general adaptation syndrome (GAS). The reactions are:

Stage 1—Alarm. When a stressor is first applied, an alarm reaction develops, during which resistance falls below normal and stress hormones are secreted more abundantly. A stressor can be anything injurious to the organism, whether physical (such as inadequate nutrition, loss of sleep, bodily injury) or psychological (such as loss of love or personal security). The stress hormones that are secreted cause an increase in heartbeat and respiration, elevation in blood sugar level, increase in perspiration, dilated pupils, and slowed digestion. In this stage the body has recognized a stressor and prepares for fight or flight. The person chooses whether to use this burst of energy to fight or flee the situation. If exposure to the stress-producing situation continues, the alarm reaction is followed by the second stage, the stage of resistance.

Stage 2—Resistance. In this stage the body seeks to develop a resistance to the particular stressor that provoked the alarm reaction. It attempts to repair any damage caused by the stress. If the stressor does not disappear, however, the body cannot repair the damage and must remain alert. Eventually, this stage of resistance will come to an end and the third stage emerges.

Stage 3—Exhaustion. If the stage of exhaustion continues for any great length of time, the person may develop one of the stress-related disorders, which include:

Migraine headaches,
Chronic neck and back aches,
Bronchial asthma,
Peptic ulcer disease,
Irritable bowel syndrome,
Acne and eczema,
Coronary heart disease,
Impotence, and
Diabetes.

It is at this stage that burnout occurs, precipitated by prolonged stress. Burnout is a syndrome of emotional exhaustion, depersonalization, and reduced personal accomplishments. J. Edelwich (1980) has identified four steps in the development of burnout.

1. Enthusiasm, when one is enthused with one's work,
2. Stagnation, when one's concern is with taking care of oneself,
3. Frustration, when one feels as if success is impossible, and
4. Apathy, when one no longer cares about anyone or anything.

Of particular importance in these findings is the fact that burnout affects certain occupations more than others and is especially common in the helping professions—those concerned with providing assistance to those in need. It is associated with interacting closely with people who hurt. High on the list of affected job categories are police officers and other criminal justice workers, nurses, air traffic controllers, clerks at complaint windows, social service investigators, and bus drivers. The syndrome tends to occur most often in work where one deals with frustrating and seemingly insoluble problems every day.

It was thought at one time that this syndrome was nothing more than depression. Eldelwich's research has proved, however, that there is a distinctive pattern that can occur to anyone in a state of fatigue or frustration brought on by devotion to a cause, a way of life, and even a relationship that has not produced the expected rewards. The symptoms (both the subtle and the obvious) include:

- Being tired and increasingly irritable;
- Feeling an increasingly heavy strain to keep up with a job load;
- Working harder and accomplishing the same or less;
- Getting tired more easily;
- Feeling blue or depressed for no apparent reason;
- Forgetting appointments, deadlines, and personal possessions;
- Socializing with friends and family less often;
- Finding it difficult to converse with others; and
- Laughing less often.

OCCUPATIONAL STRESSORS

The Superman/Superwoman Syndrome

In his research, Selye also found that it is generally accepted by the medical profession that some occupations are more likely to cause stress-related maladies (e.g., high blood pressure, cardiovascular disease, gastric ulcers, mental disturbances, etc.) than others. Crisis work is one such occupation. Many persons point to the fact that crisis interveners usually have to deal with people under adverse, traumatic circumstances. The intervention most often occurs when emotional feelings are most intense. Furthermore, the painful aftermath of crime, in terms of the victim's loss, suffering, or even death, is seen and experienced more directly by crisis interveners than by anyone else with which the victim will subsequently interact (i.e., family, friends, medical staff). Many of these crises—such as birth, accidents, crime victimization, emotional breakdowns, incarceration, and death—are social situations in which family members are not present and crisis interveners are, trying to help individuals as representatives of the community.

Other researchers conclude that for many people self-esteem is related to their sense of competency . . . and their identity is tied up with their self-esteem. Both are tied to psychological health—how we see ourselves and how we feel about ourselves. Crisis workers basically try to do their best not to make the situations worse for the victims, and will take positive steps to return them to where they were prior to the victimization. Sometimes, despite the best of efforts, things do not work out the way they should. Given this connection, what happens to the person who is in a work environment that leaves him or her with a sense of failure or a sense of helplessness?

The one pair of variables that intercedes most often and causes psychological damage and stress for the crisis intervener is that of omnipotence and its opposite, helplessness. The intervener is often confronted with the discrepancy between the horror of his personal observations—that of one person's inhumanity toward another—and the need to "make it all right again" for the victim. These intense feelings of helplessness in the face of disastrous events cause an undeniable inner conflict that surfaces as stress. At the same time, the desire to be omnipotent and solve all the problems and meet all the demands of the crisis victim emerges, causing inner conflict.

The crisis intervener must be aware that intensely dependent persons, particularly those in crisis situations, may attribute tremendous powers to the potential rescuer. Many crisis interveners will cling to this old Superman/Superwoman image, which becomes reinforced by the crisis victim's needs. Worry and anxiety about their performance looms like a guillotine over their heads. They will feel that achievement is difficult, and perfection an impossibility. Although the idea of the superperson is admirable, it is an open invitation to failure. No one can be perfect in everything. In this sense, "taking charge" has its negative side. How can it be possible to solve everyone's problems?

Dealing with Seduction

Seduction is defined in Webster's Dictionary as "the act of leading astray or to err in conduct or belief." This may involve alluring, enticing, and winning behavior, not only of a sexual nature but also conscious or unconscious behavior designed to mislead or manipulate the other person. This type of behavior may be seen in many different kinds of victims, both female and male, as well as in the crisis intervener. Sigmund Freud identified the concept of transference based on the seductive behavior of a patient of his colleague the psychiatrist Joseph Breuer. Breuer was treating the now infamous Anna O. when she called his home to announce that she secretly was "nursing" a belief that she was pregnant with his child. Breuer immediately terminated treatment and was discouraged from further psychoanalytic work. However, Freud helped Breuer to understand what was going on in the psychiatrist/patient relationship through his concept of transference, the process by which patients attribute to their helpers the feelings priorly held for their parents.

Seductiveness may be encountered as a character trait and also in the transference process between crisis intervener and victim. As a character trait it is seen most often in the hysterical personality which sexualizes all relationships because of feelings of insatiation. This person lives in a state of sexual arousal, which is reflected in the surrounding atmosphere of excitement. This person often sees him- or herself as the unwitting object of the seduction of others, unaware of his or her own provocative role. This characteristic distortion especially enters into the perceptions of the crisis intervener. The relationship is especially sexualized because unconsciously the intervener is regarded as the omnipotent parent, the superperson who has the power to rescue and satisfy all needs and undo all the negative things that have happened. The passions and longings of the helpless child are reignited, the victim seems to fall in love, and the intervener becomes the object of passions. The intervener is perceived unrealistically as if he or she were a significant childhood figure, usually a parent. The victim may then make an effort to seduce the intervener into a sexual relationship.

In other cases, the seductive transference has little to do with sex or love. Sexually provocative behavior may be used to mask or counter underlying feelings of envy, hostility, fear, depression or emptiness. The attempt at sexual seduction may really be a manipulative attempt to exert power and control over the intervener or the situation. The crisis relationship may be felt as a dangerous heterosexual or homosexual temptation. Many times, the persons are not really interested in sexual intercourse. The real intent may be to bolster self-esteem by making a conquest. They may feel worthless as people and of interest only as sexual objects. The goal may be to feel lovable or to be taken care of, or it may be to discredit the intervener and debase her- or himself. Any kindness on the part of intervener may be treated as if it were very special, as a seduction; that is, the victim's own sexual needs are projected onto the intervener. This occurs most frequently during the investigation of cases of rape or sexual abuse. The initial interview and subsequent references to sexual matters may be regarded by some victims as an expression of personal interest by the intervener. The intervener may be accused of being too preoccupied with sexual questions and inferences. If the intervener holds eye contact for too long a time, he or she may be suspected of trying to seduce the victim. If the intervener becomes defensive, he or she may then react destructively by becoming formal, cold, or brusque. The victim will then react by feeling rejected and rapport will be difficult to establish. On the other hand, during follow-up with a rape victim in an effort to gain cooperation or to strengthen the victim's self-image, the intervener may offer praise and compliments to the victim. To an already devastated victim, whose home life has probably suffered and whose self-concept may be destroyed, this positive reinforcement may be internalized to a greater degree than necessary. Also, during investigation there will be a need to telephone the victim at home during inappropriate times such as late at night. This may suggest a kind of overconcern that transcends the reality of the situation and may be misinterpreted by the victim. Interveners must be constantly aware that they are delving into areas with the victims that leave themselves open for seduction and must guide themselves on a fine line as to what is appropriate. Interveners must carefully maintain a professional stance during the interview because the victims are quite vulnerable at this time. Limiting the relationship to the professional needs of the situation, which becomes the common goal of both parties, is an absolute necessity during crisis.

Seduction may be a powerful temptation to the crisis intervener. It can come from a female or male victim, or it can come from the intervener because of problems that he or she may be having at a particular time. Different interveners are vulnerable in varying degrees to different types of seduction. If the intervener is feeling anxious, depressed, ineffective, or inadequate in self-esteem, any seductiveness may be exaggerated in his or her own mind. Sometimes the intervener may even encourage it. It may be difficult for interveners to resist victims who play on their wish to be omnipotent, famous, admired, or lovable. Interveners may respond seductively, and this will intensify the erotic transference and encourage sexual acting out. This flirtation will bolster a shaky self-concept and may be seen as evidence of personal magnetism, power, and conquest. Therefore, what may be seen as a problem with a sedutive victim may be largely created by the crisis intervener's unconscious or conscious seductiveness. Interveners must be constantly aware of their own needs, drives, and desires to fulfill unfulfilled needs through the victim, as these impulses deflect from providing the victim with constructive and professional intervention.

Self-Doubt

Many crisis situations will awaken within the intervener feelings of anxiety and self-doubt regarding his or her adequacy to handle the critical situation. While moderate levels of anxiety are appropriate, too much is debilitating, especially if it is transmitted to the crisis victim who, at this point, is depending on the intervener to help solve his or her problems. The person in crisis who is already feeling helpless and vulnerable and then perceives anxiety in the intervener may lose all hope in the possibility of being helped.

In these types of situations something in the interaction may be related to certain problems which the intervener has not been able to solve in him- or herself. This problem may be related to tensions within the department or with a supervisor, to conflicts with family members. It may be related to his or her own personal sense of striving or failure, or even to the intervener's own personal experiences of victimization. Whatever the facts in any individual case, these problems interfere with the handling of the crisis by the intervener. In essence, not only is the victim in a state of crisis, the intervener is as well. This becomes evident behaviorally as the intervener loses professional distance from the victim and becomes personally and emotionally involved in the situation. When an intervener is in a state of crisis, he or she will be unable to perceive others as separate persons and will therefore be unable to be sensitive to the victims needs, and incapable of helping adequately. Instead the intervener will react to the situation in terms of his or her own problems; and since he or she has not been successful in resolving these, whatever the intervener does for the victim will not be very effective. To illustrate this point, consider the following examples. A female detective finds that upon transfer to the sex crimes division, she experiences specific difficulty whenever she has to deal with situations of child sexual abuse. In such cases she usually becomes emotionally involved and upset, and is unable to function with her usual effectiveness. If she were to pursue these feelings, she would probably find that in the past she had had some traumatic experience in relation to sexual abuse. Perhaps when she was a child she was herself a victim, or she may have been witness to such a situation. At the time she may not have been able to understand what was going on and may also have been helpless to intervene. The memories of this bad experience may have been repressed, but her feelings of sadness and helplessness are likely to be stimulated over and over again whenever she comes into contact with a child in similar circumstances.

Another example is the crisis counselor who is feeling particularly helpless over a current conflict with upper management at his place of employment. Such a counselor may likely have some difficulty in handling the problems of a victim in any situation which involves feelings of helplessness and vulnerability. What is interesting is that the crisis counselor may not always see the obvious link between his own problems and those of the victim. However, the feeling of difficulty in handling particular cases is what presents itself.

While most of us successfully keep our private life and our professional work separate, as human beings with our own emotional problems, professional distance becomes difficult at times.

It is important to learn how to handle these emotional conflicts—to understand and accept our physical and emotional limitations. By understanding these limitations, greater control may be exercised over them. Everyone has strengths and weaknesses. Decide which things you do well, and put your major efforts into these. Everyone also functions better in some situations than in others. When possible, it is better to direct activities to those areas of life where our function is effective and comfortable, and away from those areas where we are ineffective and uncomfortable. Do not criticize yourself if you cannot achieve the impossible. Expect crisis reactions to a variety of situations. Recognize the symptoms and realize that these symptoms are not necessarily indications of unworthiness. It is important for crisis interveners to thoroughly understand that they are limited in their ability to "make everything better" for someone who has experienced a crisis.

EMOTIONAL CONTROL

Understanding people in crisis situations and being able to relate to them depend to a great degree on an understanding of yourself under stress and your own ability to deal with crisis. The productive channeling of emotional energy that is caused by stress is a goal that must be achieved by crisis interveners. The following are some suggestions that can be used for alleviating stress:

Work off stress. If you are angry or upset, try to blow off steam physically by activities such as running, playing tennis, or gardening. Aerobic exercises, jogging, pedaling a stationary bicycle, bike riding, rowing, jumping rope, running in place, skating, dancing, and swimming are all excellent stress reducers. In addition, any sport that requires nearly continuous movement will help. This includes basketball, soccer, tennis, squash, and racquetball.

Even taking a walk can help. Walking is a simple and very underrated exercise, yet walking has several physical benefits. It exercises not just the legs, but also several postural muscles, and can help prevent backaches. It also burns calories and promotes digestion. Brisk walking in particular improves both circulation and respiration.

Debriefing/talking out your worries. In crisis intervention, there will always appear, despite experience and knowledge, some cases that will arouse anxiety and tension and penetrate your so-called professional armor. One way that has been developed in order to try to handle this problem is consultation. It is truly difficult to be objective at all times in all cases. At times something may be causing difficulty in regard to some particular aspect of a case. The most constructive way to handle this difficulty and the ensuing feelings is through informal discussions and consultation with colleagues. This generally provides several solutions. Initially there is a sharing of anxiety and responsibility, but there is also the benefit from discussion of problems. Constructive comments from others are usually helpful in evaluating difficult cases and maintaining morale. Every intervener should be prepared for some failures. Mutual support and empathy derived from sharing with someone you trust and respect, rather than admitting defeat, identifies the intelligent human being who knows when to ask for assistance.

Many people still perceive psychological problems in terms of social stigma, rather than as treatable, often transient, medical problems. Every criminal justice department has its stereotypical descriptions of those with problems: "The Rubber Gun Squad," "The Loonies," "The Crazies," "The Bow and Arrow Squad," or "The Nut Squad." This is probably due to the fact that officers labeled as problems are considered a menace to themselves and others and are therefore relieved of their weapons, one of the symbols of their unique position and authority. They may then be placed on limited or light duty until they are considered able to assume regular responsibilities. Under these conditions, it is hardly surprising that few officers will willingly present themselves at the department psychological services unit. Most officers will therefore wait until their problems either disappear or become so obvious that a superior makes a referral for them. What is not realized is that stress is like any other human problem. One would not hesitate to seek help when physical injury or disease strikes, yet hesitate if the problem is psychological. Better education, improved communication, and a more enlightened attitude toward emotional trauma must be instilled in order to create a climate where it is not a shame to seek professional help when psychological distress occurs.

Avoid self-medication. Although there are many chemicals, including alcohol and drugs, that can mask stress symptoms, they do not help one adjust to the stress itself. Many are also habit forming. Medication is a form of flight reaction and can cause more stress than it solves. The ability to handle stress comes from within, not from the outside.

Get enough sleep and rest. Lack of sleep can lessen the ability to deal with stress and causes irritability. Most people need at least 7 to 8 hours of sleep out of every 24.

Balance work and recreation. Schedule time for recreation to relax your mind. Although inactivity can cause boredom, a little loafing can ease stress. This should not be a constant escape, but occasionally can be used to your advantage.

Get away from it all/self-imposed isolation. When you feel that you are overloaded by stressful contacts with people in crisis, try to divert yourself. Times like these call for some peace and quiet, uninterrupted by any human being and especially one with problems. As simple a thing as going to the movies, watching television, reading a story, or visiting a friend can help. There is no harm in running away from a painful situation long enough to catch your breath and regain the composure you need to come back and face the problem. When possible and practical, a change of scene can help. A quiet walk through the woods, for example, can bring peace and a new perspective. There are times when we need to "escape" even if it is just a brief letup from the usual routine.

Learn your limitations. Learn to accept what cannot be changed. One of the main characteristics of crisis events is the evident loss of control for the victim. As crisis interveners or "rescuers," we may tend to get upset about circumstances that are truly beyond our control. This leads to frustration. Learn that there is just so much than can be done for the victim, and that you will not be able to do it all for them.

Learn to accept rejection. While crisis workers may enjoy the reward of helping others, there are times when the victim is not grateful for your intervention. Crisis work often places the helper in the position of being the object of displaced anger and rage. Understand that these strong feelings are not directed personally but are vented because you are an available target. Associated with displaced anger is the experience of rejection and lack of gratitude. Nothing is more painful than rejection of and lack of appreciation for one's sincere attempt to help another. Very often the victim will walk away without a word of appreciation, not even a thank-you. Unfortunately, these are some of the risks of crisis work about which nothing can be done.

Reach out to department resources. Every organization has resources that may be utilized in times of need. Seek professional help when you need it. Crisis is, psychologically speaking, a high-risk profession, with crisis interveners generally among the last to seek help. Members of highly stressed professions should have periodic stress-level checkups to take stock of their lives and forestall potential problems.

Learn a drug-free method of relaxation. The importance of regular relaxation breaks cannot be overemphasized. Whether you use meditation, progressive relaxation, self-hypnosis, yoga, biofeedback, or some other technique, a relaxation break can give your mind a rest. It revitalizes coping abilities, promotes a more balanced outlook, and can give you increased energy for dealing with whatever difficulties you face.

CONCLUSION

Awareness of job stress that is inherent in crisis work or people work serves as a reducer in several ways. By becoming aware of the nature of psychological job stressors, crisis interveners can be alerted to the potential dangers facing them. In addition, they can become cognizant of the fact that stress is in part a function of the environment and not totally within and unique to themselves. Understanding and reducing stress by eliminating some of the stressors, increasing the stress intervener's ability to cope, or providing solutions for the stressed intervener are a few suggestions.

BIBLIOGRAPHY

AUTO-EROTIC DEATH

Berlyne, N., and Strachan, M. "Neuropsychiatric Sequelae of Attempted Hanging." *British Journal of Psychiatry*, 114 (1967): 411–429.

Hazelwood, R., and Dietz, P. *Autoerotic Fatalities*. Lexington, Mass.: D. C. Heath, 1983.

Resnick, Harvey L. "Eroticized Repetitive Hangings." *American Journal of Psychotherapy*, (1972):

Shankel, W., and Carr, A. "Transvestism and Hanging Episodes in a Male Adolescent." *Psychiatric Quarterly*, 30 (1956): 478–493.

Starch, Adolf Taylor. *Der Alraun, ein beitraq zur pflanzensagenkunde*. Baltimore, Md.: J. H. Furst Co., 1917.

Weisman, A. "Self-Destruction and Sexual Perverson." In E. Schneidman (Ed.), *Essays in Self-Destruction*. New York: Science House, 1967.

BURNOUT

Besner, Hilda F., and Robinson, Sandra J. *Understanding and Solving Your Police Marriage Problems*. Springfield, Ill.: Charles C. Thomas, 1982.

Cheek, F. G., and Miller, M. D. "The Experience of Stress for Correctional Officers: A Double Bind Theory of Correctional Stress." *Journal of Criminal Justice*, 11, no. 2 (1983): 105–120.

Cherniss, C. *Professional Burnout in Human Service Occupations*. New York: Praeger, 1980a.

Cherniss, C. *Staff Burnout: Job Stress in the Human Services*. Beverly Hills: Sage Publications, 1980b.

Cox, T. *Stress*. Baltimore, Md.: University Park Press, 1978.

Edelwich, J. *Burnout: Stages of Disillusionment in the Helping Professions*. New York: Human Services Press, 1980.

Ellison, Katherine W., and Genz, John L. *Stress and the Police Officer*, Springfield, Ill.: Charles C. Thomas, 1985.

Guralnik, P. "Mortality by Occupation and Cause of Death." Vital Statistics Special Report. *U.S. Public Health Service* (1963): 53.

Jacobi, J. "Reducing Police Stress: A Psychiatrist's Point of View." In William H. Kross and Joseph J. Hurrell (Eds.), *Job Stress and the Police Officer; Identifying Stress Reduction Techniques*. Washington, D.C.: United States Government Printing Office, 1976.

Kroes, William H. *Society's Victims—The Police: An Analysis of Job Stress in Policing*. Springfield, Ill.: Charles C. Thomas, 1980.

Maslach, C. "Burned Out." *Human Behavior*, 2 (1976): 16–22.

Maslach, C., and Jackson, S. E. "Burned Out Cops and Their Families." *Psychology Today*, 12 (1979): 59–62.

Nelson, Martha, and James, Pat. *Police Wife: How to Live with the Law and Like It*. Springfield, Ill.: Charles C. Thomas, 1982.

Selye, H. "Stress and Distress." *Comprehensive Therapy*, 1, no. 8 (1976); 24–31.

Selye, H. "The Stress of Police Work." *Police Stress*, 1 (1978): 7–9.

Sewell, J. D., and Crew, L. "Stress and the Police Dispatcher." *FBI Law Enforcement Bulletin*, 53, no. 3 (1984): 7–11.

Sweeney, Earl M. *The Public and the Police*. Springfield, Ill.: Charles C. Thomas, 1985.

Webb, S. D., and Smith, D. L. "Police Stress: A Conceptual Overview." *Journal of Criminal Justice*, 8, no. 4 (1980): 251–258.

CHILD ABUSE

Davis, James R. *Help Me, I'm Hurt: The Child Abuse Handbook*. Dubuque, Iowa: Kendal/Hunt, 1982.

Finkelhor, David. *Sexually Victimized Children*. New York: Free Press, 1979.

Forward, Susan, and Buck, Craig. *Betrayal of Innocence: Incest and Its Devastation*. New York: Penguin, 1979.

Gil, David G. "Unraveling Child Abuse." *American Journal of Ortho Psychiatry*, 45, no. 3 (1975): 346–356.

Giovannoni, Jeanne M., and Becerra, Rosina M. *Defining Child Abuse*. New York: Free Press, 1979.

Groth, N. "Patterns of Sexual Assault against Children and Adolescents." In Ann Burgess, and N. Groth (Eds.), *Sexual Assault of Children and Adolescents*. Denver: C. Henry Kempe National Center for the Prevention and Treatment of Child Abuse and Neglect, 1978.

Kempe, C. Henry, and Helfer, Ray E. (Eds). *Helping the Battered Child and His Family*. Philadelphia: J. B. Lippincott, 1972.

Kempe, C. Henry, and Helfer, Ray E. *The Battered Child*. 3d ed. Chicago: University of Chicago Press, 1980.

Platt, Anthony. *The Child Savers*. Chicago: University of Chicago Press, 1977.

Scroi, Susanne M. "Kids with Clap! Gonorrhea as an Indicator of Child Sexual Assault." *Victimology*, 2, no. 2 (Summer 1977): 251–267.

Walters, David R. *Physical and Sexual Abuse of Children; Causes and Treatment*. Bloomington: Indiana University Press, 1975.

Weinberg, S. *Incest Behavior*. New York: Harper and Row, 1955.

COMMUNICATION

Berlo, David K. *The Process of Communication: An Introduction to Theory and Practice*. San Diego, Calif.: Harcourt, Brace, Jovanovich, 1960.

Birdwhistell, Ray L. *Kinesics & Context: Essays on Body Motion Communication*. Philadelphia: University of Pennsylvania Press, 1970.

Mehrabian, Albert. *Silent Messages: Implicit Communication of Emotions and Attitudes* (2nd. ed.). Belmont, Calif.: Wadsworth, 1981.

Opler, Marvin K. *Culture and Mental Health*. New York: MacMillan, 1959.

Opler, Marvin K., and Singer, Jerome L. "Ethnic Differences in Behavior and Psychopathology: Italian and Irish." *International Journal of Social Psychiatry*, 2 (1956): 11–23.

Pancheri, Paolo. "Infarct as a Stress Agent: Life History and Personality Characteristics in Improved Versus Not-improved Patients after Severe Heart Attack," *Journal of Human Stress*, 4, no. 1 (March 1978): 16–22, 41–42.

Pease, Allan. *Signals*. New York: Bantam, 1984.

Singer, Jerome L., and Opler, Marvin K. "Contrasting Patterns of Fantasy and Mobility in Irish and Italian Schizophrenics." *Journal of Abnormal Social Psychology*, 53 (1956): 42–47.

Zola, Irvin K. "Culture and Symptoms: An Analysis of Patients' Presenting Complaints," *American Sociological Review*, 31, no. 5 (1966): 615–630.

CRISIS

Aguilera, D. C., Messick, J. M., and Farrell, M. S. *Crisis Intervention: Theory and Methodology*. St. Louis: C. V. Mosby Co., 1970.

Bae, R. P. "Ineffective Crisis Intervention Techniques: The Case of the Police." *Journal of Crime and Justice* 4 (1981): 61–82.

Baldwin, B. A. "Crisis Intervention: An Overview of Theory and Practice." *The Counseling Psychologist*, 8 (1979): 43–52.

Baldwin, B. A. "Styles of Crisis Intervention: Toward a Convergent Model." *Professional Psychology*, (1980): 113–120.

Banks, Hermon, and Romano, A. T. *Human Relations for Emergency Response Personnel*. Springfield Ill.: Charles C. Thomas, 1983.

Bard, M. "Family Intervention Police Teams as a Community Mental Health Resource." *Journal of Criminal Law, Criminology, and Police Science*, 60: (1969): 247–250.

Bard, M., and Berkowitz, B. *Training Police as Specialists in Intervention*. Project Report of the Law Enforcement Assistance Administration. Washington, D. C.: U.S. Government Printing Office, 1970.

Crow, G. A. *Crisis Intervention*. New York: Associated Press, 1977.

Cumming, E., Cumming, I., and Edell, L. "Policeman as Philosopher, Guide, and Friend." *Social Problems*, 12 (1965): 276–286.

Dixon, S. L. *Working with People in Crisis: Theory and Practice*. St. Louis: C. V. Mosby Co., 1979.

Everstine, Diana Sullivan, and Everstine, Louis. *People in Crisis: Strategic Therapeutic Interventions*. New York: Brunner/Mazel, Publishers, 1983.

France, Kenneth. *Crisis Intervention: A Handbook of Immediate Person-to-Person Help*. Springfield, Ill.: Charles C. Thomas, 1982.

Fraser, J. R., and Froelich, J. S. "Crisis Intervention in the Courtroom." *Community Mental Health Journal*, 15; no. 3 (1979): 237–246.

Greenstone, J. L., and Leviton, S. C. *Crisis Intervention*. Dubuque, Iowa: Kendall-Hunt, 1982.

Greenstone, J. L., and Leviton, Sharon. *The Crisis Intervener's Handbook*. Vols. 1 and 2. Dallas: Rothschild Publishing, 1978, 1980.

Hamburg, D. *A Perspective on Coping Behavior. Archives of General Psychiatry*, 17 (1967): 277–284.

Hendricks, James. *Crisis Intervention: Contemporary Issues for On-Site Interveners*. Springfield, Ill.: Charles C. Thomas, 1985.

Hendricks, James E., and Greenstone, J. L. "Crisis Intervention in Criminal Justice." In J. L. Greenstone and S. Leviton (Eds.), *Crisis Intervention*. Dubuque, Iowa: Kendall-Hunt, 1982.

Kennedy, E. *Crisis Counseling: An Essential Guide for Non-Professional Counselors*. New York: Continumm, 1981.

McGee, Richard K. *Crisis Intervention in the Community*. Baltimore, Md.: University Park Press, 1974.

Mitchel, J. T., and Resnik, H. P. L. *Emergency Response to Crisis*. Bowie, Md.: Robert J. Brady Co., 1981.

Morrice, J. K. W. *Crisis Intervention: Studies in Community Care*. Oxford: Pergamon Press, 1976.

Nemetz, W. C. "Crisis Intervention." *The Police Chief* 14; no. 4 (April 1977): 53–56.

Parad, H. J., and Caplan, G. "A Framework for Studying Families in Crisis." *Social Work*, 5 (July 1960): 74–80.

Punch, M., and Naylor, T. "The Police: A Social Service." *New Society*, 10, no. 2 (1973): 54.

Rapaport, L. "The State of Crisis: Some Theoretical Considerations." *The Social Service Review*, 36 (1962): 211–217.

Romaine, Edward V. *Crisis Intervention and How It Works*. Springfield, Ill.: Charles C. Thomas, 1984.

Rosenbaum, C. Peter, and Beebee, John E. *Psychiatric Treatment: Crisis, Clinic, Consultation*. New York: McGraw-Hill, 1975.

Rosenbluh, E. S. *Techniques of Crisis Intervention*. Louisville: Behavioral Science Service, 1974.

Schreiber, B., and Andrews, J. "Crisis Intervention Training for Police Using Civilian Instructors: A Practical Model." *The Police Chief*, 12; no. 10 (October 1975): 254.

Zusman, Jack. "Meeting Mental Health Needs in a Disaster." In Howard J. Parad, H. L. P. Resnik, and Libbie G. Parad (Eds.), *Emergency and Disaster Management*. Bowie, Md.: Charles Press Publishers, 1976.

DISASTER BEHAVIOR

Adams, P. R., and Adams, G. R. "Mount St. Helen's Ashfall: Evidence for a Disaster Stress Reaction." *American Psychologist*, 39 (1984): 252–260.

Adler, A. "Neuropsychiatric Complications in Victims of Boston's Cocoanut Grove Disaster." *Journal of the American Medical Association*, 123 (1943): 1098–1101.

Davidson, A. D. "Coping with Stress Reactions in Rescue Workers: A Program That Worked. *Police Stress*, (Spring 1979):

Davidson, L. M., and Baum, A. "Chronic Stress and Post-Traumatic Disorder." *Journal of Consulting and Clinical Psychology*.

Friedman, P., and Linn, L. "Some Psychiatric Notes on the *Andrea Doria* Disaster." *American Journal of Psychiatry*, (1957): 114–426.

Kobasa, S. C. "Stressful Life Events, Personality and Health: An Inquiry into Hardiness." *Journal of Personality and Social Psychology*, 37, no. 1 (1979): 1–11.

Lord, W. *A Night to Remember*. New York: Holt, Rinehart and Winston, 1955.

O'Brien, D. "Mental Anguish: An Occupational Hazard." *Emergency*, (March 1979): 61–64.

Raher, J. W., Wallace, A. F. C., and Rayner, J. F. *Emergency Medical Care in Disasters* (Disaster Study No. 6). Washington, D. C.: National Academy of Science, National Research Council, 1956.

Uhlenhuth, E. "Free Therapy Said to Be Helpful to Chicago Train Wreck Victims." *Psychiatric News*, 8, no. 3: 1, 27.

Wallace, A. F. C. *Tornado in Worcester*. Washington, D.C.: National Academy of Sciences, National Research Council, 1956.

Wilkinson, C. B. "Aftermath of a Disaster: The Collapse of the Hyatt Regency Hotel Skywalks." *American Journal of Psychiatry*, 140 (1983): 1134–1139.

DOMESTIC VIOLENCE

Bard, M., and Zacker, J. "The Prevention of Family Violence: Dilemmas of Community Intervention." *Journal of Marriage and the Family*, 33, no. 4 (1971).

Bard, M., and Zacker, J. "How Police Handle Explosive Squabbles." *Psychology Today*, 10, no. 6 (1976): 71–74, 143.

Bell, D. J. *The Police Response to Domestic Violence: An Exploratory Study*. Paper presented to the Society of Police and Criminal Psychology, Nashville, Tenn.: 1982.

Berk, S. F., and Loeske, D. R. "Handling Family Violence: Situational Determinants of Police Arrests in Domestic Disturbances." *Law and Society Review*, 15 (1981): 317–346.

Dobash, R. E., and Dobash, R. *Violence against Wives*. New York: Free Press, 1979.

Fleming, Jennifer Baker. *Stopping Wife Abuse*, Garden City: Anchor Books, 1979.

Gelles, R. J. *The Violent Home: A Study of Physical Aggression between Husbands and Wives*. Beverly Hills, Calif.: Sage Publications, 1972.

Goode, W. "Force and Violence in the Family." *Journal of Marriage and the Family*, 33, no. 4 (1971): 624–636.

Homat, R. J., and Kennedy, D. B. *Battered Women and the Police: A Comparison of*

Perceptions. Paper presentation at the Academy of Criminal Justice Sciences Meetings, Louisville, Kentucky, 1982.

International Association of Chiefs of Police. *Wife Beating.* Training Key No. 245. Gaithersburg, Md.: International Association of Chiefs of Police, 1976.

Langley, R., and Levy, R. *Wife Beating: The Silent Crisis.* New York: E. P. Dutton, 1977.

Liebman, D. A., and Schwartz, J. A. "Police Programs in Domestic Crisis Intervention: A Review." In J. R. Snibbe and H. M. Snibbe (Eds.), *The Urban Policeman in Transition: A Psychological and Sociological Review.* Springfield, Ill.: Charles C. Thomas, 1973, pp. 421–472.

Loving, N. *Responding to Spouse Abuse and Wife Beating.* Washington, D.C.: Police Executive Research Forum, 1980.

Martin, D. *Battered Wives.* San Francisco, Calif.: Glide Publications, 1976.

Oppenlander, N. "Coping or Copping Out: Police Service Delivery in Domestic Disputes." *Criminology,* 20 (1982): 449–465.

Parnas, R. I. "The Police Response to the Domestic Disturbance." *Washington Law Review,* 4 (1967): 914–960.

Paterson, E. J. "How the Legal System Responds to Battered Women." In D. M. Moore (Ed.), *Battered Women.* Beverly Hills, Calif.: Sage Publications, 1979.

Pizzey, E. *Scream Quietly or the Neighbors Will Hear.* Middlesex, England: Penguin Press, 1974.

The Police Foundation. *Domestic Violence and the Police.* Washington, D.C.: The Police Foundation, 1978.

Rittenmeyer, S. D. "Of Battered Wives, Self-Defense and Double Standards of Justice." *Journal of Criminal Justice,* 9 (1981): 389–395.

Schonborn, Karl L. *Dealing with Violence: The Challenge Faced by Police and Other Peacekeepers.* Springfield, Ill.: Charles C. Thomas, 1975.

Steinmetz, S. K., and Straus, M. A. (Eds.). *Violence in the Family.* New York: Dodd Mead and Company, 1974.

Straus, M. A. *Violence in the Family.* New York: Harper & Row, 1974.

Straus, M. A. "Wife Beating—How Common and Why?" *Victimology,* 2, nos. 3–4 (1978): 443–458.

Straus, M. A., Gelles, R., and Steinmetz, S. K. *Behind Closed Doors: Violence in the American Family.* Garden City, N.Y.: Anchor, 1980.

Thorman, George. *Family Violence.* Springfield, Ill.: Charles C. Thomas, 1983.

Walker, L. E. *The Battered Woman,* New York: Harper & Row, 1979.

Walter, J. "Police in the Middle: A Study of Small City Police Intervention in Domestic Disputes." *Journal of Police Sciences and Administration,* 9 (1981): 243–260.

ELDER ABUSE

Block, M., and Sinnott, J. *The Battered Elder Syndrome: An Exploratory Study.* College Park, Md.: University of Maryland, 1979.

Cavan, R. S. *The American Family.* New York: Crowell Press, 1963.

Fuller, S. S. "Inhibiting Helplessness in Elderly People." *Journal of Gerontological Nursing,* 4 (1978): 18–21.

Lau, E., and Kosberg, J. "Abuse of the Elderly by Informal Care Providers." *Aging*, (1977): 299–300: 11–15.

O'Malley, H., Segars, H., Perez, R., Mitchell, V., and Kneupfal, G., "Elder Abuse in Massachusetts: A Survey of Professionals and Paraprofessionals." Boston: Legal Research and Services for the Elderly, 1979.

Steinmetz, S. K. "Battered Parents." *Society*, 15 (1978): (7–8): 54–55.

Steinmetz, S. K., and Straus, M. A. (Eds). *Violence in the Family*. New York: Harper & Row, 1974.

U.S. Senate, Committee on Aging. *Abuse of Older Persons*. Washington, D.C.: U.S. Government Printing Office, 1981.

GRIEF

Kubler-Ross, E. "On Death and Dying." *Journal of the American Medical Association*, 221 (1972): 174–179.

Lindemann, E. "Symptomatology and Management of Acute Grief." *American Journal of Psychiatry*, 101, no. 2 (1944): 141–148.

Parkes, C. *Bereavement: Studies of Grief in Adult Life*. New York: International Universities Press, 1972.

MALE SEXUAL ABUSE

Awad, G. "Father-Son Incest: A Case Report." *The Journal of Nervous and Mental Disease*, 162, no. 2 (1976):

Burgess, A., and Groth, N. *Sexual Assault of Children and Adolescents*. Denver: C. Henry Kempe National Center for the Prevention and Treatment of Child Abuse and Neglect, 1978.

Cairns, P. *Sexual Addiction*. Minneapolis: Compcare Publications, 1983.

Chaneles, S. *Sexual Abuse of Children: Implications for Casework*. Denver: The American Human Association, 1967.

Cotton, D. "The Male Victim of Sexual Assault: Patterns of Occurrence, Trauma Reaction, and Adaptive Responses." *Dissertation Abstracts International*, 41, no. 9B (March 1981): 3568–3569.

DeFrancis, V. *Protecting the Child Victim of Sex Crimes Committed by Adults*. Denver: The American Humane Association, 1969.

Ellerstein, H., and Caravan, W. "Sexual Abuse of Boys." *American Journal of Diseases of Children*, 134 (March 1980):

Finkelhor, D. *Sexually Victimized Children*. New York: The Free Press, 1979.

Finkelhor, D. *Child Sexual Abuse: New Theory and Research*. New York: Free Press, 1984.

Fritz, G., Stoll, K., and Wagner, H. "A Comparison of Males and Females Who Were Sexually Molested as Children." *Journal of Sex and Marital Therapy*, 7 (1981): 54–59.

Krulevitz, J. "Sex Differences in Evaluation of Female and Male Victims Responses to Assault." *Journal of Applied Social Psychology*, 11, no. 2 (1981): 460–474.

Masjleti, M. "Suffering in Silence, The Male Incest Victim." *Child Welfare*, 59, no. 5 (May 1980):

Pierce, A., and Pierce, L. "The Sexually Abused Child: A Comparison of Male and Female Victims." *Child Abuse and Neglect*, 9 (1985).

Raybin, J. "Homosexual Incest." *The Journal of Nervous and Mental Disease*, 148, no. 2 (February 1969).

Tick, E. "Male Child Sexual Abuse: The Best Kept Secret." *Voices* (Fall 1984).

RAPE/SEXUAL ASSAULT

Amir, M. *Patterns of Forcible Rape*. Chicago: University of Chicago Press, 1971.

Bard, Morton, and Ellison, K. "Crisis Intervention and Investigation of Forcible Rape." *Police Chief* 51, no. 5 (1974): 68–74.

Burgess, A. W., and Holmstrom, L. L. "The Rape Victim in the Emergency Ward." *American Journal of Nursing*, 73 (1973): 1741–1745.

Burgess, A. W., and Holmstrom, L. L. *Rape: Victims of Crisis*. Bowie, Md.: Robert J. Brady Company, 1974.

Burgess, A. W., and Holmstrom, L. L. *Rape: Crisis and Recovery*. Bowie, Md.: Robert J. Brady, 1979.

Halleck, S. "The Physician's Role in Management of Victims of Sex Offenders." *Journal of the American Medical Association*, 180 (1962): 273–278.

Hayman, C., and Lanza, C. "Sexual Assault on Women and Girls." *American Journal of Obstetrics and Gynecology*, 109 (1971): 480–486.

Holmstrom, L. L., and Burgess, A. W. *Rape: The Victim Goes on Trial*. Paper read at the 68th annual meeting of the American Sociological Association, New York, N.Y., August 27–30, 1973.

Holmstrom, L. L., and Burgess, A. W. *Rape: The Victim and the Criminal Justice System*. Paper read at the First International Symposium on Victimology, Jerusalem, September 2–6, 1973.

McDonald, J. *Rape: Offenders and Their Victims*. Springfield, Ill.: Charles C. Thomas, 1975.

STRESS

Piaget, J. *Adaptation and Intelligence: Organic Selection and Phenocopy*. Chicago: University of Chicago Press, 1980.

Selye, H. *The Stress of Life* (2nd. ed.). New York: McGraw-Hill, 1978.

SUDDEN INFANT DEATH SYNDROME

Beckwith, J. D. The Sudden Infant Death Syndrome. U.S. Department of Health, Education, and Welfare, Publication No. (HSA) 77–5251, 1977.

Harper, R. M., Leake, B., Hoffman, H., Walter, D. O., Hoppenbrouwers, T., Hodgman, J., and Sternman, M. B. "Periodicity of Sleep States Is Altered in Infants at Risk for the Sudden Infant Death Syndrome." *Science*, 213 (1981): 1030–1032.

Lipsett, Lewis. "Conditioning the Rage to Live." *Psychology Today*, 13, no. 9 (1980): 124.

Lipsitt, Lewis. "Infant Learning." In T. M. Field, A. Huston, H. C. Quay, L.

Troll, and G. Finley (Eds.), *Review of Human Development*. New York. Wiley and Sons, 1982.

Naeye, R. L. Brain-Stem and Adrenal Abnormalities in the Sudden Infant Death Syndrome. *American Journal of Clinical Pathology*, 66 (1976): 526.

Raring, Richard H. *Crib Death*. Hicksville, N.Y.: Exposition Press, 1975.

Steinschneider. A. "Prolonged Apnea and the Sudden Infant Death Syndrome: Clinical and Laboratory Observations." *Pediatrics*, 50 (1972): 646.

Steinschneider, A. "Nasopharyngitis and Prolonged Sleep Apnea." *Pediatrics*, 59: (1975): 967.

SUICIDE

Beebe, John E., "Evaluation of the Suicidal Patient." In C. Peter Rosenbaum and John E. Beebe (Eds.), *Psychiatric Treatment: Crisis, Clinic, Consultation*. New York: McGraw-Hill, 1975.

Calista, Leonard V. *Understanding and Preventing Suicide*. Springfield, Ill.: Charles C. Thomas, 1967.

Davis, Patricia A. *Suicidal Adolescents*. Springfield, Ill.: Charles C. Thomas, 1975.

Durkheim, Emile. *Suicide, A Study in Sociology*. Glencoe, Ill.: Free Press, 1960.

Farber, M. *Theory of Suicide*. New York: Funk and Wagnalls, 1968.

Freud, S. "Mourning and Melancholia." In *The Standard Edition of the Complete Psychological Works of Sigmund Freud*, Vol. 14. London: Hogarth Press, 1957.

Hendin, H. *Suicide; Comprehensive Textbook of Psychiatry*. Edited by A. M. Freedman and H. I. Kaplan. Baltimore: Williams and Wilkins Company, 1967, pp. 1170–1179.

Hendin, Herbert, *Suicide in America*. New York: W. W. Norton and Co.

Litman, R. E. "Actively Suicidal Patients: Management in General Medical Practice," *Calif. Med.*, 104 (1966): 168–174.

Prentice, Ann E. *Suicide: A Selective Bibliography of Over 2,200 Items*. Metuchen N. J.: The Scarecrow Press, 1974.

Richman, J. J., and M. Rosenbaum. "The Family Doctor and the Suicidal Family." *Psychiatric Medicine* 1 (1970): 27–35.

Shneidman, E. S. *On the Nature of Suicide*. San Francisco: Jossey-Bass, 1969.

Shneidman, E. S., and Farberow, N. L. *Clues to Suicide*. New York: McGraw-Hill, 1957.

Shneidman, E. S., and Farberow, N. L. "Statistical Comparison between Attempted and Committed Suicide." In N. L. Farberow and E. S. Shneidman (Eds), *The Cry for Help*. New York: McGraw-Hill, 1961, pp. 19–47.

Schneidman, Edwin S., and A. D. Pokorny. "A Scheme for Classifying Suicidal Behaviors." In A. T. Beck, H. L. P. Resnk, and D. J. Lettieri (Eds.), *The Prediction of Suicide*. Bowie, Md.: Charles Press, 1974.

Shneidman, Norma, L. Farberow, and Robert Litman (Eds.), *The Psychology of Suicide*. New York: Science House, 1970.

Stengel, E. *Suicide and Attempted Suicide*. London: MacGibbon and Kee, 1965.

Weissman, M., Fox, K., and Klerman, G. "Hostility and Depression Associated with Suicide Attempts." *American Journal of Psychiatry* 130, no. 4 (April 1973).

TRANSACTIONAL ANALYSIS

Berne, Eric. *Games People Play*, New York: Grove Press, 1964.

Berne, Eric. *What Do You Say after You Say Hello?* New York: Grove Press, 1972.

Harris, Thomas. *I'm OK—You're OK—A Practical Guide to Transactional Analysis*. New York: Harper & Row, 1969.

Hendricks, J. E. "Transactional Analysis and the Police: Family Disputes." *Journal of Police Science and Administration*, 5, no. 4 (1977): 416–420.

James, M., and Jongeward, D. *Born to Win*. Reading, Mass.: Addison-Wesley, 1971.

Jongeward, Dorothy. *Everybody Wins: Transactional Analysis Applied to Organizations*. Reading, Mass.: Addison-Wesley, 1973.

Romano, Anne. *Transactional Analysis for Police Personnel*. Springfield, Ill.: Charles C. Thomas, 1972.

Steiner, Charles. *Games Alcoholics Play: The Analysis of Life Scripts*. New York: Grove Press, 1971.

VICTIMOLOGY

Amir, M. "Victim Precipitated Forcible Rape." *Journal of Criminal Law*, 58 (1967).

Burges, A. W. "Family Reaction to Homicide." *American Journal of Orthopsychiatry*, 45, no. 3 (1975).

Burgess, A. W., and Holmstrom, L. L. *Rape: Victims of Crisis*. Bowie, Md.: R. J. Brady Company, 1974.

Drapkin, Israel, and Viano, Emilio. *Victimology: A New Focus, Society's Reaction to Victimization*. Lexington, Mass.: Lexington Books, 1974.

Kroes, W. *Society's Victim*. Springfield, Ill.: Charles C. Thomas, 1976.

Lanborn, Leroy. "The Culpability of the Victim." *Rutgers Law Review*, 22 (1968): 760–765.

McDonald, William. *Criminal Justice and the Victim*. Beverly Hills, Calif.: Sage Publications, 1976.

Schaefer, Steven. *The Victim and His Criminal*. New York: Random House, 1968.

Viano, Emilio C. *Victims and Society*. Washington, D.C.: Visage Press, 1974.

Virkkunem, Matthew. "Victim Precipitated Pedophilia Offender." *British Journal of Criminology*, 15 (1975): 175–180.

Wolfgang, Marvin. "Victim Precipitated Homocide." *Journal of Criminal Law—Criminology and Police Science*, 48 (1957): 1–11.

INDEX

Abuse: characteristics of abusers, 109, 117; of children, 129‹ the elderly, 106

Acquaintance rape, 116

Active listening, 99

Adolescence, 15, 17, 22, 134; and retaliatory homicide, 133; statistics in suicide, 93; and suicide, 93

Advocates, 5, 154

Alarm stage of stress, 159

Alcoholism: and domestic violence, 143, 154; as an escape from stress, 167; and suicide, 89, 92

Amish and suicide, 90

Anal stage (Freud), 14, 15

Anatomically correct dolls, 139

Andrea Doria, 18

Anger, 40, 64, 67, 74; in crisis intervention, 158; in domestic violence, 151; in hostile situation, 142; as motive for suicide, 90, 100; in rape, 115; in suicide, 93

Anxiety, 40, 68

Apathy, 67, 74, 159

Arbitrary, 20

Assault, 78

Attacks in rape, 116

Attitudes, 34

Authoritarianism, 50

Authority, 50

Autoerotic death, 94

Automobile accidents, 17, 19

Balance, 13, 15, 65

Barriers to anger, 67

Barriers to communication, 30, 34

Battered spouses, 147

Batterers programs, 154

Bereavement, 78–81; crisis intervention, 79; emotional side effects, 80; normal stages of, 81; in SIDS families, 86

Bias, 151

Blaming, 65, 74, 86

Blitz rape, 116

Bluffing the caller, 103–5

Body language, 26, 38–41

Bridges to communication, 44

Burglary, 21, 59, 71

Burnout, 157; symptoms of, 160

Calming, 11, 25, 104
Case history: cultural differences, 36; in male rape, 117; in rape, 4, 5
Catastrophe, 18, 21
Catharsis, 51
Chaos, 23
Child abuse, 129; by child molesters, 135; incest as, 135; violence related to, 137
Child victim, 129; of sexual assault, 135
Clergy, 103
Cocoanut Grove fire, 17
Cognitive development, 131
Communication, 29; effective methods of, 54; elements of, 31; model of, 32; in suicide, 90
Community reaction to rape, 121–23
Commuter train crash, 17
Components of intervention, 52–53
Compromise, 21
Conceptual models, 3–10
Confidence rape, 116
Confidentiality, 9, 120, 138
Conflict, 15, 21
Confrontation, 21
Confusion, 23
Contacting victim's social network, 52
Coping behaviors, 11, 12, 17, 42, 55
Coping mechanisms, 20, 21
Counseling, 154
Counselor approach, 4, 5
Courtesy, 37
Credibility, 74
Crib death. *See* SIDS
Criminal justice system: applications of crisis, 21; and blaming, 66; and domestic violence, 143; image of, 43; intervener, 49; police and court role, 122; and rape, 122; and SIDS, 81; and victim, 62
Crisis, 11: contagiousness of, 25; crisis behavior, 23; definition of, 12; flow of, 12–14; stages of, 13; typology of, 14–18
Crisis resolution, 53
Crisis-solving partnership, 51
Culture, 30, 35, 152

Date rape, 116
Death, 78; in adolescence, 93–94; of child, 81; as crisis, 77; in suicide, 87
Decision-making abilities, 26
Decoding messages, 31–33
Defense mechanisms, 65, 152
Denial, 23, 64, 65, 74
Dependency, 23
Depression, 12, 20, 40, 69; case history, 5; in domestic violence, 152; in suicide, 101
Developmental differences, 130–32
Differing perspectives, 208
Dignity, 55; loss of, 62; in rape, 120
Disaster, 17, 21
Disaster syndrome, 18
Discharge of anger, 12
Disequilibrium, 12
Disillusionment, 68
Disorganization, 14, 15
Display of confidence, 58
Disrespectful mode of address, 37
Distortions, 33
Dolls, use of, 139
Domestic violence, 30, 142; types of, 145

Effective listening, 45–46
Eight stages of man, 14–16
Elderly, 70, 79, 106; abuse of, 108; diseases of, 107; financial problems of, 108; and suicide, 91
Emergency room, 30, 103, 119
Emotional control, 165
Empowerment, 54; elements of, 55
Encoding messages, 31–33
Equilibrium, 13, 14, 57
Erikson, Erik, 14–16
Erotic literature, 95
Eustress, 12
Exhaustion, 159
External crisis, 14, 17

Facial expressions, 26
Fact finding, 26
Family as resource, 102; reactions to rape, 123–25; and violence, 143

Feedback in communication, 30, 44; necessity of, 58–59
Female police officers, 43
Freud, Sigmund, 14–16, 161
Friends as resource, 103
Fright, 65, 74

Gang rape, 117
General adaptation syndrome, 12, 158
Generalization, 35
Giving hope, 52
Giving information, 52
Goals, 13
Grief, 40, 77–81. *See also* Bereavement
Guilt, 19, 26, 74; in children, 140; and crisis intervention, 157; in death situation, 80; and domestic violence, 149; in rape, 118; reduction of, 74

Hangings, 95
Heightened emotions, 30
Helplessness, 5, 23, 67, 148
Homeostasis, 17
Homicide, 70
Hopelessness, 5, 21
Hospital, 30, 103, 120
Hostile situations, 141
Hyatt Regency Hotel, 18

Identification of crisis, 49, 52
Identity crisis, 15
Imitative behavior, 52
Improving listening skills, 46
Incest, 135
Infant botulism, 83
Inferences, 37
Information gathering, 26; in crisis intervention, 49
Integration, 68
Internal crisis, 14
Intervention in crisis, 49, 53
Investigation, 53, 150

Judgmental behavior, 30, 104, 128, 140

Language, 97; of child interview, 139
Latency stage (Freud), 14
Life changes, 21

Listening: active, 99; effective listening, 45; improving skills, 46; practice of, 47
Long term symptoms of crisis, 69
Loss, 80; as suicide motive, 91

Male police officer, 43
Male victim of rape, 125
Mastery of feelings, 53
Masturbation, 93
Medical approach, 4, 6
Medical examination in rape, 119–21
Medical illness in stress, 159
Medical information, 154
Mentally disturbed, 70, 92
Mentally retarded, 109; crisis intervention with, 111; situations of, 110
Mistrust, 23
Misunderstanding, 33
Moral development, 131–32
Mother of SIDS child, 85
Mt. Saint Helens disaster, 18, 21
Multidimensional approach, 2

Natural disasters, 17
Non-verbal communication, 38–41

Opportunity of crisis, 13
Oral stage (Freud), 14

Pain, expressions of, 36
Paraphrasing, 59
Perception in communication, 34
Perceptions of crisis, 13
Perceptions of criticism, 74
Personality, 17
Personalized statements, 100
Phallic stage (Freud), 14
Physical conditions in communication, 34
Physical movement, 26
Physical symptoms from rape, 119
Posttraumatic stress syndrome, 19, 69
Power, 54, 62, 115
Pregnancy of SIDS mother, 85
Prejudices, 34
Prison Family Anonymous, 6
Professional resources, 101

Property, crimes against, 71; crisis intervention in, 74; misunderstanding of, 72–73
Psychiatric approach, 3, 5, 6
Psychiatric hospital, 103
Psychiatrists, 18; and cultural differences, 36
Psychological casualties, 62
Psychological distance, 58
Psychologic approach, 3, 5, 7
Psychologists: and domestic violence, 155; and rape, 117
Psychosexual stages, 14
Puberty, 17

Rape, 31, 65, 162; approaches to care, 4–8; case history, 4–7; definition, 114; male victims of, 125; myths of, 115; trauma of, 118; typology of rapists, 115
Reassurance, 57
Recognition in crisis intervention, 51
Recoil stage, 133
Referral, 9, 128, 153
Regression, 23, 25
Rejection, 80; in seduction, 162; in stress, 166; in suicide, 90
Repression, 23
Resignation, 68, 74
Resistance, 159
Resolution stage, 13, 19, 64, 68, 74
Resources, professional and non-professional, 101, 167
Respect in crisis intervention, 51
Responding non-directly, 12
Response, 13
Responsiveness, 51, 104
Robbery, 71

Safe houses, 154
Schizophrenia and suicide, 92
Security, 55; loss of, 62
Seduction, 161–63
Self-destructive behavior, 21
Self-disclosure, 98
Self-doubt, 163–65
Selye, Hans, 12; and stress reaction, 158

Sex offenses, 4, 29, 31, 70; against children, 135; crisis intervention with, 114; incest, 135; non-violent, 113; rape, 31, 65, 114, 118, 162; with retarded people, 111
Sexual abuse, 113–29, 135–39; behavioral indicators, 136; crisis intervention with, 137; patterns of, 135; rape, 114; violence and, 113
Shame, 80
Shared feelings, 99
Shelters, 154
Shock, 17, 19, 64
Situational crisis, 14
Sleeplessness, 69, 92, 166
Social approaches to crisis, 5, 7; to sex roles, 144; to suicide, 89; to victims, 62
Social development, 15
Social environment, 15
Source, message, channel, receiver model (SMCR), 31
Spouse abuse, 144–55
Stages of crisis, 13
Stages of Freudian theory, 16
Stages of man (Erikson), 16
Stereotyping, 34
Stress, 12, 158
Sudden infant death syndrome (SIDS), 81–87; causes, 83; crisis intervention and, 86; factors of, 85; guilt of parents, 82. *See also* Crib death
Suicide, 87; rates of, 89; social variables of, 89; talking of, 96
Superman/Superwoman syndrome, 160

Techniques of crisis intervention, 56
Telephone counseling, 97
Theme identification, 100
Titanic, 18
Tone-of-voice, 23–25
Trauma, psychological, 26
Traumatic external event, 17
Two-way barriers to communication, 42
Typology of crisis, 14

Unexpected life events, 19, 20
Unpredictable, 20

Validation of crisis situation, 51
Ventilation, 51, 57, 67; in SIDS death, 86
Verbal cues, 41–42
Verbal disputes, 146
Verbal expressions, 24, 25; in crisis intervention, 53
Victimology, 61; definition, 61; flow chart, 63
Victim-precipitated crimes, 62
Victims: of assault, 78; of burglary, 21, 59, 71; of child abuse, 129; female, 5, 117, 147; of homicide, 70; of incest, 135; plight of, 62; of rape, 116; of violence, 113
Victim services agencies, 6, 154
Vitullo kit, 119
Violence in family, 143

Wife abuse, 149. *See also* Spouse abuse; Domestic violence
Withdrawal, 21, 40
Words: and emotions, 41, 46, 47; for child victims, 139

About the Author

ANNE T. ROMANO is Adjunct Professor in the Department of Criminal Justice at C. W. Post College and the Department of Behavioral Sciences at Kingsborough Community College in New York. She is also the author of several books on human relations training for 911 operators and police personnel and has published articles on spouse and child abuse patterns, terrorism, drug-related homicide, and international crime patterns including espionage, drug trafficking, arms trafficking, and rebellion.